PRAISE FOR FROM TEACHING TO THINKING

"Finally, and not too soon, a manifesto for progressive pedagogues who have a social justice orientation, a love for children and their limitless potential, and a passion for the craft of teaching. Pelo and Carter invite us into their hearts and minds for the sole purpose of inspiring us to inspire children to change the world. A must read for people who care about the future and about early childhood education."

—*Maurice Sykes, Author,* Doing the Right Thing for Children: Eight Qualities of Leadership

"Ann and Margie paint a different picture of what it means to be a leader in this time when standardization, assessment, and compliance are creating a vortex, a strong 'undertow' that has diminished the joy, the intellectual challenge, the surprises that nourish us all. They offer an antidote. Ann's portrait, enhanced through the dialogue with Margie that weaves through the book, is of a thoughtful, sensitive pedagogical companion who walks alongside educators and children. As I read the book, I felt strong empathy with the desire to interrupt what Peter Moss refers to as the 'gravitational pull' of the dominant discourse."

—*Karyn Callaghan, President, Ontario Reggio Association*

"A book by two old friends who invite us into their engaging conversation about the role of early childhood education in creating the world in which we would like to live. A book full of lively stories and important questions. A book that makes clear that early childhood education *is* rocket science—intellectually rigorous, demanding of creativity and passion, and best done in a team. A book that reaffirms that early childhood education must be grounded in democracy and social justice. A book for pedagogical leaders whose mission is to support teachers in discovering or rediscovering the complexity, joy, and wonder of being with young children."

—*Ben Mardell, Principal Investigator, Project Zero at the Harvard Graduate School of Education*

"This lovely collaboration between Ann Pelo and Margie Carter invites us to consider what is missed in opportunity and human life for both children and adults when we proceed with teaching as usual. They give us well-researched alternatives, practical guidance, and ample stories of a teaching philosophy and practice that nurtures and develops the creativity, intelligence, spirit, and wholeness of everyone who goes to school—children, teachers, and parents."

—*Louise Boyd Cadwell, Co-Founder of Cadwell Collaborative, and Author of* Bringing Reggio Emilia Home

"The thinking teacher needs a thinking provocateur, a thinking companion. *From Teaching to Thinking* offers a powerful narrative for leaders and teachers to walk together building new understandings and possibilities. Pedagogy is a matter of choice, a process that is informed by continual questioning, reflection, and research, leading to many possibilities. As a centre leader, let's 'inquire together' with our teachers. Let's explore and construct new protocols to make change happen for our pedagogical practice. If learning becomes an issue of growth not outcomes, and we elevate the child above the product, can we also elevate the teacher above the outcomes? Yes, of course we can! Let quality become something we construct together in communities of learning, not something that we respond to.

He aha te kai ō te rangatira? He Kōrero, he kōrero, he kōrero. What is the food of the leader? It is knowledge, it is communication."

—*Lorraine Manuela, Centre Leader, Tots Corner*

from Teaching *to* Thinking

A Pedagogy for Reimagining Our Work

Ann Pelo and Margie Carter

ISBN 978-0-942702-96-5

Printed in the United States by Sheridan.

© Dimensions Educational Research Foundation, 2018

Cover and interior design by Kaitlyn Nelsen. Editing by Tina Reeble and Emily Rose.

Typeset in Baskerville and Iowan Old Style BT Pro typefaces.

For more information about other Exchange Press publications and resources for directors and teachers, contact:

Exchange Press
7700 A Street
Lincoln, NE 68510
(800) 221-2864 • ExchangePress.com

from
Teaching
to Thinking

If you want to build a ship, don't drum up people to gather wood, divide the work, and give orders. Instead, teach them to long for the vast and endless sea.

—Antoine de Saint-Exupéry[1]

Table of Contents

We are all partners in a quest by Elie Wiesel

The Courage to Teach by Parker Palmer

Ordinary Resurrections by Jonathan Kozol

Down the Great Unknown by John Wesley Powell

Martin Marten by Brian Doyle

The aim of life is to live by Henry Miller

For the Children by Gary Snyder

Foreword

by Pam Oken-Wright

What is it to be fully human? This is the existential question Ann Pelo and Margie Carter place dead-center in a conversation (between each other and with us) about education in this book. Where better to start to think about what education should be, and about what teachers and children have the right to be? It is the compass-question for those of us who guide and support teachers, both the beginning and the purpose.

As a pedagogical consultant trying to support teachers and schools to be all they can be, I am lucky enough to work with educators at two ends of a continuum: teachers who have taught and learned alongside children for years, listening exquisitely to the children's ideas, questions, wonders, and emotions. They have been blessed with freedom to do what they believe is best for the children and are able to exercise autonomy, but they may not quite know how to take the next step toward possibilities they know exist. On the other end of the continuum are those who have been caught, some for decades, in a sea of requirements, data, seemingly random mandates, and reductionist demands on classroom time, and who, in some cases, are mourning a loss of connection with children and with their own potential as intelligent, creative human beings. They receive instructions ("This is the new _____ curriculum") and must respond to the expectation that the data reflect that they taught the content well. Teachers on both ends of the continuum know there can be "something more," but often don't know what that might be.

Enter Pelo and Carter, who, with this book, address pedagogical leaders—principals, pedagogical coaches, and others charged with supporting teachers to pursue that "something more": to create conditions for teaching that are consistent with the environment we want teachers to create for children. I use the word environment loosely here. It includes the *physical* environment: a place of beauty where adults and children want to spend their days, a place that inspires curiosity and provokes thinking; the *social* environment, where both children and adults are treated with respect and honored for the contributions that they bring to the classroom; and it also includes the *inner* environment, where children and teachers are encouraged to act on curiosity, to think, and to imagine. It is in that inner environment that teachers engage in inquiry alongside children and colleagues, make their process transparent, and (re)discover the pleasure of learning.

Of course, this cannot happen through more mandates, more requirements, and frequent external evaluation. But how to support teachers in the way we want them to support children? How does a pedagogical leader help teachers become all they can be? This is different from supervising teachers to make sure they give the right assessment at the right time or meet district benchmarks. The thinking teacher needs a thinking pedagogical companion.

From Teaching to Thinking takes us up above the mundane practicalities and asks us to re-examine our assumptions about teaching and learning and, in particular, about teachers and those who support them. And then it leads us back down, through reaffirmed or new assumptions, to protocols for making change happen. I am particularly inspired by the way that Pelo and Carter bring forth culture, emotion, and imagination as central to the education of humans. This begs a new definition of "education," doesn't it? No longer can we separate the mind from the heart in the classroom. And what wonders occur when we don't! In my decades of teaching young children, I witnessed a consistent reciprocity between intellect and emotion/imagination that took the learning (and the joy) so far beyond what traditionally might have been expected of young children, that to try to tease them apart is unimaginable.

Perhaps this story will illustrate what I mean …

———

The context: An outdoor classroom and a group of five-year-old girls whose teachers are accustomed to seeking out children's embedded intent (see Chapter 10). The teachers are observing the children playing with what they think is one worm that keeps presenting itself to them, day after day. They call him "Wormy," and they make habitats for him, create adventures for him, and send him back into his earthy home at the end of each day's play. The teachers observe that the play repeats, but the entire class is not engaged every day, nor does one small group seem to have a consistent shared purpose. They have decided to continue to observe and see where the play goes.

One day, as one of the players is holding Wormy, a child who has not been interested in the game before and who, the other children know, does not always control her movements well, asks to hold the worm. The first friend hesitates … should she include this friend and risk harm to Wormy, or should she protect Wormy and hurt the feelings of the friend who wants to hold him? She made her decision and let the friend hold Wormy, reminding her not to squeeze him. And yet, her hand closed, surprising both girls and Wormy most of all, squishing the poor creature. A great cry went out, other children came running, and I worried about the blame and shame I thought would come. But before I could say anything, one of the children ran to the fence, pointing to a long, thin, worm-like cloud in the sky. "It's Wormy's cloud!" she announced. "He's in Heaven!" "He's OK!" the children cried. All was forgiven. From that moment on, things were different. The intense emotion of Wormy's demise served to energize the topic for all. Suddenly everyone was engaged in thinking about worms.

The children brought worms into the classroom, studied them through drawing, observed their anatomy and the way they moved, imagined and represented their lives underground, and created stories (and a collaborative mural) about a complex worm kingdom. We teachers brought the children's words and representation to our meetings with the children, where the children decided to make a playground for worms (so the worms would come above ground and share space with the children). They negotiated plans (should a playground for worms have things that children like to play with or things that worms can use? Could worms use monkey bars, for example?) and material (clay, it was decided after some discussion), divided labor, and constructed the playground. But, they reasoned, luring the worms above ground could put the creatures in danger from birds. So they created an alternate attraction for birds, with clay worms and signs that said, "Birds Allowed" for the bird attraction and "No Birds Allowed" for the playground for worms. But, they problematized, birds don't understand our language. So they invented languages for birds and wrote the signs in both "human language" and bird language. And so on, for many weeks.

———

The turning point in this sustained investigation was, I believe, the moment of great emotion and imagination, when the children lost Wormy and found him again in the cloud. Whether emotion and imagination jump start an investigation or re-energize one right in the middle, they hold great power as catalysts for intellectual engagement. So, if in the early childhood classroom emotion and imagination are dismissed as "not what we are about," how will children become deeply engaged in intellectual pursuits?

Pelo and Carter favor inquiry over instruction, for children and for teachers. They urge us to "embrace the intellectual project of education: the development of an investigative attitude towards life—in ourselves and in children; the cultivation of curiosity, persistence, and intellectual agility; an outward expansiveness of thought in ourselves and in children" (p. 39).

In my years of teaching and learning in the classroom, I came to marvel at the power of the Awake Mind. When in a physical environment that offers materials (rather than activities), which they decide for themselves how to use in order to represent their ideas and grow an understanding of the world, children develop a sense of agency. When children learn in a social environment in which they are asked, "What do you think?" and in which they are supported to figure things out together and in which they do more talking than adults, they tend to develop a certain sense of agency. They seem to tell themselves, "I can do whatever I put my mind to." That sense of agency leads to what I call "awake minds."

Year after year, class after class, I watched minds awaken, and when they did the children became adept at making choices and using the environment, asked more questions of themselves, took on more problem-solving tasks, sought out intellectual challenges, and found pleasure in inquiry. A side effect of awake minds was academic growth; everything seemed to make more sense, and learning what the school/district required came easily.

Pelo and Carter believe that educators, like children, "—have a vast capacity for deep dives of mind, heart, and spirit. Their thoughts are 'ample and greedy'; they seek substantive questions and complexity. Their work is challenging and exhilarating and demands their full intellectual and emotional attention. Educators deserve—and are sustained by—professional learning that strengthens their development as thinkers, researchers, innovators, and constructors of knowledge" (pp. 27-28). This is what teachers can be, but for external or internal reasons, often are not.

What Pelo and Carter are proposing is that teachers learning to teach children in such settings deserve the same support from their pedagogical leaders that they are expected to give the children. Indeed, teachers who are accustomed to being told what to do may have learned to put aside their sense of agency. They may not have learned to approach teaching as an act of inquiry, or research, and may never have experienced the pleasure of it. It may have been more comfortable to stifle their own imaginations, though they value it in the children. And if the teacher does not have a mind awakened to all the possibilities, if he feels stuck with the lesson plans and assessments required, how will he support the children's awakening minds? Not only does this book pose the problem and expose the need, but it also offers a framework for action, with protocols a thinking pedagogical leader can use (flexibly) to support teachers' awakening minds.

From Teaching to Thinking is full of essential questions. Questions are the heart of inquiry and research. Wrestling with questions leads to awake minds, which generate more questions, whereas receiving answers tends to terminate inquiry. For those accustomed to receiving answers, being presented with questions instead can be uncomfortable. But what if the pedagogical leader frames support by asking open-ended questions, questions that may not have "available" answers? Then it becomes the pedagogical leader's job to help teachers embrace the discomfort of disequilibrium and fight the impulse to avoid uncertainty, while sustaining an environment of emotional safety within a culture of inquiry.

What does a classroom look like when the adults and children approach the teaching and learning from a thinking stance instead of a mandate-following stance? What if the foundation of the teacher's work is listening? What if teachers and children walk together on the paths of inquiry? And what if pedagogical leaders, whom the authors call "pedagogical companions," walk beside teachers along their own paths of inquiry? This is the paradigm that Pelo and Carter present in this important book. But it is no utopian fantasy. They give us a framework, a lexicon, and protocols to consider as we work toward living a thinking school life. And it all relies on thinking, sensitive "pedagogical companions."

I offer this story of pedagogical companionship ...

I am the pedagogical companion for the Kindergarten teachers in a local Title One public school. One teacher with whom I work, Jen Miller, recently made her first foray into seeking the intent in children's play. Until now, she interpreted play through the interrogative lens, "What's being learned here that is required on a county assessment?" But one day she commented, "The children (girls and boys, a group large enough to fill the area) are playing 'travel' again. This has gone on all year (Sept.–Dec.)." Here was my opening to ask the questions I'd longed to ask. What do you think this is about? What are the possibilities? What is your initial hypothesis? Jen wondered if the play was about packing, or about leaving home and safety, or about other places. After we reviewed her notes on what she had observed over time and brainstormed a bit about the possibilities, I invited her to continue to watch the play with her hypotheses in the back of her mind.

"But I am alone with 19 kids. I can't just watch Magic Play (the children's own name for the dramatic play area)," she said. In truth, once she set an intention to do so, she was able to watch and listen to the play, though her observation was interrupted often. I invited her to prop her phone near the area and record or video, then review later. The next day, she reported that the children had played "North Pole," working for an hour to transform the Magic Play area into the North Pole. They made ornaments for the tree that's always there and covered the space with "snow." They created a story for the North Pole for their play. Later she observed the children creating the North Pole in other contexts, for example with Magna-Tiles® and "polar bears" on the Small Building table.

We revisited her observations. "I think it's more about being there," she proposed. With each conversation, with each new set of hypotheses, Jen observes the children's play with a new lens. That new lens reveals previously unseen layers of the children's meaning. One thing she knows: it is not about the North Pole. She knows to keep observing, documenting, and wondering. Eventually Jen will offer invitations to the children in response to what she thinks might be underlying the children's recurring, passionate play. In our conversations, we generate possibilities of where such an investigation might go.

Is it about Place? If so, is it about understanding the identity of a place? What is the child's relationship to "place?" What is the relationship of place to geography, and how can a child represent that? Are places alive? How do I feel when I'm in a particular place? And how does a place feel when I'm in it? What is the relationship between "other place" and home?

———

One must engage the imagination in order to generate such questions. Many teachers, perhaps especially in the public sector, have let their imaginations atrophy in order to endure teaching in an environment that does not require it. Or perhaps they have invested their imaginations in "cute" activities or displays that bring some small satisfaction. But the imagination is a greedy thing. It wants all of us, and it knows when we are giving it lip service.

What if a pedagogical leader were to recognize that emotion and imagination are just as important to the intellectual life of a teacher as they are to a child's? What if teachers brought documentation of children's persistent, passionate and/or contagious play, or representation to staff meetings and imagined with each other what the children's embedded intent might be? What if they generated questions for their own teacher research around children's play? What if they observed children's play, conversation, and representation from the child's perspective? Might the same intellectual growth—and the pleasure in it—that children experience also inspire the teachers?

Try to remember how pleasurable it felt when you were deeply engaged in play as a child. That is not a childish circumstance. Teaching with an awake mind and active imagination is equally pleasurable, and when you can hitch it to the imagination of a child, it's pure joy. Joy that every teacher deserves to experience.

And so, pedagogist, principal, pedagogical leader, this book is, I believe, a first. It will facilitate your work supporting teachers to bring awake minds and full hearts to the children and each other. So read it, refer to it, wrestle with the questions that resonate with you, and adapt the protocols to your own settings. It will help you become the pedagogical companion your teachers need and complete the cycle of joy in learning—child, teacher, and you.

Foreword

THE DARK MOUNTAIN MANIFESTO

It is through stories that we weave reality.

—Dougald Hine and Paul Kingsnorth[2]

Preface
Writing a New Story

A story, from Ann ...

———

Energized by my first couple years of teaching 3-, 4-, and 5-year-olds in a child care center, I applied to graduate school, eager to better understand the ways of children and the underpinnings of the child care and early education arenas. I enrolled in the PhD program at a well-regarded university and moved to the Midwest, keen to dive in. I loved being in school; I relished the study of educational philosophy, of theories about teaching and learning, of child development and family systems, of the historical roots of child care in labor struggles and second wave feminism. But even as I savored the rigorous coursework and wide-ranging intellectual conversations, I missed my days with young children. I realized that I didn't want to make a life in higher education; I was captivated by the practice of early education, and was eager to return to the joyful challenge of learning side by side with children.

I re-routed myself from the PhD to the Master's track, filing the necessary paperwork to shift my course of study. The forms chugged their way through various required offices, until they landed on the desk of the department chairperson for final approval—and landed me a summons. The head of the department called me into her office to chastise me, and to urge me to reconsider my change in plans. "You're smart," she said, "and you're going to waste your intelligence and your education by working with children. Do you really think you'll make an impact on children's lives by working in child care? Stay in the academy and do research; that's the way to make a difference."

This moment in the department chairperson's office was clarifying and consequential; it laid out a potent story about early childhood education, laden with assumptions, values, and convictions. Early childhood educators needn't be "smart" or "educated"; they have no use for theory, history, cultural study, or political and social analyses.

Children's bright, loud, untidy lives are secondary in value to the order and precision of scholarly research. The work of caring for young folks happens in an intellectual ghetto, removed from the impactful, erudite life of the academy.

———

What reality does this story weave? A reality that has come to dominate our field, in which curriculum is created to be "teacher-proof" because teachers are seen as the weak link between learning goals and measurable achievement on assessments. A reality in which professional development is focused on health and safety mandates, compliance issues, and accountability to state rating systems. A reality in which children's days are overrun with activities that orient them towards learning outcomes on which they'll be evaluated in the name of "quality."

What happens if we reimagine our work and tell a different story? What other reality might we access, what other meaning might we make of our work, of children's lives?

The setting for this story is Italy, 1945 …

———

The Second World War is over; the fascist dictator of Italy, Benito Mussolini, is dead. The country is physically shattered and the people are emotionally and psychologically worn down. Worn down, but not broken, for in that devastated country was the strong political will that sustained the Resistance and that will fuel the rebuilding of Italy.

In the spring of 1945, the citizens of Reggio Emilia, a small town in northern Italy, came together determined to remake their community in such a way that the fascism that had led to their country's disintegration would not find a foothold again. They scraped together the few resources available in their devastated village: an army tank, six horses left by the retreating Germans, and three trucks. They sold these, which gave them some initial funds. They salvaged bricks and beams from bombed houses and began to build a school on land that a farmer donated—the first secular school in Italy—a school run not by the church or the state, but created by and in service to the community. This was the community's response to the danger of totalitarianism and tyranny: create a school for the youngest children.

Here's how Loris Malaguzzi, the first pedagogical leader in the Reggio schools, describes the beginning: "Finding support for the school in a devastated town, rich only in mourning and poverty, would be a long and difficult ordeal, and would require sacrifices and solidarity ... rage and strength to survive."[1]

What sort of teaching and learning would take place in this school founded to oppose fascism? It would, by necessity, emphasize critical dialogue, collaboration, subjectivity, and inquiry. What would be the goal of this educational project? Nothing less than changing history. Malaguzzi, again: "We are part of an ongoing story of men and women, ideals intact, who realize that history can be changed, and that it is changed starting with the future of children."[2]

What did this beginning feel like? This ambitious project to change history by creating a new way of teaching and learning? Here's how Malaguzzi describes the first teachers: "Their thoughts were ample and greedy and their energy boundless ... We felt both enthusiasm and fear ... We were able to imagine the great challenge, but we did not yet know our own capabilities nor those of the children."[3]

From these beginnings grew the schools that we know of today in Reggio. There was more activism done to garner the support of the city government: parents and teachers held school on the stairs of city hall, and in the central piazza, and in city parks, determined to make the school visible in the community, part of the civic consciousness. They occupied an abandoned building in the center of town, transforming it from war rubble into a home for the serious and joyful work of inquiry and investigation. Every gesture, every act was in service of the goal of changing history: "The first philosophy learned from these extraordinary events, in the wake of such a war, was to give a human, dignified, civil meaning to existence, to be able to make choices with clarity of mind and purpose, and to yearn for the future of mankind."[4]

———

What reality does this story weave? What meaning does it offer for the work of early childhood education? Our work is bigger than standardized curriculum and high stakes testing; it is part of the vital and substantive project "to give a human, dignified, civil meaning to existence."[5]

• • • • • • To do this work, we must hold a clarity of mind and purpose, we must yearn for the future of humankind, we must commit ourselves to changing history by our daily engagement with young children.

Two stories, laying out choices to make about the meaning and purpose of early childhood education. Two stories, offering vastly different understandings of who educators are—and who ought to be an educator. Two stories, two ways to weigh the value of children's lives. Two stories, each with a corresponding reality.

Considering these stories side by side reminds us that there are many ways to understand and configure our work, and each of those ways grows from and sustains political, social, and cultural commitments. Education is a political act, and through it, we weave reality.

The Convictions at the Heart of this Book

- In the face of the suffocating press of accountability requirements, we align ourselves with the courageous educators and administrators living from a place of hope rather than despair. We strive to tell a story about education and its purposes that invigorates our commitments to justice and to joy: a story about listening, about intention, about humility and critical discourse. A story that welcomes a multiplicity of experiences and acknowledges a multiplicity of truths. A story that interrogates assumptions and habits. This story holds a vision of education to which we are eager to be held accountable, as it invites us to reimagine our work.

- We believe that educators—like children—have a vast capacity for deep dives of mind, heart, and spirit. Their thoughts are "ample and greedy";

they seek substantive questions and complexity. Their work is challenging and exhilarating, and demands their full intellectual and emotional attention. Educators deserve—and are sustained by—professional learning that strengthens their development as thinkers, researchers, innovators, and constructors of knowledge. This book grows from our deep regard for educators, and our resolve to stand steady at their side.

• Our thinking about early childhood education is informed by our commitment to challenge racial and economic injustice and the ongoing assault on democratic principles in the United States, and by our grief at the growing evidence for irreversible global warming. Scholar Peter Moss writes that a story about early childhood education "that blithely speaks of investing in the future or preparing children to succeed in the global race without interrogating what that future might be or the sustainability of that global race, that story just will not do."[6]

Like Moss, we believe that new stories are necessary, stories that "offer hope that another world is possible, a world that is more equal, democratic and sustainable, a world where surprise and wonder, diversity and complexity find their rightful place in early childhood education, indeed all education."[7] To move towards these new stories, we believe that we must intertwine considerations of culture, racism, white privilege, and power into conversations about pedagogy. We must weave the necessary dispositions and skills for citizenship into our discussions about teaching and learning. We must move beyond efforts towards "greening" our schools, and seek to know our places with a humility that recognizes that we humans are not the center of the story of the Earth. In these ways, we can begin to tell a new story about early childhood education, and in the words of Moss, education's "potential to amaze and surprise, to invoke wonder and passion, to emancipate and experiment."[8]

What convictions drive *your* work? What story are you making of your life? For what do you want to be known?

How did we Come to this Book?

We met nearly thirty years ago, on Ann's first day of work in a child care center in Seattle. She was long on enthusiasm, and astoundingly short on experience. Margie was the visiting staff coach; she threw Ann a lifeline on that first day, gathering the children for a story (a story!) that quieted the chaos. From that first day, we've been writing a story together, bound by our shared political and pedagogical commitments and by deep pleasure in our rigorous collaborations. We've led seminars together; we've made videos together; with our colleague, Deb Curtis, we crafted the Thinking Lens together. But we hadn't written together, not until now. With this book, we offer our current understandings of intellectually rigorous, full-hearted teaching and learning that braids theory and practice.

This book's format draws on the practice, common in Australia, New Zealand, and Canada, of active engagement with and response to texts both spoken and written. Ann offers theory, story, and core concepts in her writing, and Margie offers a response that speaks to the ideas that especially stand out to her, and the questions for practice with which she wants us to engage. With this format, we aim to model active reading, as though Margie were making notes in the margin, lacing the pages with sticky notes, and carrying on a lively conversation with Ann. We invite you to join the conversation as you read this book—and to invite your colleagues to read and think with you. Pedagogical practice is not a solitary act, nor should reading and learning be; we urge you to read and think with others.

The essayist and short-story writer Barry Lopez says that "The responsibility of the storyteller is to the culture of the community."[9] We write this book for those who refuse to betray themselves or to betray children by adhering to marketplace outcomes and assessment-driven configurations of teaching and learning. We write this book for those who will not be complicit in the narrowing of education to the too-easy formula that says "quality" is achieved by lists of learning goals or by rating scales. We write this book for those who are ready to reimagine our work, and write a new and renewing story of early childhood education.

—*Ann Pelo and Margie Carter*

FOR LONGING

Blessed be the longing that brought you here
And quickens your soul with wonder.
May you have the courage to listen to the voice of desire
That disturbs you when you have settled for something safe.
May you have the wisdom to enter generously into your own unease
To discover the new direction your longing wants you to take.

—John O'Donohue[3]

The Heart *of* Education

At the heart of education are two questions: What kind of people do we want to be? What kind of world do we want to live in?

Our answers to these questions help us answer a third question: What is the purpose of education, and how do we go about achieving it?

What answers might we deduce from the current pressures to inscribe early childhood programs with standardized, scripted curriculum that emphasizes literacy and numeracy at the cost of vigorous play and rigorous exploration? Pressures to administer a barrage of assessments to three-, four-, and five-year-old children?

We can read, in these pressures, the conviction that early education is about school readiness, and that school is significant because it prepares young people for work. This understanding of education arises from particular answers to the two core questions: What kind of people do we want to be? Productive workers. What kind of world do we want to live in? A society in which success is measured through competition and achievement is calculated in the currency of the marketplace.

Something in us recoils from those answers. We demand a more generous and far-reaching vision for the purpose of education—a vision that relocates the meaning of education from school readiness to authentic intellectual development, relational and emotional capacity, and attention to social and ecological justice.

• • • • • • What kind of people do we want to be?
What kind of world do we want to live in?

I'll give you my answers with a story …

———

The early arrivers to my child care classroom lay on the carpet with books, reading and chatting. Shifting her position as she lounged with her buddies, Maia noticed the heater vent along the wall of the room, and scooted close to it, peering into it. Her casual interest sharpened to alertness, and she called to the other children, "Look in here! There are Legos in here!"

Aaron hurried to look. Nose pressed close to the vent, he said, with no small relish, "This is kind of yucky in here." Dylan, joining Maia and Aaron at the vent, affirmed, "Yeah, it's stinky."

I checked out the vent with the children and was taken aback by how grubby it was. There were, indeed, Legos in there, and cracker crumbs, old Band-Aids, and other less recognizable bits of flotsam from our classroom life. "I'll get that cleaned out," I assured the children, though they seemed more intrigued than concerned.

Maia, not acknowledging my housekeeping promise, declared, "There must be a skunk in there. That's why it's stinky!"

There was a chorus of assent. "Yeah, that's it! There's a skunk in our warmer!" "Stinkiness means skunks."

I was startled. I'd been on a trajectory towards cleaning the vent so we could move on to more substantial and interesting matters; the three children's serious consideration of the source of the stinkiness stopped me in my tracks. I stifled my desire to haul out the vacuum and deal with the dust bunnies, and threw in my hat with the children and the skunk. "How do you suppose a skunk got into the vent?" I asked.

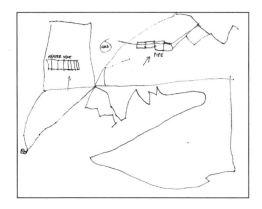

The children didn't leap into fantasy, as I'd half-expected they would. Instead, they began to study the vent and the surrounding circumstances.

Aaron stood at our second-story window and looked down at the ground below. He noticed a capped-off pipe, something I'm not sure that any of us had consciously seen before. Aaron asked me about that round iron piece, and I told him what I knew: that it was a lid covering the open end of a pipe. "Aha!" he exclaimed. "That's how the skunk got in! She opened the lid, crawled into the pipe, and followed the pipe all the way to the heater vent."

Dylan had a different notion. He thought the skunk had simply climbed the stairs to our classroom on the second floor of the building, as we all do each day.

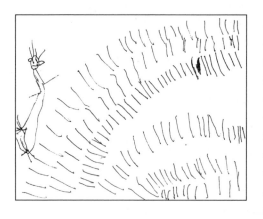

His idea was met with skepticism by Aaron. How would the skunk open the doors that she encountered—the front door of the building, the door at the top of the stairs, the door of our classroom? Skunks are certainly too short to reach the doorknobs, and they don't have hands to turn them. Dylan responded to Aaron's challenge by improvising: "The skunk had rope with her," he said, fingering the collection of twine, old tape, a handful of screws and nuts that he carried with him in his pocket most of the time, ready for any happy accident that would require creative engineering. "The skunk made a lasso with the rope and threw it onto the doorknob and pulled hard, and the door opened. Every door."

Maia was quite linear in her articulation, laying out a crisp sequence of events without worrying too much about the details. "The skunk walked through the front door, up the stairs, into the hallway, and into the vent. The doors were probably open."

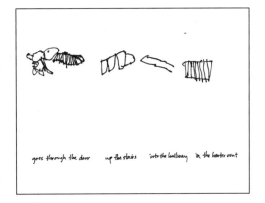

goes through the door   up the stairs   into the hallway   in the heater vent

Other children arrived as Aaron, Dylan, Maia, and I were considering the presence of a skunk in the heater vent; each new arrival was oriented to the news. After their exclamations of delighted dismay, the conversation turned to what we ought to do about the skunk. The children were quick in their consensus: Send the skunk away They dictated a letter for me to inscribe:

Dear Skunk,

Don't go in the hole, because it stinks. Please don't go in the hole, Skunk. Go back in your hole.

Love from Maia, Dylan, Aaron, Emma, and Jack

P.S. What is your name?

The children folded the letter into a small bundle, taped it closed, and set it on the heater vent. Some of the children went on to create additional offerings to the skunk: sketches of their theories about how the skunk had made her way into the vent; drawings of themselves; additional notes to the skunk, most of which said, simply, "Dear Skunk." By the end of the day, the vent was mounded with letters and gifts, a small shrine to the skunk.

My co-teacher, Tim, and I sat together to figure out what, if anything, we ought to do about that pile of offerings. I was charmed by the children's response to the stinky

heater vent: by their leap of imagination and logic—"stinkiness means skunks!"—and by their gestures of relationship. Even as they told the skunk to beat it back to her own hole, they asked her name, and then made gifts and wrote messages to this stinky creature, extending themselves in friendship. I thought we should write a response to the children in the persona of the skunk. I didn't have a clear idea of what that letter ought to say, but it seemed to me a lovely opportunity to explore the ways in which friendships are established across significant differences.

Tim really disagreed with me. He was touched by the children's outpouring, certainly, but thought it would be a betrayal of the children's dignity if we wrote a note from the skunk. He saw a manufactured letter from the skunk as a deceit, although well-intended, on par with urging children to believe in Santa or the Easter Bunny. He didn't want us to muck around with the children's whimsy and imagination, the integrity of their conversation, their capacity to straddle the fanciful and the real.

I was taken aback, and humbled. I'd been ready to jump in with a correspondence; it hadn't occurred to me that there was anything objectionable about that, other than, perhaps, the too-cuteness of it.

Tim and I continued to think together, seeking a third space: neither my space, in which we'd write a letter, nor Tim's space, in which we'd leave the children to their play, but a third space, a new space, that we would create together. We found our way to a plan that we each felt curious about, one that increased the complexity of the situation with the skunk, allowed for the existence of multiple understandings about the skunk, and that held open the invitation for the children to continue to construct the story. We'd simply take the children's letters and gifts off the heater vent.

From Tim's perspective, this allowed for the possibility of human intervention by the custodian or by us teachers, as we tended to the order and cleanliness of the room, keeping the experience firmly anchored in the terrain of the real. From my perspective, removing the letters allowed for the possibility that the skunk existed and had received the offerings, keeping the experience joyfully connected to the landscape of the children's imaginings.

Emma was the first to arrive the next morning. She made a beeline to the heater vent. She greeted each new-arriving child with an announcement of what she'd found there: "When I came to school, I saw that the letter and the presents were gone and now I know there is a real skunk!"

Alex mused, "It was very stinky. Maybe it's a dead skunk."

Jack protested, "No, it's not dead, because it took away the letter and the presents, so it's alive."

Emma suggested, "It maybe chewed on the letter because skunks don't know what to do with letters. It's not sending us a letter back—maybe it's working on a letter right now."

Maia asserted, "She's gonna send a letter back; you have to wait. I think she's working on a letter now."

Rowan posited, "I think the letter says, 'Dear Garden Room, I'm sorry that I chewed up your letter and took your presents away. I'll send you a letter soon. Dear Skunk.'"

———

What a dazzlement this experience was for me—the children, Tim, and me coming together to embrace this moment, with careful observation and thoughtful reflection, with the insight of experience and the joy of conjecture, in the eager anticipation that comes with the beginning of a friendship. Does this story capture why you became an educator? Does it remind you, wonderfully, of children's and educators' creative and collaborative capacities, insightful thinking, leaps of understanding, innovation?

This story is my answer to the questions: What kind of people do we want to be? What kind of world do we want to live in?

What kind of people do we want to be? Thinkers, collaborators, dreamers, inventors; people committed to community and to meaningful engagement with each other; people who embrace the fullness of emotion and who welcome challenging questions like: What is friendship? How do we embrace mystery and the magical? What do we do when a skunk arrives in our heater vent?

What kind of world do we want to live in? A community characterized by the lively exchange of ideas, in which many languages are spoken: the languages of art, science, and literature; ecology and justice; logic, imagination, and action. A society in which the expressions of heart, mind, and spirit are equally prized as necessary components of a fully engaged human life. A community distinguished by intentional action, by deliberate and thoughtful efforts, by purposefulness and attentiveness.

There's a song by the musician Tom Hunter that says, "This world is changing so fast we can't see what's coming before it arrives./To think passing tests will get our kids ready is a gamble we play with their lives./How can we prepare our children for a world we cannot yet see?/I say we work hard so they can become as human as they can be."[1]

What kind of people do we want to be? As human as we can be, in support of children being as human as they can be.

From Instruction to Inquiry

Educators are eager to teach, and to teach, we think, means to talk: to question, to nudge, to instruct, to challenge. During a conversation with educators in Halifax, Nova Scotia, my attention was caught by an insight from a teacher of four- and five-year-olds: "We talk too much," she said. "We think that the children aren't learning if we don't ask them questions."

She hit the nail on the head. We fling questions at children, one after another, a rapid-fire sequence of queries that bear little relevance to a child's pursuits and that hold little interest for us or for the child. What color is that? How many blocks are in your tower? What letter does your name start with? Our intention is to teach, but our verbal quizzes reduce learning to a recitation of superficial facts.

As my conversation in Nova Scotia continued, teacher educator Carrie Melsom suggested a way out of this stale and dead-end orientation. She said, "We ought to join our attention to the children's attention, rather than asking the children to join their attention to what we think they ought to pay attention to, or to the learning goals and assessment benchmarks that have our attention."[2]

What a transformative invitation Carrie offers! What a startling and liberating shift in perspective!

• • • • • We can re-shape our intention from *teaching* to *thinking*—from *instruction* to *inquiry*. We can join the children in their consideration of substantive and intriguing ideas, join them in their search to make meaning—their search *to know* rather than *to learn*.

We can strive to understand children's thinking, tune ourselves to children's intricate dance of committed study. We can refuse to be seduced by the simplistic and superficial recitation of facts. We can sidestep the snares of checklists and accounting. Instead, we can embrace the intellectual project of education: the development of an investigative attitude towards life—in ourselves and in children; the cultivation of curiosity, persistence, and intellectual agility; an outward expansiveness of thought in ourselves and in children.

From teaching to thinking. From instruction to inquiry. What does this intellectual project look like, for children, for us?

Another story that captures the spirit of inquiry at its most graceful and potent …

———

In early autumn, a few years ago, a four-year-old child at the child care program where I worked asked why leaves change color. Her question launched her teacher, Sandra, a small group of three-, four-, and five-year-old children, and myself, the mentor teacher, into a study of the changing colors of leaves, their fall from trees, their death, and their springtime re-emergence. That year, I inhabited the seasons with a consciousness that I'd not before brought to a year's unfolding.

Sandra and I heard Madeline's question, not as a request for scientific explanations, but as a query into mystery. Madeline asked her question as she encountered the burst of autumn color for only the fourth time in her life. The first year that she experienced leaves' red and orange drift to the ground, she was a baby, and everything was bright and new and sensual. When she was two, out in the leaves that her parents raked, they were a new terrain for play. At three years old, she may have had a sense of a familiar return: she'd seen this change in the leaves before. Now, at four, she understood leaves' change from green to gold as a seasonal tide, and wondered about it: What is this mysterious transformation that happens every year? Help me make sense of this beautiful, inexplicable change.

Sandra and I invited three children to join Madeline and us in exploring the lives of leaves (you can read a detailed description of our study in The Language of Art[3]*). We began by considering the role of color in the lives of leaves.*

> *Ana suggested, "In the fall, more things are happening to leaves, so they're changing. Leaves get frosty-cold in the fall, and they need to comfort themselves."*

> *Alex disagreed. "I don't agree with you, Ana," he said. "Color doesn't do anything. It just decorates the leaves. It just makes things pretty."*

> *Beck offered another understanding. "The color is the mommy and the leaf is the baby, he mused.*

> *Alex tried on Beck's idea. "Maybe color says 'Okay, trees, time to go to bed,' like the color is the mommy. The color lets them know it's fall and time for trees to go to bed and sleep through the winter. And in spring, they'll wake up again and move like the wind."*

What is the role of color? Comfort, or beauty, seasonal alarm clock, or seasonal lullaby? We didn't come to any consensus, but I no longer looked at the autumn leaves without a bow to the mystery of their wild color. Inquiry ought to unsettle us, carry us to questions we'd never considered before and to a gladness for the contradictory and complex possibilities held by those questions.

Eventually, the trees were bare-limbed, their fallen leaves mounded below them, brown corpses dissolving in the winter rain. The children recognized that winter is a hard season, that it brings a rough-edged cold—that this sharp season is a season of death. We wondered about the sodden leaves left dead and rotting on the ground.

"In the coldness they fall down, and in the darkness they fall down," Madeline said. *"When a leaf drops on the ground, it feels sad, and wants to be alive again."*

"The leaf needs comfort," Ana offered. "A hug would help a leaf, and being with the leaf. Maybe you could stay with it. You just give it comfort before it dies."

The children didn't end their conversation with the leaf desolate and dying on the ground. They imagined it into the next season—into spring's rain.

"When a leaf gets water, it feels happy because it knows it is going to grow," Madeline declared. *"Water grows the leaves. The leaf starts to be green again and a person puts the green leaf back up, if they can reach. Anyone can do it. If there's a little tree, a kid can do it, and if it's a tall one, a grown-up can do it. It stays there always, and if it falls you put it back on. It lays there until water comes on it."*

Ana: *"When it's spring, Mother Nature comes in the middle of the night and put the leaf back on the branch. She's the one who controls the Earth. She flies up and puts the leaf on the tree."*

———

Life reborn! But the source of rebirth is unclear: Is a leaf's green renewed by the replenishing rain? Do we have a role in this regeneration, or is it in the steady care of Mother Nature? Are leaves, in fact, eternal, always existing, always renewing, falling to the ground only to be re-attached to tree limbs only to fall to the ground again, in an ever-spinning cycle of life and death?

All these considerations seem foolish and fanciful, though charming. If our educational effort is to teach information, this conversation would sound alarm bells. But if our educational effort is to cultivate an outward expansiveness of thought, this conversation is an affirmation of children's capacity for innovative and insightful contemplation of the mysteries of the Earth.

Read on: there is another season's instruction in the way of inquiry …

———

One morning in late winter, Ana rushed into the classroom with big news: she'd seen tiny leaves unfurling on a tree near the child care center. We hurried out to look, and to consider what was happening to the trees we'd come to know through the fall and winter—this astonishing arrival of bright, new leaves on winter-bare branches.

We found the budding tree that Ana had seen, and leaned close to study its green-silked branches.

Madeline suggested, "I think they won't stay like this. I think they'll show more leaves."

Beck was excited. "Now I know how leaves come onto branches! They come from inside the branches. They don't come from the ground. Those dead leaves are just on the ground. There are really, really, really little leaves on the branch."

Beck's delight was energizing; I jumped in with him. "That's a big discovery! How can you tell that the leaves come from inside the branch?"

"Because they're attached," Beck replied. "The leaf is inside the branch. The whole tree is holding the leaf."

Madeline captured Beck's idea in the language of story. "The leaf is inside the branch. The branch is curled around the leaf. The leaf digs and finds its way out—it sees a light hole and it finds its way out. The baby comes out of the branch when it's big enough, and keeps getting bigger on the branch. The baby leaf grows into a big sister. Then it's almost going to die, when it's a mother."

I wanted to understand more about this trajectory of thought, and asked, "How do leaves know when it's time to grow out of the branches?"

Madeline had a hypothesis. "All the leaves fall down, and then new leaves grow on the tree."

To remind the children of their earlier conceptualization of the leaves' cyclic transfer from branch to ground to branch, I asked, "What about the leaves that are dead and get water on them and turn green—the leaves that people put back on the tree?"

"They stay dead on the ground until the other leaves fall off," Madeline hedged.

Alex didn't talk much about his understanding of the origins of the budding leaves. He communicated eloquently in a sketch that traced the seasonal cycle of trees: from full-leaved summer, through autumn's diminishing foliage, into winter's bareness, and then to spring's first flowering into fullness.

He created five sketches, though, not the obvious four. The additional sketch fit between winter and spring, and captured a tree without leaves, but with movement rising inside the trunk. In the stark lines of a late-winter tree, life bubbled up from the ground and flowed into the tree. Alex said, simply, "The tree gets life from the earth to make leaves again."

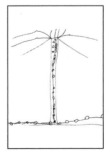

What a complexity of thought these children offer! Beck linked the life cycle of leaves to the life cycle of humans, with the tree holding a leaf as a pregnant mother nurtures the child in her womb. Madeline expands this understanding to include the changing roles in a family dynamic: from baby to big sister to mama—the life course that she knew in her family life. Alex introduced circularity to the seasonal cycle that echoed Madeline's and Ana's earlier ideas of leaves' cyclical fall and replacement. And he exploded the other children's articulated hypothesis of a one-way trajectory from birth to death with his notion that the tree engages life even in winter, an inward and invisible flow of energy drawn up from the dark, damp soil.

The Life Cycle of Inquiry

When our course is set for inquiry, we will offer hypothesis, then let them go, as new evidence compels new understanding and new questions. Our thinking is fluid and spacious, imagination braided with observation braided with metaphor braided with lived experience. We move from question to observation to hypotheses to further questions to revisions of thinking.

Inquiry: a consideration of questions that move us and questions that matter. Questions that explore essential aspects of life, like the compassionate witness of dying, and the origin of leaves, and the forward flow of our lives from baby to big sister to mama. Questions that open into new questions. Questions that carry us forward into a community engaged in shared wondering, shared marveling, shared seeking, shared discovery.

Inquiry: a seeking for knowledge; an investigation; the act of seeking understanding by questioning. So says Webster's dictionary.[4] Synonyms for inquiry include *study, delving, exploration, research*. Antonyms: *answer, reply, response*. This formal definition illuminates the difference between inquiry and instruction. "Inquiry" has movement and flow and unpredictability: *delving, exploring*. "Answer" ends the movement; it's orderly and static and complete.

We are pressed, as early childhood educators, to focus on answers—to prepare children to meet learning goals and to endure assessments. Elliot Eisner, an education professor at Stanford University, calls out the dead-end trajectory of such a course in his essay, "The Satisfactions of Teaching:"[5]

Great teaching traffics in enduring puzzlements, persistent dilemmas, complex conundrums, enigmatic paradoxes.

On the other hand, certainty is closed, and closed streets don't interest the mind.

Great ideas have legs. They take you somewhere. With them, you can raise questions that can't be answered. These unanswerable questions should be a source of comfort. Puzzlements invite the most precious of human abilities to take wing. I speak of imagination, the neglected stepchild of American education.[6]

"Closed streets don't interest the mind." "Great ideas have legs." With these two phrases, Eisner fingers an elemental tension in our field: the tug between an emphasis on answers and outcomes, and an emphasis on imagination, intuition, inquiry, insight, and innovation. Learning goals are bound into accountability to funders. But educators are not bound into a narrow focus on learning goals. Programs for young children need not lose themselves—and children—in the closed streets of mandated assessments, but can commit to striding out of those closed streets into the spacious landscape where imagination lives.

With this book, we commit ourselves to imagination and inquiry—to investigation into the lives of leaves, and the insights about our human lives that come from intuitive puzzling about living and aging and dying. Standing with Eisner, we call this *"great teaching."* It's great for children, and it's great for educators.

Bridging a Divided Life

Margie Carter

My heart leaps when Ann starts this book with the questions: What kind of people do we want to be? What kind of world do we want to live in? How often are these questions on our minds as we approach a mentoring session with an educator, plan a professional learning conference, or assess learning outcomes from children? I think our education settings would take a different trajectory if questions such as these were our guiding framework.

As I look back on my decades as an educator, I have to search hard for examples of when the purpose of education was explored with any depth in my own teacher preparation or my work as a teacher educator in community colleges. Certainly, there were provocations along the way. Reading John Dewey's *Democracy and Education* had a strong impact on me, but Dewey's ideas quickly slipped into the background as I tried to survive my first few years of teaching primary school.[7]

When I became a kindergarten teacher, I was eager to come to know who each child was, to share a heart connection with each child, to find a window into how each child put together ideas and made meaning out of their early encounters with the physical world and the world of ideas. In 1964, I didn't have the fierce pressures for instruction toward assessment and school readiness that exist today, but neither did I have thinking partners or mentors to move me into deeper considerations for my work. I wanted the sorts of conversations and collaborations that we hear in Ann's stories of skunks and leaves, but I didn't know how to make them happen.

As a new teacher, mostly left to my own floundering devices, I fell into looking for effective techniques to "manage" my classroom. I lost track of my earlier philosophical considerations for daily teaching, and neither my peers nor supervisors nurtured that as a foundation for an educator's decision-making. Before long, I became discouraged, my longings and vision for my work dislodged. I found myself simply doing what was required, no longer fueled by philosophical questions or coming home with lively stories.

What would have helped me find my footing, kept a fire in my belly, and not narrowed my thinking to a search for strategies? How could I have stayed focused on meeting up with children's minds, rather than their behaviors? I needed an environment with colleagues and leadership that shared questions and stories like Ann's to marvel and wonder about. All teachers need an organizational culture where there is space to find your intentions, your questions, and agency.

In the 1960s and 70s, it was in community organizing, not my teaching, that I found my footing. The civil rights, women's, and anti-war movements kept questions of "What do we value?" implicitly, if not always explicitly, in front-page headlines. As I found comrades eager to talk about the problems of our country's political directions and our culture of consumerism, violence, and racial and gender inequities, I realized these were key issues to think about in educating young children. Out in my community meetings, I felt enlivened by a sense of possibility. At my workplace, everyone was isolated in her own classroom, watching the clock until it was time to go home. At school, I longed for these fierce conversations about unpacking our values and beliefs about the purpose of education, paralleling the informative and enriching community conversations in my life outside of work.

Alongside my community organizing, I continued to teach, and to learn. The writing of Maria Montessori, Jonathan Kozol, Sylvia Ashton-Warner, and then Paulo Freire's book *Pedagogy of the Oppressed*, helped me explore the intersection of education and social justice.[8] It was in this writing that I discovered what Freire described as replacing the "banking method" of education with a pedagogy that treats "learners as teachers" and "teachers as learners."[9] Freire described Brazil's literacy campaign sweeping the country by abandoning pre-planned, direct instruction, and instead, building learning opportunities based on stories and vocabulary generated from the people participating in the literacy classes. I recognized that this is what Ashton-Warner had invented in her teaching of Māori children in Aotearora New Zealand, when she had children develop "word boxes" with words they wanted to be able to read and write.[10] Freire's work was strongly political, as people learned to "read the world as they read the word."[11] I think today we would use terms like pedagogical inquiry and social constructivism, but talk of pedagogy and inquiry was not part of the average teacher's thinking or vernacular in those days. Widespread interest in the theories of Vygotsky and in the schools of Reggio Emilia hadn't yet arrived on the scene.

Decades later, I heard Parker Palmer describe my early teaching experience of behaving one way, but believing another way as an aspect of "a divided life," awash with internal dissonance.[12] Not a healthy habit, or a useful one for connecting with children and families in a meaningful way. Living a divided life is one of the numerous habits educators must dismantle in order to bring the fullness of ourselves as humans into the teaching and learning process.

What approach to teaching can we champion that gives permission to—and indeed, invites—educators to be full participants in crafting their unique art of teaching? Thinking about my own experience, I wonder how dismantling a divided life might have happened. What if someone had been at my teaching side, learning about my passions, mentoring me to find my bigger questions, connecting me to conversations and ideas to deepen my thinking? Perhaps my journey to bring Freire's pedagogical approach into my work with children and teachers would have been a shorter trek. I'm left with further questions for how we could make teaching and teacher education a different journey for today's educators.

What kind of teacher education and work place culture will support educators to have integrity in their work?

What specific practices help educators hold on to intellectual engagement with their work?

How can we give legs to the great ideas of children and teachers so that they become visible?

What You Missed that Day You Were Absent from Fourth Grade

Mrs. Nelson explained how to stand still and listen
to the wind, how to find meaning in pumping gas,

how peeling potatoes can be a form of prayer. She took
questions on how not to feel lost in the dark.

After lunch she distributed worksheets
that covered ways to remember your grandfather's

voice. Then the class discussed falling asleep
without feeling you had forgotten to do something else—

something important—and how to believe
the house you wake in is your home. This prompted

Mrs. Nelson to draw a chalkboard diagram detailing
how to chant the Psalms during cigarette breaks,

and how not to squirm for sound when your own thoughts
are all you hear; also, that you have enough.

The English lesson was that I am
is a complete sentence.

And just before the afternoon bell, she made the math equation
look easy. The one that proves that hundreds of questions,

and feeling cold, and all those nights spent looking
for whatever it was you lost, and one person

add up to something.

—Brad Aaron Modlin[4]

Creating a
Culture *of* Inquiry

From teaching to thinking. From instruction to inquiry. How do we support the development of an investigative attitude towards life? What does a culture of inquiry look like? How do we begin telling a new story that will transform how we think and work? We can learn from the children standing nose to nose with the budding branches of a new-greening tree in springtime.

A culture of inquiry prizes questions and the process of investigating them, more than arriving at answers. From a simple question about why leaves change color came provocative and unexpected questions: What is the role of color for a leaf? What is it to anticipate one's death and to long for life? Where is not-yet-born life held?

A culture of inquiry values complexity, not-knowing, uncertainty, divergent and contradictory ideas: Does each leaf have an eternal cycle of death and renewal, fueled by water, and aided by humans or by Mother Nature? Or are leaves, like humans, born into a life that includes aging and death?

A culture of inquiry holds as its project the shared construction of knowledge and understanding, rather than the transmission of information and topical knowledge. What a closed street we'd have been on, the children and Sandra and me, if we'd turned to a science book to find the "correct" answer to Madeline's question about why leaves change color.

A culture of inquiry honors imagination and creative leaps, gestures of intuition and spirit and heart: color is the mother of a leaf; a leaf grieves its death and welcomes the renewal that rain brings; a leaf not only grows in size, but as it grows, its family relationships change; a tree draws vital energy from the earth, even in the bleakest days of winter.

A culture of inquiry is rooted in the immediacy of what is unfolding, rather than narrowly focused on the achievement of learning goals, or the eventuality of assessments, or the replication of routines. The immediacy of what's unfolding—leaves bright in the autumn sun, then dead on the winter ground, then budding into spring's brightness—and the questions that these leaves spark, the thinking they stimulate, the sense of living in a particular place in a particular season that they strengthen. Weigh all that against a list of learning outcomes and the assessments meant to measure children's knowledge: Where will we find the richer insights into how and what children think and wonder and communicate and imagine?

These characteristics of inquiry stand true for educators and for children. In early childhood programs committed to inquiry, educators value (and are valued for) their questions about the meaning of children's play, and about the complexities of learning. Educators embrace their uncertainty, and seek out divergent perspectives in order to add to the complexity of their thinking. They come together in the shared project of constructing new understandings and uncovering new questions about their work. Educators look to their intuition and listen to their hearts with as much regard as they tend to their formal knowledge. They are fully present in the moment-by-moment unfolding of life that they share with each other and with children, leaning forward with eager curiosity and with glad engagement, confident that what offers itself is worthy of their full attention. This is what it means to be an educator in a culture of inquiry.

Children know about inquiry. They stride across the terrain of questions as explorers in a wondrous world, moving with nimbleness and grace. They steer clear of the closed streets of certainty where adults tend to congregate. Listen to the way that educator Carla Rinaldi, from Reggio Emilia, Italy, describes children's instinct for inquiry:

> The young child is the first great researcher. Children are born searching
> for the meaning of life, the meaning of the self in relation to others and

to the world, the meaning of their existence, the meaning of conventions and customs, and of the rules and the answers we provide.

If we know how to listen to them, children can give back to us the pleasure of amazement, of marvel, of doubt ... the pleasure of the 'why.' Children can give us the strength of doubt and the courage of error. They can transmit to us the joy of searching and the value of research as an openness toward others and toward everything that is new.[1]

As we tune ourselves to inquiry, this is what we can learn from children pressed close around a stinky heater vent, from children leaning into the branches of a springtime tree: the willingness to feel deeply—to be amazed, to marvel, to doubt. Courage to make mistakes. Openness to others, characterized by curiosity and humility rather than the conceit of certainty. From children, we can learn to be researchers about questions that matter.

What Gets in the Way?

We have habits to dismantle and new muscle to develop when we commit to cultivating a culture of inquiry in our programs. There are inherited practices that we need to question—things that we do because the teachers before us did them, things that we do because, well, that's just what teachers do. Carol Anne Wien has written about what she calls "teacher scripts," which are unexamined views of what teachers ought to do; these teacher scripts get in the way of a culture of lively, engaged inquiry.[2]

Teacher scripts direct us to make sure children follow rules and routines and stick to the time schedule. They tell us to manage children's behavior—to correct it, direct it, affirm it. Scripts instruct us to plan learning activities linked to outcomes. They orient us towards getting children ready for the culture of school by coaching them to stand in line when there's somewhere to go and to raise their hands when they have something to say. Teacher scripts tell us to prioritize health and safety, and keep us busy sanitizing tables and toys, in between admonishing children to walk instead of run, to build block towers only as tall as their knees, and to stay off the monkey bars.

We hold onto teacher scripts, in part, to "prove" that we are real teachers; they help us demonstrate that we're actively doing something for, with, or to children. Teacher scripts get bound into our identities as early childhood educators, but in a way that narrows and constrains our role to rule enforcement, classroom management, and instruction. You might think about your work, and ask yourself if there's a default script that shapes how you engage with children, educators, or families. How does your script serve you? How does it get in the way of the relationships you long to have with children, educators, and families?

If we extend the metaphor of scripts to their theatrical opposite, improvisation, we discover playful insights into our work as educators committed to inquiry, imagination, insight, and innovation. Improvisational theater is created at the moment it's performed; it's a collaboration in real time and space by the people involved, who don't fall back on a script written in advance. The overarching rule of improvisation is to say "yes" to what you're offered by another participant, and then to add your best offering—something new, a provocation, a gesture, a musing, or a question intended to keep the exchange going.

How does this rule speak to our work as educators—as people striving to be as human as we can be in order to support children to be as human as they can be? If we unpack this invocation to say "yes," here's what we can learn from improvisation:

Improvisation is deeply relational: each person leans towards the other, offering and receiving; it is a creative collaboration, a co-constructed experience.

Improvisation requires nimbleness of mind and alert curiosity: participants listen closely, respond generously, and listen some more; a phrase used in improvisation urges participants to "play to the top of their intelligence."

Improvisation is an exercise in non-attachment: participants make an offering and let it go to another participant's creative energy; they don't try to force a story line or an outcome.

Improvisation asks that we are fully present: improvisational comic Chris Gethard says that we must "let this present, small moment be enough."[3]

Improvisation is unscripted, but participants can rehearse: Chris Gethard, again: "You can't practice the content, you can't plan what you're going to say. But you can learn how your brain responds, and you can tune yourself to the other people."[4]

Improvisation asks that we accept silence: there are pauses in the exchange for thinking, inventing, reaching into an offering to see what's there, waiting for an offering while it's being created; participants mustn't rush to fill the silence.

Improvisation asks that we allow ourselves to be changed by the exchange: something new is created by the participants, and in that act of creation, a new insight or deeper self-awareness or unexpected question is born.

When we lay down the scripts that prescribe our behavior as educators, and instead, take up the precepts of improvisation, we begin to cultivate the dispositions that will support our work in the creative culture of inquiry. As improvisational players, we join our attention to the children's attention, and together, we set off on a journey into new terrain, creating the map as we go.

Teaching as Pedagogical Practice

We can translate the shift from teaching scripts to improvisation into educational language by considering teaching as pedagogical practice. Pedagogy means, simply, the art of teaching; in its daily use, it has wide-ranging connotations. The word—and its resonance—was brought to life for me during a conversation with a colleague, Nina LaBoy. She focused on "ped" and played with other words that contain that root: pedestrian and pedals, words that involve using our feet for movement. "We could think of pedagogy as 'walking,'" Nina suggested. "'Walking with children.'" What an exhilarating and provocative image for our work! Walking with children—not instructing, drilling, or assessing them. Walking with them.

What is it to walk with a child? We're side by side, companionable, maybe chatting, maybe quiet together. We pause to pick up a stone and feel its heft and texture, or we squat to peer at the ants lining their way out of a crack in the sidewalk, or we stop to watch the flow of rainwater along the curb. Our course is meandering and attentive; we are engaged by each other and by the world around us. Walking with a child is not speed walking for exercise, it is slow walking for companionship and discovery.

The verb tense of *walking* is the present participle—it refers to things that are still happening, to life in motion. Walking is journey, not destination. It is slow-moving, an unfolding forward. We look ahead and side to side, we gaze back at where we've been.

We're present to the immediate offerings, and we're delighted or puzzled or unsettled by them. We reflect on when we've encountered such offerings before, or we wonder at their newness and unfamiliarity. We allow what we see and smell and touch and hear to have their full resonance. If we look at a map, it is only briefly and for reference; we don't keep our heads bent over the map, our eyes on the GPS, ignoring what's around us.

Pedagogy offers an invitation to walk with children, fully present and engaged, not relying on activity books or pre-determined curriculum to shape our days, but drawing on our own insight, self-awareness, critical thinking, and innovation. Drawing on our capacity to be thinkers alongside the children.

When we understand our work to be pedagogical practice aimed at sustaining a culture of inquiry, educators listen, wonder, and reflect; we're surprised, delighted, and moved. We are willing to be challenged and changed by our experiences with children and families. We're more attentive to creating possibilities than pursuing predefined goals, focusing on what Peter Moss calls "the organization of opportunities rather than the anxiety of pursuing outcomes."[5] We embrace complexity and its companion, uncertainty.

Now, this may not be anything like what you were taught about being an educator. I was taught that being an educator is about being an expert, being in charge, knowing the answers, and helping children find their way to those answers. It was not about "walking with children." It was not about being what Loris Malaguzzi called "a professional marveller," constructing knowledge alongside children, experimenting and making mistakes, seeking and delving.[6] But it isn't very interesting to be the expert in charge all the time, charting one's course with lesson plans and checklists of learning goals. It's a drawback that gets in the way of delight and astonishment, and unexpected, rich inquiry.

Carla Rinaldi writes that "The potential of the child is stunted when the endpoint of their learning is formulated in advance."[7] *Our* potential as educators—and as humans—is equally stunted when we teach from a place of pre-determined activities linked to learning outcomes that are, in turn, linked to assessments.

In a pedagogy of inquiry, is *anything* formulated in advance? Yes. With thoughtfulness and intention, we consider our values and beliefs about the purpose of education: about the kind of people we want to be and the kind of world we want to live in. We make commitments for our learning and for the children's learning—not in the hyper-specific language of learning outcomes, but broader and deeper, with more nuanced commitments to relational and emotional learning, perspectival and intellectual learning, dispositional learning, and ecological and social justice learning. We establish an approach to the inquiry we'll do side by side with children that is about substantive and meaningful ideas like friendship with skunks and the birth of leaves. We develop a protocol for the research we'll do as educators, in collaboration with colleagues and with families, about how children think and theorize, feel and dream, imagine and wonder, communicate and reflect. These are elements of pedagogical practice that sustain a culture of inquiry.

Professional Learning as Pedagogical Practice

To cultivate a pedagogical approach to education, we must formulate professional learning as pedagogical practice.

In early education, it's typical for in-service learning and professional development offerings to take the shape of workshops organized around make-and-take activities, ideas for lesson plans that align with learning goals, and protocols for assessment. Alongside this, the day-to-day emphasis of organizational leaders and program administrators is too often configured around monitoring staff compliance with health, safety, and licensing regulations; helping educators plan activities to meet mandated learning goals; and improving scores on rating scales.

These approaches to organizational leadership and professional learning seem to say that we believe the purpose of our work in early education is to keep children safe and healthy, and to prepare them for school by offering pre-planned activities that correspond to learning goals and assessment measures. In this understanding of the purpose of education, we train educators to be technicians, teaching them the regulations, and giving them lesson plans to follow and tests to administer.

If we believe, however, that the purpose of education is to cultivate dispositions for critical thinking, glad collaboration, imagining, inventing, questioning, and investigating, then we direct our educational leadership and professional learning towards creating opportunities for exploration, reflection, and collaboration. We strive to honor educators' capacities to be professional marvellers, to be researchers curious about and compelled by children's thinking.

Consider this distinction between *pedagogy* and the typical word that we use in our field as shorthand for teaching and learning, *curriculum*. We can define *pedagogy* as "how we think." In *The Early Years Learning Framework of Australia*, *pedagogy* is defined as "educators' professional practice, especially those aspects that involve building and nurturing relationships, decision-making, teaching and learning."[8] Contrast that with *curriculum*, which refers to "what we do," the lessons we plan. Again, from the *Australian Early Years Learning Framework*: *curriculum* means "all the interactions, experiences, activities, routines and events, planned and unplanned, that occur in an environment designed to foster children's learning and development."[9]

Traditional in-service learning and professional development often sidestep thinking and emphasize strategies and techniques—the planning of curriculum and the "doing" of activities and the managing of routines and events. This shortchanges educators' rights to be supported as thinkers, researchers, co-constructors of knowledge, and participants in a culture of inquiry.

Curriculum ought to be an expression of pedagogical thought.

· · · · · · · · When we bring our curriculum close to our pedagogy, we insert space for reflection and meaning-making into the usual trajectory from observation to action. We make *thinking* rather than *doing* our priority.

This, then, carries us to a new understanding of our work as organizational leaders and teacher educators responsible for in-service learning and professional development. When we reconfigure our professional learning to be pedagogical practice, we are called to be pedagogical leaders, with a commitment to supporting educators' *thinking* rather than their *teaching*, and their embrace of *inquiry* rather than *instruction*.

The Work of Pedagogical Leaders

The focus of the work of pedagogical leaders is to help educators become researchers who watch and listen to children with delight and curiosity, noticing the details of children's play and conversation in order to plan responsively. Pedagogical leaders embody the dispositions for inquiry, and call these dispositions forward in educators: dispositions to marvel, to doubt, to make mistakes, to stand open to others and to everything that is new. Which is to say, pedagogical leaders invite educators to be fully human and present, engaged in the unfolding, unpredictable, perplexing, delighting life that we share with children and families. This is an invitation into a way of being in the world, not a transmission of teaching techniques and strategies.

Pedagogical leaders invite reflective, contextual thinking, and a willingness to linger in questions and not-knowing. Pedagogical leaders view teaching as experimentation. They encourage educators to seek out divergent points of view in order to increase complexity. Pedagogical leaders engage questions of ethics, emotion, and imagination as surely as they do matters of intellectual learning and skill development. They walk with educators, and invite educators to walk with children.

Our work as pedagogical leaders is the work of culture-making. Our focus is on pedagogy, on the practice of teaching and learning. Our attention is given to the ways in which children, educators, families, and administrators live into a commitment to inquiry as a way of being in the world. Our aim is not compliance, but creativity, critical thinking, cultural connection, and co-constructed knowledge.

Larry Daloz draws an instructive distinction between leadership and authority.[10] Authority, he says, is aimed at maintaining equilibrium. Leadership, in contrast, facilitates a continual movement from equilibrium to new, deeper, more fluid expressions of community identity.

This can be the aim of pedagogical leadership: to unsettle the habitual, to spark disequilibrium, to challenge educators to think rather than to teach, to provoke conversation about the purpose of education and how best to accomplish it. To move a learning community into an ever-unfolding identity rooted in joyful, participatory inquiry.

Margie Carter

An Invitation to Walk Beside

Ann and I share a love of playing with words, and Nina LaBoy's suggestion that pedagogy could mean *walking alongside* makes me smile. It makes me think of the phrase "We make the road by walking," an adaptation of a proverb by the Spanish poet Antonio Machado, "se hace camino al andar," or "you make the way as you go."[11] *We Make the Road by Walking* became the title of an edited book of conversations between Myles Horton and Paulo Freire.[12] The book explored participatory education—the idea that teaching can be shaped by calling forth student voices and experiences as the focus of examination for learning skills and content. Doesn't that sound relevant to Ann's writing about how a pedagogical leader works?

In Freire's Brazilian adult literacy educational campaigns, teachers were literally sent to the fields to ask peasants to teach them about their lives. The teachers culled out themes from the workers' hopes and dreams, in contrast to their current conditions. These themes shaped their literacy instruction. (Imagine doing that with the educators with whom we work!)

In the United States, Horton worked with disenfranchised African Americans in the South and their uneducated white counterparts in the Appalachian Mountains using the same pedagogy. Teachers in all these settings connected their students' experiences to a larger examination of the oppressive conditions of their lives. This participatory education approach created an emergent curriculum of "read the word in order to read the world." Their empowerment motivated these hungry learners, and as a result, they acquired not only literacy, but critical thinking and analytical skills to become agents of social change.

This understanding of education can be contrasted in just about every way with the common "banking" approach to education, which sees education as a way of filling up students' minds with content that an educator, school system, or curriculum developer has decided has merit. But if education is only a banking process, how do you expand your thinking and become more creative?

• • • • • • How do you sustain hope and uncover choices
not yet imagined?

The language of participatory education may be different than our early childhood discourse, but I think the concept speaks directly to our early childhood education practices. Today it is common to hear both children and teachers in the United States complain that they hate their days in school. With imposed lockstep lessons and scripted curriculum, both groups are subjected to a banking method of being taught, which oppressively deadens their spirits and their eagerness to learn. Is this really what we want as outcomes?

Robbed of their inherent exuberance for living and learning, children are virtually powerless in the world of adults. Rarely do schools, especially publicly funded ones for low-income communities, offer children the opportunity to explore and articulate their learning interests, and thus demonstrate their competency. Teachers, though adults with more potential power, are viewed as marginally competent technicians, treated as low-wage workers mandated to deliver a curriculum. Increasingly, they are losing any sense of agency or hope for shaping their teaching approach. Oh, how different this could be if we trusted and unleashed children and educators to identify problems they want to solve, contributions they want to make to improve the world—not to mention their own lives.

Ann offers a picture of participatory education when she describes sustaining a culture of inquiry with listening, wondering, and openness to being changed in our work with children in families. She writes:

> We're more attentive to creating possibilities than to pursuing predefined goals, focusing on what Peter Moss calls 'the organization of opportunities rather than the anxiety of pursuing outcomes.' We embrace complexity and its companion, uncertainty.

Giving attention to creating possibilities is a mindset that enables one to move through fears to embrace complexity and uncertainty. As you start on that pedagogical journey you'll uncover the road forward. In an education climate in which funding is tied to pre-defined outcomes, this can be a particularly bumpy road with many roadblocks and detours. There really isn't a universal map or GPS system for getting around barriers. We make the road by walking, discovering things in ourselves that need to change, how to work collaboratively, and asking useful questions to propel us forward.

Structures for Openness

I love the phrase "habits to dismantle" that Ann uses and, indeed, recognize some of my own predispositions that need attention. For instance, I'm the kind of person who doesn't usually like to travel without a map. I think of myself as flexible, open minded, and willing to take risks, but I still tend to want a clear plan or agenda. So, why in my early work as a coach trying to change teaching practices, did I unwittingly pull the rug out from teachers, suggesting they abandon what was secure and familiar without yet having a firm grasp on what else might be more rewarding? I did this when I asked Johanna to try not posting a curriculum plan in advance and start focusing her curriculum on what the children were doing. I suggested to John that he stop limiting the number of children allowed in different learning centers, and give them more opportunities to negotiate. Instead, I might have offered Johanna a suggestion to write some notes about how she saw the children engaging (or not) in her curriculum activities as a way to talk about what help she was looking for from her coach. As John's director, I could have asked for his thinking about the value of children negotiating their conflicts and suggested some ways we might gather evidence about that.

My teacher education work began to shift when Betty Jones gifted me with the notion of creating "structures for openness." Rather than telling educators how to set up a classroom, I began to offer principles to incorporate in designing their environments. Instead of saying, "Here's what I would do," I began offering considerations for how to think through decisions to make. Ann suggests this same change in approach when she contrasts definitions of curriculum and pedagogy, a shift from "what we do" to "how we think."

The structure offered by a set of principles or "approaches to thinking" usually serves as a scaffold for reaching towards a goal, along with releasing tension about "getting it right." Ann offers the principles of improvisation. When she speaks of "moving with nimbleness and grace," I'm reminded of the principles of mindfulness, a form of spiritual practice which asks practitioners to pause, pay attention, appreciate the details, and consider a gesture that makes the moment more sacred. I hear echoes of this when Ann writes that we must give attention to spirit and heart in our teaching. My mind scans for what I know about this from experiences I've had.

Once when I was assigned as a coach in a center, two teachers always asked for time with me. I regularly found them discouraged and sometimes at wit's end. They repeatedly complained about children's behavior and constant eruptions, and their difficulty in managing faithfulness to classroom rules. Because of my decades of thinking and experience in early childhood education, I could often scan the room and spot several changes that would probably make life easier for the children *and* the teachers. But before offering any suggestions, I wanted to acknowledge the weariness on the faces of these caring educators, and my appreciation for how they were always seeking ways to improve their classroom. I wanted to offer something to help them think more deeply about the children's ability to engage with interest in the environment. I wanted my offering to support a growing confidence in their own ability to be reflective teachers who can figure things out—who can make the road by walking.

What would help them learn to take a deep breath, signal to each other a need for support, and take a risk to improvise, rather than focus on rules? I called on my own tentative improvisational skills and rummaged in my bag for the remaining sticky notes left after a meeting earlier in the day. "Here's a tool you might try. Each time you find the children's behavior starting to annoy or distract your focus, grab one of these sticky notes and pop it up in that part of the room. Leave them there until I return in two weeks and let's see what we discover."

My improvised tool created the structure of openness that I was seeking. On my next visit, the teachers had fewer wrinkles in their brows, the energy of being pleased with themselves, and an eagerness to report what they'd uncovered. The majority of the sticky notes were in the block area, with the discovery that far more children wanted to play there than their posted sign of only four children at once. After some conversation, they decided to expand the block area to make room for more children. Though they hadn't gotten around to making a sign for the new number allowed in the block area, the children seemed to be managing just fine and the overall disruptions in the room were subsiding. Challenging myself to continue to improvise, I responded, "Yes, and now you can catch your breath and use those sticky notes to jot down notes about how the children use the block area, their conversations, efforts, and accomplishments."

From Reaction to Reflection

I've worked to move from reaction to reflection in my own coaching and mentoring practice, and that's been my focus for educators as well. One strategy that's helped me dismantle the habit of reaction is to change the words we use in daily practice. Rather than defaulting to the complaint that "The children are misbehaving," we might wonder instead, "What are they trying to tell us?" Rather than saying, "Our curriculum this week is … ," we can, instead, make visible "Questions that we're focused on this week in response to the children's play." This suggests another phrase that Ann uses: "muscles to develop."

• • • • • • The muscles of inquiry focus our attention, and mobilize our curiosity and search for meaning; we stretch to find connective tissue between ideas and additional perspectives. We move from reflex to reflection as our first instinct.

As the term "reflection" becomes more common in our early childhood education vernacular, I appreciate how educator/author William Ayers reminds us that we aren't reflecting for reflection's sake, but rather for decision making:

Reflection is more than thinking, although thinking and thoughtfulness are essential to begin. Reflection is thinking rigorously, critically, and systematically about practices and problems of importance to further growth … Reflection is a disciplined way of assessing situations, imagining a future different from today, and preparing to act.[13]

Ayer's words are useful to consider not only for working with children, but for those of us working with educators as supervisors, coaches, or college instructors. His call to think critically about practices and problems of importance to further growth is essential for the work of providing pedagogical leadership. Our habits of being "fixer-uppers" may undermine an educator's self-awareness or disposition to be self-reflective. Preparing to act should involve finding the most important questions to ask, and this requires practice with that rigorous thinking and disciplined assessment that Ayers calls out.

Sparking the Spirit of Inquiry

I find so much of what is done in the name of training both disheartening and demeaning. We could, instead, immerse educators in a culture of inquiry, with structures that support them to think together, nudge new perspectives, and take initiative. Our professional learning can focus on "the organization of opportunities," and invite educators to see their work in new ways.

Deb Curtis and I invented activities with metaphors that characterized the roles of a teacher, wanting to scaffold educators' thinking away from the banking model of "drill and fill" (which also rhymes with kill).[14] We'd invite educators to consider how they would use the skills of a *gardener, knitter, architect, newscaster,* and *forensic detective* in their work as teachers. We'd explore what dispositions they would need for each of these roles. As teacher educators and coaches, we were engaged in the pedagogical practices Ann describes.

Most states across the United States have developed Quality Rating and Improvement Systems (QRIS) that offer trainings to raise scores on rating scales defining quality. Increasingly, coaches are part of the QRIS approach, which creates an opportunity for more imaginative practices. A shout out to those QRIS organizations that separate the roles of monitor and coach. When we separate the notion of monitoring from coaching, we move a step closer to Freire's idea of participatory education and this book's idea of pedagogical leadership. A monitor has "power over," while a coach, divested from that role, has the opportunity to exercise "power for," and perhaps, "power with," educators. *Power with* is working side by side to improve the teaching and learning experience. What if the role of a coach were described along these lines?:

> As a coach, your role is to craft an inquiry process, working with program administrators to nurture this as their culture. You will work with educators to explore questions like 'What do you want to be known for?' and 'How would you like to see our profession grow?' Your job is to walk beside these administrators and educators to grow their identity and their personal agency to bring about change.

In the organization of opportunities, there is a role for each person in a program to shape a culture of joyful, playful inquiry. Mr. Banks, a Head Start custodian, ended his cleaning of the outdoor sandbox each day by raking beautiful designs into the sand for the children to discover the next morning. Cheryl, a cook at a child care center, lobbied for a window from the kitchen to the hallway so she could catch the children's attention with the aromas of the food she prepared and entice them with baskets of colorful vegetables. Director Michael set up a messaging system outside his door with photos and questions to engage the children in his work. The administrative team of a large agency held discussions of books by philosophers, artists, and teachers as part of their process of developing organizational values. All of these people were growing a culture that values relationships, thinking about and delighting in children together, and believing that what we do makes a difference. Everyone in a learning community has something to offer and to learn. How is that message conveyed where you work? Ann says:

> Pedagogical leaders invite educators to be fully human and present, engaged in the unfolding, unpredictable, perplexing, delighting life we share with children and families. This is an invitation into a way of being in the world, not a transmission of teaching techniques and strategies.

Making a commitment to joyful, participatory inquiry. I think this was what Freire and Horton had in mind as they invented empowering pedagogical practices, reminding us that we make the road by walking. If I were a teacher educator or center administrator today, I would try to unsettle the habitual with conversations focused on questions like these:

. . . .

What do you most long for in a workplace focused on children and families?

. . . .

Can you describe an experience with children that changed your thinking?

. . . .

How might the phrase "we make the road by walking" be useful to your thinking and teaching practice?

. . . .

What organizational structures could support your unfolding identity as an educator?

. . . .

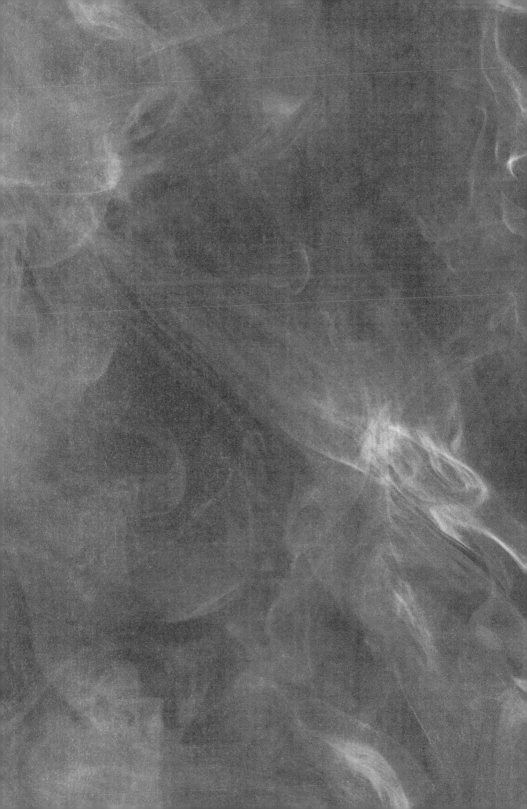

FIRE

What makes a fire burn
is space between the logs,
a breathing space.
Too much of a good thing,
too many logs
packed in too tight
can douse the flames
almost as surely
as a pail of water would.

So building fires
requires attention
to the spaces in between,
as much as to the wood.

When we are able to build
open spaces
in the same way
we have learned
to pile on the logs,
then we can come to see how
it is fuel, and absence of the fuel
together, that makes fire possible.

We only need to lay a log
lightly from time to time.
A fire
grows
simply because the space is there,
with openings
in which the flame
that knows just how it wants to burn
can find its way.

—**Judy Brown**[5]

3

Rethinking Professional Learning

Professional learning as pedagogical practice is aimed at nurturing educators to be thinkers: self-aware, reflective and responsive, creative and curious, excited by complexity, comfortable with uncertainty, energized by inquiry—their own and children's. In this conceptualization of professional learning, administrators, coaches, and teacher educators strive towards supporting the full participation of educators in a community bound together by shared values for critical thinking, glad collaboration, imagining, inventing, and questioning.

In his book, *The Courage to Teach*, scholar Parker Palmer offers this analysis of the typical conversation about professional development:

> The question we most commonly ask is the 'what' question—what subjects shall we teach?

> When the conversation goes a bit deeper, we ask the 'how' question—what methods and techniques are required to teach well?

> Occasionally, when it goes deeper still, we ask the 'why' question—for what purpose and to what ends do we teach?

But seldom do we ask the 'who' question—who is the self that teaches?[1]

Palmer calls us to hold the "who" question with attention and devotion—to tend carefully and caringly to educators as complex, contrary, passionate, full-hearted, thoughtful, deep-feeling, uncertain, bold, anxious, eager, always-evolving human beings.

Not to teaching strategies. Not to curriculum activities. Not to learning goals and assessment benchmarks.

To human beings.

Palmer goes on to say: "Good teaching cannot be reduced to technique; good teaching comes from the identity and integrity of the teacher."

Our work as pedagogical leaders is to call educators into their fullest selves, which is to say, into the generous expression of identity and integrity.

Beyond Mentoring and Coaching: The Role of a Pedagogical Leader

What does this look like, this honoring of identity and integrity?

We can turn to a fable—a teaching story—for insights into the potent role of a pedagogical leader. Tove Jansson's story of Moomintroll awake in midwinter helps us envision the relationship we can call forward with educators. Here's my retelling ...

———

Moomintroll, a child of an uncertain age, typically sleeps in gentle hibernation through the winter with his family. But one winter's night, a streak of moonlight on his sleeping face awakens him, and he finds himself in the wildly unfamiliar world of winter. Moomintroll makes his way out of the slumbering house and steps into "the first snow of his experience. It felt unpleasantly prickly, but at the same time his nose caught a new smell. It was a more serious smell than any he had met before, and slightly frightening. But it made him wide awake and greatly interested."[2]

———

Listen to how he begins to change, right away, without even recognizing the change ...

———

"Without Moomintroll knowing a thing about it, at that moment his velvet skin decided to start growing woolier. It decided to become, by and by, a coat of fur for winter use. That would take some time, but at least the decision was made. And that's always a good thing."

———

When educators are stirred into awareness of new possibilities—as Moomintroll is awakened by the moonlight—they begin, right then, to change. That moment of being "wide awake and greatly interested" is a tender moment, and unsettling ("unpleasantly prickly"!), and sets the course for transformation to come ...

———

Moomintroll is unsettled—he's alone and lonely and afraid, and he sets out into the winter night in search of companions, knowing that he "would feel worse if he were the only one awake among the sleeping."

Eventually, he comes across a track of small footprints in the snow, and follows them to a campfire, where Too-Ticky, a bemusing creature, sits whistling to herself. Moomintroll introduces himself and asks about the song that Too-Ticky is whistling. He receives this perplexing reply: "The refrain is about the things one can't understand. I'm thinking about the aurora borealis. You can't tell if it really does exist or if it just looks like existing. All things are so very uncertain, and that's exactly what makes me feel reassured."

———

And with that, Moomintroll has found his mentor. Educators, awakening into new possibilities, need companions who understand that disequilibrium is a gift, companions like Too-Ticky who embrace uncertainty and not-knowing. Pedagogical leaders can be these companions. We keep company with educators as they find their way into new understandings of their work—not teaching them what they ought to do or directing their journey, but standing at their side, with provocative questions and generous listening ...

———

Moomintroll begins to learn the language and gestures and rhythms of wintertime by simply and wonderfully and achingly living through the season with Too-Ticky at his side. Winter unfolds forward, through the long, dark nights and brief, dim days of the far North, and, at last, spring arrives.

Moomintroll welcomes spring with a fuller sense of life: "Now I've got the whole year," he says. "I've got winter, too. I've lived wide-awake through an entire year."

———

Ah, this is something to wish for the educators with whom we work! May they live into new, more expansive understandings of education and of their role, and may those new understandings offer them "a fuller sense of life" ...

———

One spring afternoon, Too-Ticky reminds Moomintroll of the glories of swimming in the sea in the summer, and Moomintroll chides her:

"Why didn't you talk like that in the winter? It'd have been such a comfort. Remember I said once: There were a lot of apples here. And you just replied: But now there's a lot of snow. Didn't you understand that I was melancholy?"

Too-Ticky replied, "One has to discover everything for oneself. And get over it all alone."

And the book ends there, with Moomintroll looking out at the sea, knowing the ocean now both in its winter ice and summer pulse. "The end and the beginning," writes Jansson, capturing what it is to step from disequilibrium into a life that is changed, expanded, made more whole and more challenging.

———

This is the work of pedagogical leaders: to call educators forward into new terrain, and to keep steady company with them as, together, we contemplate the enduring puzzlements and enigmatic paradoxes which are a source of comfort and reassurance. Our encounters with the new, serious, and unsettling awaken and enliven us, and open us into an expanded awareness of forward-flowing life. We inhabit our lives more generously and fully, and our living becomes a deeper expression of identity and integrity.

In the dynamic between pedagogical leader and educator, there is both the full-hearted companionship of exploration and the solitary inwardness of discovery. There is provocation and persistence. There is collaboration of the sort that Elizabeth Jones and John Nimmo write about, collaboration that "requires risk-taking with some passion about it [and] that begins with someone's act of provocation and the willingness of another to become engaged."[3]

A Meeting of Minds

In early education, we've embraced the concept of mentoring as a useful approach to connecting more experienced with less experienced educators. In the last few years, the role of coaches has been highlighted. Typically, in early education, mentors and coaches give advice and make suggestions about behavior management and curriculum activities. They're charged with helping educators develop their facility with assessments and prepare for evaluative visits related to standards and rating scales. Their focus is typically on standards, lesson plans, and paper work, on accountability to current definitions of quality.

This typical framing of the work of mentors and coaches does not support the sort of pedagogical practice that turns a community towards inquiry, and that invites educators to be thinkers.

This analysis from Lilian Katz about the relationships between educators and children offers insight into the relationships between mentors and coaches and educators:

> The content of the relationships between teachers [in the United States] and their pupils tends to be dominated by information about the child's conduct and level of performance. Thus, it seems that the content of relationships between teachers and children in our early childhood settings, when not focused on mundane routines, is about the children.
>
> In contrast, my impression of Reggio Emilia is that the content of teacher-child relationships is focused on the work itself, rather than mainly on routines or the children's performances on academic tasks. Adults' and children's minds meet on matters of interest to both of them.[4]

This could be written about the relationships between program supervisors, mentors, and coaches and educators. Too often, the focus of our interactions with educators is administrative and logistical—the "mundane routines" that Katz references, and educators' compliance with standards-related tasks.

But as pedagogical leaders striving to support educators as thinkers and researchers, we don't squander our interactions with educators on discussions of paperwork and scheduling, which surely don't invite educators into inquiry. As pedagogical leaders, we understand that every interaction we have with educators is professional learning and communicates what we value in their classroom practice.

As pedagogical leaders, we shape the content of our conversations with educators to focus on thinking about children and about the process of learning. We pose questions that we're genuinely curious about, we ask for a story about children's play, we invite a meeting of minds about ideas of interest to all of us. This communicates to educators that what we care about is thinking and wondering—more than whether they've disinfected their tables recently, submitted their leave requests on time, or have begun their assessment entries. Those logistical considerations have a place, but they do not move us closer to achieving what we've articulated as the purpose of education: to grow a culture of inquiry.

Pedagogical Leaders as Necessary Companions

Pedagogical leadership is directed towards cultivating the practice of teacher research, helping educators develop "a habit of mind and a set of tools" that allow them to "stop reacting" and, instead, to observe mindfully, reflect expansively, and act with intention.[5] Pedagogical leaders do not play a supervisory or evaluative role, but, rather, the role of a necessary companion, or *critical friend*.

The go-to definition of *critical friend* comes from Arthur Costa and Bena Kallick: "a trusted person who asks provocative questions, provides data to be examined through another lens, and offers critique of a person's work as a friend."[6] Too-Ticky is a critical friend to Moomintroll, just as a pedagogical leader is a critical friend to educators, a necessary companion on the journey from equilibrium and its habitual ways of thinking into the rigorous terrain of new puzzlements and unfamiliar perspectives.

The work of Larry Daloz and Sharon Parks, senior fellows of the Whidbey Institute and scholars in the field of adult learning and leadership, can inform our understanding of what it is to be a pedagogical companion. A critical friend, they write, "sees you in the fullness of who you are and who you can become."[7] There is surely the feel of risk, of vulnerability, when an educator steps from the familiar and predictable into a transformed and transforming landscape of new questions about and understandings of teaching and learning. One aspect of our role as pedagogical friends is to bear steady witness to the full human capacity of an educator to sustain complexity; we serve as a generous and unwavering companion as an educator takes her first tentative steps into that prickly snow and its serious smell that startles her "wide awake and greatly interested."[8]

But a pedagogical companion is more than compassionate witness. A critical friend acts as a provocateur, offering challenge alongside support. Too-Ticky whistles a song "about the things one can't understand … All things are so very uncertain, and that's exactly what makes me feel reassured."[9] What a puzzlement to offer just-awakened Moomintroll, eager for certainty, for something to hold onto as a comforting reference in a changed world. A critical friend, trusting in an educator's capacity to be challenged, suggests new perspectives and questions old assumptions; presses the dichotomies and invites contradictions; asks keen questions and holds the space for not-knowing.

Parker Palmer writes that "If we want to deepen our understanding of our integrity, we must experiment with our lives."[10] A pedagogical companion invites this experimentation and the accompanying practice of thoughtful self-examination: "Why do I think what I think?" "How do I know what I know?" Like Too-Ticky, a critical friend understands that "One has to discover everything for oneself." Rather than offering innocuous reassurance to Moomintroll's melancholy midwinter heart, Too-Ticky makes an observation that keeps Moomintroll present to his disequilibrium: "Remember I said once: 'There were a lot of apples here.' And you just replied: 'But now there's a lot of snow.'"[11]

Pedagogical Leaders Stand Side by Side with Educators

It serves us well, as pedagogical leaders and critical friends, to consider Eve Trook's descriptions of three kinds of relational power:

We use *power on* when we are trying to prevent, stop or change something.

We use *power for* on behalf of another person's power through our planning, coaching, and scaffolding.

We use *power with* when we share power side by side with curiosity— allowing, even enjoying, rather than guiding, another's behavior or action.[12]

Eve Trook developed this framework to help educators think about how they use power with children. I believe it holds deep resonance for us as pedagogical leaders, as well. When we approach educators in the spirit of telling them what to do or not to do, we exercise *power on*, which surely does not invite an educator into a journey into new understanding. As pedagogical leaders, our intention ought to be *power for* and, most especially, *power with*.

• • • • • • • We stand side by side with educators, companions with them on their journey to the fullest expression of their identity and integrity.

We think with them about teaching and learning, about children, about their delights and puzzlements and challenges and longings. We don't set out to mold educators into some pre-established notion of who we think they ought to be or how we believe they ought to think or feel. Our aim is to strengthen educators' identity as thinkers and researchers, as people engaged by inquiry rather than beholden to instruction.

A couple of insights into *power with*, from two skillful pedagogical leaders:

My goal is not to get teachers to respond the way I would, but to have them consider their goals and values, along with the body of early childhood knowledge, as a reference point for deciding what to do. In some cases they might benefit from seeing how I might respond, but only if they consider my thinking with regards to their own thinking. I want to promote self-reflection, not imitation.[13]

—*Margie Carter*

When someone comes in and just tells or persuades educators to do something, it may work for a bit, but the impact fades. What has greater impact is when educators change their thinking and this new thinking changes their practice.[14]

—*Ijumaa Jordan*

Carter and Jordan remind us that the aim of a pedagogical companions is to invite self-reflection and intentional action that express the identity and integrity of an educator. A pedagogical leader, acting as a critical friend, seeks to cultivate in educators the practice of watching and listening to children, capturing details of the children's play and conversation in order to understand children's thinking and wondering. We offer intriguing perspectives that add complexity and contradiction to the process of making meaning of children's play and conversations. We help educators plan offerings to children intended to spark new questions and puzzlements for both the children and the educators. And we work with educators to make visible the stories of their own and children's inquiry.

Pedagogical Leadership in a Community of Practice

This discussion of the role of critical friend may create the sense that the work of a pedagogical leader takes place in a one-on-one relationship with individual educators. Certainly, there is abundant exchange between a pedagogical leader and individual educators, but the focus of a pedagogical leader is to grow a community of learners, and, over time, a community that learns.

"Self as learner" is a familiar notion to us. The idea of a community of learners adds the spark that comes from engagement with a range of perspectives and experiences: "Who we are together is different from and more than who we are alone," writes organizational development consultant Tenneson Woolf.[15] "Not just a summing-up, but a different entity with different resources that become visible and available."[16] From this coming-together, we grow into the shared identity of a community that learns. Again, Woolf: "A community that learns pays attention in an on-going way. A community that learns has a disposition for and an awareness of learning through all that changes and in its full complexity. Less grandstanding. More understanding. Less blame. More compassion. Less judgment. More curiosity."[17]

Tiziana Filippini captures the lively intellectual feel of a community that learns in her description of pedagogical practice in the schools of Reggio Emilia, Italy:

> We reflect on our practice—a reflection that moves toward theory—or start from a theoretical assumption and compare it to what we have seen in practice, to redefine its meaning … We consider what has happened and search for its interpretation; we negotiate to construct a collective understanding. Without these reciprocal relationships and

processes of sharing, each one of us would remain isolated within his or her own perspective.[18]

A community that learns is in continual construction of collective understandings born of multiple perspectives coming together. This isn't easy! The give-and-take of authentic exchange does not mean happy-dappy, easy-as-pie congeniality. Authentic relationships ask that we offer ourselves to each other; that we consider difficult and complex circumstances together; that we argue, we make mistakes, we disagree. We join together with comrades and collaborators, yes, and also with people quite different from ourselves, people who challenge and vex us.

I recently encountered a re-framing of the way that we have typically conceptualized relationships in a community that learns in an article by Brian Arao and Kristi Clemens. They suggest that we need to move from the idea of "safe spaces" to the goal of creating "brave spaces."[19] They write about this in the context of conversations about social justice and identity; I find it is also deeply resonate when carried into consideration of a community that learns. In safe spaces, we expect to be free from risk, difficulty, discomfort, but when we come together in the midst of our differences, committed to a shared life, we are sure to encounter difficulty and discomfort. We need our communities to be brave spaces—brave, because we are going to be vulnerable and exposed. Brave, because we are going to take risks with each other. Brave, because there will be conflict and discomfort and rigorous challenge.

Listen to this insight by Elizabeth Jones and John Nimmo: "Dialogue is not simply 'talking to each other'—swapping points of view and leaving to 'make up your mind.' It involves being prepared to wrestle with another's perspective. Dialogue is a collaborative act."[20]

This sort of dialogue is at the heart of a community that learns—dialogue about "persistent dilemmas, complex conundrums, enigmatic paradoxes … unanswerable questions."[21] It is a courageous act in a brave space in a culture of inquiry that prizes questions more than answers, values complexity and uncertainty, honors insight and imagination, and is committed to the shared construction of knowledge and understanding. Genuine collaboration requires brave space, and a community that learns requires genuine collaboration.

Courageous collaboration is at the heart of pedagogical practice. Filippini is describing a community that learns when she says "we negotiate to construct a collective understanding."[22] Pedagogical practice is born in dialogue; it calls on humility and frank speech, it both nurtures and reflects a capacity for disagreement and wrestling with other perspectives, it calls for courage, and finds its home in brave spaces.

Leadership Principles for Reimagining Our Work

Rather than delivering "training," a pedagogical leader strives to bring educators together in a community of learning and practice anchored in the shared construction of knowledge. A pedagogical leader sees her work as culture-making rather than the guidance and development of individual educators, or the achievement of high scores on the state quality rating. This culture-making takes place informally, through conversations and stories about children's and educators' learning. It happens in the context of organizational structures like staff meetings, in-service learning days, and staff retreats. It is strengthened by protocols for thinking about learning and by the on-going practice of pedagogical documentation—the cycle of observation, study, and action that spins children and educators into deeper and more expansive inquiry.

From this broad conceptualization of pedagogical leadership, we can distill four principles to guide us as we live into the culture-making role of a pedagogical leader:

1. **Anchor organizational systems in vision and values.**
   At the heart of a culture of inquiry is intentional and deliberate attention to what our lives express. A community that learns stretches always towards fluid and generous alignment with deep-held values about inquiry and wonder, curiosity and inventiveness, persistence and paradox. The organizational systems that undergird such a community are built on strong and continual consideration of vision and values.

2. **Hold an organizational focus rather than a focus on individual educators.** A community that learns calibrates its growth and learning to the scale of years rather than weeks or months. It takes up sustained study of substantive ideas over a long stretch of time. It holds as its aim the development of shared understandings about teaching and learning invigorated by wrestling with differing perspectives and diverse experiences about how best to express those understandings in daily lived practice.

3. **Engage educators in ways that parallel how we hope they will engage with children.** Louise Boyd Cadwell calls forward this orientation towards inquiry in educators: "We want to know what the children think, feel, and wonder. We believe that the children will have things to tell each other and us that we have never heard before. We are always listening for a surprise and the birth of a new idea. This practice supports a mutual quest for understanding."[23] Pedagogical leaders hold this same orientation about educators. We're curious to know what they think, feel, and wonder. We expect to learn from them, as well as with them. We anticipate that they will give birth to new ideas—not just new to them, but new to us. We join educators on a mutual quest for understanding, just as they join children on such a quest.

4. **Come together with families as collaborators, colleagues, and critical friends.** We talk about collaboration with families a fair amount in our field, but we tend to mean that in the most superficial way. In a community that learns, educators join with families in the sort of collaboration that Jones and Nimmo write about, collaboration that "involves more than a coming together. It requires more from the participants than simply sharing their perspectives. At best, it requires that the participants reach a new level of understanding—a perspective that was not apparent before."[24] Families are as central as educators, administrators, and children in the effort to live into our vision, values, and practices.

We'll take up these principles in the next chapters, as we continue to explore the nuanced and complex practice of pedagogical leadership.

Communities that are Brave Spaces

Margie Carter

The pedagogical practices that Ann inspires us with require that we deeply know ourselves and open ourselves to new perspectives. Educators are often remarkably skilled facilitators at interpreting and addressing children's feelings, spicy interactions, and desires to be seen in all their humanity. These teachers carefully craft a classroom culture that is respectful and responsive, that acknowledges differences, and engages the perspectives and longings of all children and families. Can we use what we know to support equally complicated communities of practice among ourselves as adults? What skills and dispositions do we need to actively pursue to make it so? What will make it possible for us as humans, living in a world of realistic fears, to approach our living and learning with uncertainty as a source of enlivenment? How do we mobilize bravery so as to not diminish our learning by staying only where we feel comfortable and safe?

Pedagogical practice is born in dialogue, and dialogue is a collaborative act. Ann's call for humility and frank speech most certainly requires a brave space. Our courage falters, though, when we encounter perspectives and experiences sharply counter to our own. We want to stay comfortable, we want folks to like us, we want our workplaces to feel warm and congenial—we have many impulses that carry us away from direct engagement with those who seem too different from us, in the hopes of staying comfortable and safe.

The democratic principles of our country and, indeed, our professional code of ethics, compel us to respect diversity. We ought to move beyond diversity—which is having all sorts of people at the table—to equity, ensuring that those traditionally silenced or marginalized are heard and taken seriously. Conversations in diverse groups aiming for equity require emotional safety, but the idea of safety shouldn't be conflated with comfort. The expectation of safety is a manifestation of privilege because our country has never been truly safe or equitable for people of color. If you are white, this may be a new understanding to face. If you are a person of color, you may be tired, angry, or living in despair with that reality.

Most white people don't like to be pushed out of our comfort zone, and we allow all the discomfort and courage to be transferred to our colleagues of color and to families of color, who may not be emotionally or physically safe out in the world. One aspect of creating a brave community means that white people listen with humility to and learn from the frank and real truths of living in a racist system. In such a community, courage and commitment will grow on all sides.

We can no longer avoid talking about the dynamics of racism, power, and privilege, as they inform the perspectives we bring to our teaching practices, and are always at play in our wider communities. For those of us who are white, I pass along the question of Terasa Cooley, "What emboldens us to step out of safety and into the light of demanding justice?"

Pedagogical leaders can both serve as and seek out critical friends, as they work towards creating brave spaces. The term "critical friend" doesn't mean someone who criticizes, but rather someone who is critically essential to our learning. The relationship must be one of mutual trust. Ann offers us a window into how a necessary companion, as a critical friend contributes to an organizational culture of courage and humility. She describes the mindset of trusting in another's capacity to be challenged, the process of formulating questions that invite self-examination and experimentation. This can occur because an emotional, social, and intellectual climate has been created that "holds the space for not-knowing."

In using the fable of Moomintroll to illuminate the role of a pedagogical leader, Ann provokes our thinking by calling us into new terrain. Perhaps by exploring this terrain of fables, we can each construct our understanding of the mutual trust that a pedagogical leader must develop to be an effective critical friend.

• •

Here's a challenge: Consider developing a story, perhaps as a fable, about Trust going on a journey and encountering Risk.

• •

. . . .

How might that story unfold when Urges jump in the path—urges to retreat to safe space—with suggestions on how to avoid risk?

. . . .

Share your fable with someone you know and ask what they see as the moral of the story.

. . . .

I think my fable includes some critical friends named Courage and Bravery.

. . . .

WINGS OF THE SAME BIRD

We hear the voices of our parents,
our elders, our teachers,
those that came before us
and with us

We were kids
who cared about justice
We are freedom fighters,
resistance
resistance

We are teachers for transformation
Workers, in this for the long haul

We are not only undoing,
We are building something strong

We are all wings of the same bird

that bird is called …
hope, survival, movement, mentoring,
power, empowerment, generativity,
change, stubborn,
life-giving
victory
And she will fly.

——Katie Kissinger[6]

4

A Principle *for* Reimagining Our Work:

Anchor Organizational Systems in Vision and Values

Three core elements shape the life of a community that learns:

- **Vision** that guides it: Who are we as a community?
- **Values** that serve as touch-points for decisions: How will we live into our vision?
- **Systems and practices** that embody and amplify vision and values: How will we express ourselves?

We do a complex dance with these three elements. We're biased towards systems, quick to think in practical terms about logistical details, about doing and fixing, about acting and responding. As organizational leaders, a focus on systems can consume our days; we live with daily pressure to be solvers of problems, efficiently navigating the structural and practical challenges that arrive in our programs with dependable frequency. Vision and values can be overshadowed by systems.

As pedagogical leaders, though, striving to nurture a community that learns, our great work, our important work, is to tend as diligently to vision and values as we do to systems—to let systems be an outgrowth of deliberate attention to vision and values. This is where the dance begins. It's not enough simply to articulate a vision and values for a program: it is essential to create the organizational circumstances in which vision and values are lively and in motion. Yet a concentrated focus on systems can distract us from thoughtful, regular consideration of vision and values. When we do the dance well, we are attentive, thoughtful, and deliberate, constantly braiding vision, values, and organizational systems.

Who Are We as a Community? Living with Vision

Vision guides an intentional culture. To get at vision, we ask questions like:
- What is the nature of the community we hope to be?
- What is the role of educators in children's learning?
- What do we want children to learn?
- What sort of teaching and learning will best serve what we believe to be the purpose of education?

Vision is a declaration of what we care about and who we strive to be. It is our statement about the purpose of education, our answer to the questions about what kind of people we want to be and what kind of world we want to live in. Vision is an expression of potential: we look beyond what is to what could be.

Consider the various meanings of the word vision. It connotes "sight," as in "20-20 vision." It suggests something that appears in a dream or trance, a revelation. Some cultures embrace the practice of vision quest, a journey away from the everyday to discover one's life direction and spiritual calling. Taken together, these meanings of vision speak of discovery, of dreaming one's way into clear seeing and into a direction revealed.

How practiced are we at dreaming? We're often mired in the mundane and logistical; we don't linger much in the arena of dreams. We sometimes talk about longings, about needs unfilled that we badly want filled—enough money to pay staff what they deserve, or new playground equipment to replace the splintering wooden climber. But those aren't dreams; those aren't visions that set our direction, that speak to who we want to be and how we want to live. They're solid practical desires, helpful when fulfilled, perhaps even transformative—but they're grounded in the immediate and tangible, more linked to systems and structures than to dreams.

To dream is to aspire, conceive, imagine. It's derived from the Old English word meaning "to rejoice, to play music." We sometimes braid the idea of "hope" into the notion of "dream"—hope, which shares its etymology with the word "hop," meaning "leaping in expectation," cherishing a desire with anticipation.

• • • • • • • • When did you last dream in a way that had you leaping in expectation? That had you joyfully making music, so delighted were you with what you had imagined?

We can define *vision* as the fullness of dreaming with hope. Full-bodied and generative, drawing on and fueling inspiration, *vision* offers a picture of what we want to create. *Vision* integrates imagination, passion, and delighted anticipation of the possible. *Vision* sets our course.

Vision is distinct from mission. Mission is a statement of services, it's what we do. Vision is our most actualized way of being in the world; it grows beyond how things are to describe how we would like them to be. It's the expression of a community's purpose, its aim and intention.

Pedagogical leaders committed to creating a culture of inquiry carry a vision of a community that learns, characterized by lively questioning and experimentation, and inhabited by thinkers committed to meaningful engagement with each other and with substantive ideas. We dream towards coming together as people who are as human as we can be, curious and inventive, patient and humble. And we live into our dream with hope and muscle, finding our way forward through our values as we create systems that sustain and amplify our vision.

Peter Block, an organizational consultant, writes that, "The most compelling dialogue we can have is about our vision. Leadership is keeping others focused on the vision, and this means that we have to get comfortable talking about it."[1] Pedagogical leaders keep others in the community focused on vision, and keep vision at the heart of the dialogue about the community's practices and pursuits.

How Will We Live into Our Vision?
Finding Direction from Values

Our values animate our vision. Values are the principles and beliefs that guide our decision-making about how we'll realize our vision—how we'll understand and enact relationships; how we'll address social justice and ecological concerns; how we'll construct curriculum and design our physical space and allocate money and time. Values embody what we stand for, they reflect our ideals, and, so, they provide the basis for decisions and direction.

I spent some time poking around on the web to read how people write about values. Several websites, focused on ethics in the workplace, listed an array of values that an organization might adopt. Look at this quite varied list: ambition, competency, individuality, equality, service, responsibility, accuracy, dedication, diversity, improvement, enjoyment, loyalty, credibility, honesty, teamwork, accountability, empowerment, efficiency, dignity, collaboration, stewardship, accomplishment, courage, independence, security, compassion, friendliness, discipline, generosity, persistence, optimism, dependability, flexibility.

As I read this list, I had an immediate visceral response to each of these words—"yes, yes!" or "no way." Values are deep-rooted and carry potent imagery and resonance. They grow from our vision of who we want to be, and speak to how we aim to become who we envision. Articulated, our vision begins to breathe us alive. We can deliberately call forward the particular values that will carry us towards our vision and consciously consult them as we chart our course.

A fair amount of daily practice in early childhood programs is inherited: circle time, for example, and naptime customs, and activities centered on holidays and seasons. We do what we do because that's what has always been done. These proceedings have become untethered from vision and values. Pedagogical leaders act as provocateurs, asking "Why?" We interrogate inherited practices, asking if the values that they express are, indeed, the values that our community wants to embody.

Pedagogical leaders wake a community into conscious conversations about the values we hold at the center of our shared life as the expression of who we strive to be. Our shared values, in turn, help us develop the practices, policies, and organizational structures that determine the shape of our days together.

How Will We Express Ourselves?
Crafting Organizational Systems

Alongside pedagogical practice, organizational systems embody and amplify vision and values: What specific organizational structures, practices, and policies will allow us to become the program we want to be? What systems will hold our program accountable to our commitments about the purpose of education?

When we talk about systems, we mean what we'll do, concretely, to become the program we aspire to be. Systems means behavior, guided by values and vision. Systems means decisions about how we distribute resources of time, money, and leadership.

We strive to align organizational systems with our pedagogical vision and values, and seek to put systems in place that weave together our classroom, administrative, and family practices. In this way, we create a unified and unifying expression of community identity.

The role of pedagogical leaders is to ask questions aimed at lining up organizational systems in this way, questions like:

- How will we structure our welcome and orientation for new staff, so that it parallels how we hope educators welcome and orient new children and their families?

- How will we arrange our physical space so that there is room for educators to meet in reflection and study, and for families to come together to share stories and insights, and for children to give over to investigation, play, and contemplation?

- How will we plan the content of staff meetings and retreats and family gatherings, so that it parallels how we hope educators plan curriculum for children?

- How will we organize consistent and substantive planning time for educators, so that it parallels how we hope educators offer children meaningful time for reflection and meaning-making and how we hope educators and families come together for study and the shared construction of understanding?

- How will we structure staff evaluations, so that the process parallels how we hope educators invite children to reflect on their learning?

- What practices will we put in place to provide educators and families with opportunities to expand their leadership in our program and in the field of early education—practices that parallel the ways we hope educators invite children to stretch into new terrain and take on new roles?

The systems and practices that we have in place for educators, families, and children each contribute to answers to the question, "Who are we as a community?" When we align our systems with our values, those answers speak with congruency, illuminating organizational integrity, the wholeness that comes when *what we do* unfolds from *what we care about*, on all fronts. Our practices, then, become an expression of community identity, rather than simply a bunch of policies to follow.

Pedagogical leaders call a community into integrity by holding the community's values as the measure for decisions about systems, policies, practices. They ensure that organizational conversations are anchored by consideration of the community's values, offering those values as touchstones for decision-making and course-setting. In this way, pedagogical leaders help a community grow into an always more integrated expression of their vision for who they are.

A Systems Example: Structures for Welcoming

Consider this cornerstone question: How will we structure our welcome and orientation for new staff, so that it parallels how we hope educators welcome and orient new children and their families?

It's tempting to hand piles of paperwork to new staff members, full of details about staff schedules and break times, how payroll is managed, how leave requests and sick days are handled, copies of lesson plan forms and expectations for record-keeping. After handing over this paperwork, we could show new staff members where the bathrooms and the break room are, where they can drop their coats and bags, and then send them off to work.

We would cringe—and rightly so—if that was how educators greeted children and families as they began their time in our program.

What if, in our first exchanges with new staff members, we welcomed "the self that teaches?" What if we invited conversations about what we hope our center stands for—the values and vision that anchor our community? What if we made time for thoughtful observation and those vulnerable first steps into relationship—just as we would for a child as she joins our center? …

———

My first day as an educator at Hilltop Children's Center was full of paperwork—but with no time to read it, only to sign the necessary legal forms—and a tour of the building, a quick introduction to the educator with whom I'd be working, and then I was on duty.

This was our typical welcome to new staff for many years. We had a change in leadership, though, and that change set us on a trajectory for change. The director, who served in the role as pedagogical leader, challenged us to re-make our orientation process, streamlining the orientation to employment logistics and developing a new orientation to values, vision, and pedagogy. She called out our commitment to be a community of people who feel deeply, dream boldly, and who bear generous and kind witness to each other as thinkers, innovators, seekers, and players. "Nowhere in that vision does it say we're a community of people who fill out paperwork efficiently," she said. "Our vision is all about relationship and reflection, self-awareness and collaboration. What values will help us actualize that vision in our orientation process?"

Through a series of conversations facilitated by our pedagogical leader, we named what we'd longed for ourselves, when we'd each joined the staff. And we called forward core aspects of our collegial relationships, elements of our work together that we hoped would be seeded during a new staff member's first days. Through that process, we articulated the values that would guide us as we created a new orientation process:

- *We value protected time for planting the seeds of relationship and connection.*
- *We value the reflective practice of observation and discussion.*
- *We value the discipline of study and writing.*
- *We value the generosity of collegiality.*

From those values, we constructed a new welcome and orientation system. We arranged a paid three-day period for a new staff member to come to know our community before she or he had any responsibilities with children. During that time, a new educator spent time in guided observation of a range of classrooms; working with the pedagogical leader, she explored the meaning of her observations. A new educator moved through an orientation handbook that addressed our core values and vision with observation practices, readings, and questions for study. She also met for the first time with her peer mentor, a long-time staff member who would be her informal partner during her first year on staff, an ally she could turn to with her questions, musings, discoveries, and uncertainties.

We continually revisited this welcome and orientation process, as we learned from new staff what worked well about it and what left them overwhelmed or confused or at loose ends. Our overarching intention, called forward by our pedagogical leader, was to engage educators as we hope they engage children and families, with a warm and thoughtful welcome into a rich and lively community.

———

Integrating Vision, Values, and Systems

When we make systems-focused decisions based on values that express our vision, we stay tuned to the pedagogical process of teaching and learning rather than to regulations and assessment. We create an integrated and integrating culture of inquiry in which curiosity and conversation, research and reflection, saturate our days and seep into all aspects of our program.

Here's a glimpse into how we approached this integrating practice at Hilltop over several years. We began by working together to craft a vision statement that articulated our aims and intention. From there, we called forward the values that would help us live into our vision. Finally, we set out the practices that we would take up to express our values. We began with this overarching vision statement describing the community we wanted to be ...

———

Hilltop Children's Center: A Learning Community for Children and Adults

Where children are valued for their ability to do meaningful work, their wonder and curiosity, their perspectives, and their ability to play—

Where families are valued for their bonds and traditions, their ability to play, their commitment to work, home, and community, and their dreams for their children—

Where staff are valued for their vision, their delight in children, their skill, heart, and knowledge, their commitment to families, and their ability to play—

We cherish what we learn from each other.

———

From that beginning, over the course of several years, we amplified that vision statement into its component elements: our vision, our values, and our practices for each group in our community—children, families, educators ...

———

Our Vision for Children
We regard children as compassionate and generous friends, reflective thinkers, thoughtful solvers of problems, breathtakingly alive in their bodies, and skillful

collaborators. We seek to honor those qualities in them, nurturing their developing understandings of themselves in relationship with others. We want children to honor their feelings and ideas, to be reflective and self-aware, and to explore many perspectives. We invite children to see themselves as members of a community and to take responsibility for the shape of that community. We encourage children to notice and speak out about unfairness and to act to change it.

Values at the heart of our program for children

We value questions and the process of investigating them, more than arriving at answers.

We value complexity, not-knowing, uncertainty, divergent and contradictory ideas.

We value the process of constructing knowledge and understanding through collective experimentation, dialogue, and study.

We value the influence of the classroom environment, the thoughtful use of time, and the intentional organization of routines on children's play and relationships.

We value the role of imagination and intuition, of spirit and heart, as surely as we value intellect.

Practices that express our values

The values we hold for children's experiences at Hilltop are reflected in the day's flow and emphasis. We want children's time here to be characterized by:

- *long stretches of uninterrupted time, in which children's questions, understandings, emotions, relationships, and explorations serve as the foundation for our curriculum;*

- *many opportunities and substantial adult support for children to form relationships with each other, creating a community shaped by playfulness, inquiry, and affection in which conflicts are seen as opportunities to strengthen connection and in which collaboration is a core practice;*

- *opportunities for children to use many media to represent and revisit their theories, experiences, and feelings, and to communicate those ideas, experiences, and feelings to others;*

- *encouragement for children to inhabit their bodies' sensuality and muscle, perceptivity and movement, balance, stillness, and speed; time, space, and supplies for children to transform materials, making, shaping, taking apart, recreating; and*

- *adults moving with respect and quiet gentleness in the classroom, acknowledging with our voices, our movements, and our demeanor that the rooms are the children's work spaces, dreaming spaces, feeling spaces, living spaces, and that we are there to listen and to support and to listen some more.*

Our Vision for Families

We want Hilltop to be a vital, vibrant community, characterized by rich relationships and thoughtful dialogue. We aim to create an environment that reflects and honors children's families, building bridges between home and Hilltop that allow children to move easily and fluidly between these two central arenas of their lives. We understand families to be:

- *eager to understand, grow, discover, and investigate;*

- *curious to discover both the power and fragility of their children; powerful in their bonds with their children; competent to reflect on and rethink their experiences; and*

- *able to consider their own children and all children.*

We offer ourselves as resources for families about child growth and learning, and see families as resources for educators about their children's cultural contexts, passions, and developmental journeys. We recognize that families balance work and home, and seek to support them in their efforts to hold those substantial responsibilities.

Values at the heart of our program for families

We value families' devotion to ensuring their children's safety and well-being, to knowing, in particular and intimate detail, about their children's moment-to-moment lives, and to playing a primary role in each unfolding day and each wakeful night.

We value the trust that families place in us, as they share their children's lives with us.

We value shared decision-making, educators and families together shaping the daily life and the curriculum of the classroom.

We value mutual intimacy, in which educators and families offer themselves to each other as full human beings, not locked into the confining roles of "parent" and "teacher."

Practices that express our values

Central in our classrooms are tangible markers of home: framed family photos, photo albums, tea cups made by parents for children, treasure boxes in which families leaves surprises for their children, nap pillows decorated by families for their children.

We share stories of children's play and work at Hilltop in journals that travel between home and Hilltop. We invite families to add to their children's journals, responding to what we've written and writing their own entries.

We create space in our classrooms for families to linger, providing adult-sized seating in couches and comfortable chairs where they can snuggle with their children, read their children's journals, and chat with each other.

We hold frequent gatherings for children, families, and educators: monthly community sing-alongs, informal social gatherings on weekends and evenings, occasional educational forums for families, community rituals marking passages like birth and death, and celebrations like tea parties for no particular reason, just because it's a joy to come together.

We meet with families in small groups for collaborative conferences to study traces of children's pursuits in order to understand children's thinking and questioning, and to plan our next offerings to children.

Our Vision for Educators

We want educators at Hilltop to be on fire about their work; to feel competent, excited, curious, and profoundly attentive to the children. We strive to be a program in which educators move between theory and practice, with a solid understanding of the thinking underneath our teaching practices and with lively teaching practices that set each classroom alight. We commit to knowing the children intimately, and to living alongside them in ways that communicate our affection, delight, and regard.

Values at the heart of our program for educators

We value attentiveness to, curiosity about, and delight in children's play.

We value self-awareness about the ways in which our beliefs and cultural perspectives shape what we notice and don't notice.

We value relationships anchored in glad witnessing, authentic exchange, and curiosity about others' perspectives.

We value the practice of teacher research, and the experience of collaborative study, meaning-making, and planning.

We value the contributions of child development knowledge and early learning theories to our learning, as well as the insights offered by poetry and literature, the physical arts, and the arenas of science, ecology, and technology.

Practices that express our values

We emphasize teaching practices grounded in the pedagogical cycle of observation, study, and planning. We gather observation notes and collect photos and work samples of children's pursuits, and come together regularly with colleagues and families to explore children's perspectives. We plan offerings to children intended to support and extend their intellectual, emotional, and social pursuits.

We meet in teaching teams for weekly study and learning, and monthly as a full staff. Our pedagogical leader crafts a year-long focus for our professional learning related to the central tenets of our pedagogical practice.

We create visual and written documentation that analyzes the meaning of children's play and that tells the story of our thinking about children's thinking.

We invite educators into leadership roles in our programs, facilitating visits by professionals to Hilltop, leading orientation workshops for new staff, partnering with new staff as mentors, and writing for publication.

———

The process of weaving together our vision, values, and practices called us into integrity. It helped us steer a course through the shoals of compliance and assessment by keeping us focused on the core questions: Who are we as a community? How will we live into our vision? How will we express ourselves?

We didn't write this statement all at once. It grew out of several years of conversation, exploration and provocation, as we wrestled our way to shared commitments for our work, aiming always to ensure that *what we did* reflected *what we valued*. And it continues to evolve; the staff revisit it regularly, considering what continues to be resonant and what's changing, so that it both reflects and shapes the on-going growth of the center.

In this, as in other formative processes, the pedagogical leader keeps the dynamics of vision, values, and practice in continual motion. When there's a decision to make, the pedagogical leader anchors the discussion in consideration of vision and values, asking questions like "How will this decision amplify or disrupt our vision?" The pedagogical leader notices when habit creeps into practice or when regulations become the measure for action, and sounds the call to revisit and refresh the braiding of vision, values, and systems.

Dreaming and Vision Building for Professional Learning

Margie Carter

The principle that this chapter offers for pedagogical leadership captivates me like the song of a rare bird. So different from how typical administrators or coaches see and describe their work! Lingering on each paragraph of Ann's writing, I noted phrases that could serve as a playlist we might write the music for, composing a new approach to leadership and professional learning:

- Our vision is the fullness of our dreaming with hope;
- Carrying a vision of a community that learns;
- Waking a community into conscious conversations;
- How will we become ourselves?
- How will we express ourselves?
- Structures determine the shape of our days;
- Systems embody and amplify our values and vision;
- Systems mean decisions about how we allocate our resources of time, money, and leadership.

Ann describes a shift that happened in the culture of her child care center when the director began to see herself as a pedagogical leader, beyond the notion of a manager or supervisor. That in and of itself may be new thinking and terminology for a director struggling to stay afloat every day. In our book *The Visionary Director,* Deb Curtis and I tried to offer administrators a framework for conceptualizing this possibility for themselves.[2] Working with directors, we found ways to guide the process of clarifying values and collaboratively developing a vision statement. We also discovered that without structures and systems to help programs live into their dreams, even the most eloquent vision statement won't grow legs. Time and time again we saw teachers and administrators stall out, burn out, or become cynical about efforts to make significant changes. We came to understand a reversed wording of the principle Ann offers—vision and values must be anchored in organizational systems. Both wordings are trying to sustain the practice of dreaming with hope.

Across town from Hilltop Children's Center, I watched another director, Luz Casio, invent her way into pedagogical leadership, as she shaped her vision of a community that learns at her early childhood center, the Refugee and Immigrant Family Center (RIFC), a program that served a population very different from that at Hilltop. This community primarily spoke Spanish as their first language, and was made up of newly-arrived immigrants and second- and third-generation immigrant families. Their aspirations were to raise their community out of the troubles of poverty, secure their cultural values and language in a happy future for their children, and make a meaningful contribution to their adopted country. Honoring the identity of this community, Luz, the center director, cultivated a program culture focused on these organizational values:

Social Justice: We value cultural democracy, overcoming bias, and undoing racism, and we believe that children and adults can only thrive in a world where inequities are noticed and actively challenged.

Collaborative Relationships: We value mutual respect, reciprocity, and collaborative decision-making among children, families, staff, and educators, and we believe that this builds strong and equitable communities.

Intentional Practice: We value pride in our work, innovation, and going beyond conventional ideas of quality experiences for children, and we believe this creates a sustainable quality of life for ourselves and generations to come.

Joyful Work: We value playfulness, purpose, and passion in the classroom as well as in the office, and we believe that adults can draw inspiration from children's lively minds.

Watching Luz at work brings to life Ann's phrase about waking a community into conscious conversations about values. Despite the pressures of accountability to different bureaucratic funding streams, Luz focuses her educators on living into their values, not limiting their thinking to compliance with regulations. She hands out lists of tasks related to their accountability, asking, "How will you organize getting these done for yourself so that they don't get in the way of the real focus of your work here? We have systems that might help, examples others have used, but these are only possible ways. Who might need a mentor and who could offer mentoring leadership? Let me know if you need some time off the floor for this."

Staff meetings at Luz's center take up Ann's questions, "How will we become ourselves? How will we express ourselves?" Luz asks educators to bring photos of children's pursuits that make them curious; she guides the educators in puzzling out their questions about and enchantments with the children's play, and invites them to identify their own childhood memories related to the play. Often, a staff member's baby attends the meeting, nursing for a time with his mama and then enjoying the arms and laps of other educators while his mama guides discussion of an assigned book chapter. The reading may be in English, but the lively conversation is primarily in Spanish, and Luz prompts educators to consider the text in light of their own observations and experience. These are educators becoming confident in themselves and trusting in their right to question what seems culturally off-putting about strategies or theories in their reading. Isn't this an expression of what Ann suggests?

> As pedagogical leaders, we carry a vision of a community that learns, characterized by lively questioning and experimentation, and inhabited by thinkers committed to meaningful engagement with each other and with substantive ideas. We dream towards coming together as people who are as human as we can be, curious and inventive, patient and humble. And we live into our dream with hope and muscle, finding our way forward through our values as we create systems that sustain and amplify our vision.

You can read more about Luz's approach to pedagogical leadership and the outcomes she describes for children, families, and teachers in my *Exchange* interview with her.[3] For now, consider these questions for yourself:

· ·

What has your heart singing and dreaming with new hope for your work?

· ·

What muscles do you want to develop toward bringing that to life?

· ·

What process could you put in place to ensure each decision you make amplifies, rather than diminishes your vision?

· ·

The Best in Art and Life

The best in art and life
comes from a center
something urgent and powerful
an ideal or emotion
that insists
on its being.

From that insistence
a shape emerges
and creates its structure out of passion.

If you begin with a structure,
you have to make up the passion,

and that's very hard to do.

—**Roger Rosenblatt**[7]

5

A Principle *for* Reimagining Our Work:

Understand Professional Learning as the Work of Culture-Making

A culture of inquiry encompasses the full gamut of how we live together, the many daily expressions of our vision for who we want to be and the values by which we want to live. More than an organizing principle for staff meetings and curriculum planning, a culture of inquiry comprises the way we think about our use of space and time, the way we approach the rhythms of classroom life, the way we align budgets, the way we organize administrative roles and responsibilities, the way we orient our relationships with families. Culture is part and parcel of everything we do. A culture of inquiry is integrated into the fullness of our days together, not set apart as "professional development," but acting as the overarching and defining way that we live together throughout all aspects of our program.

A culture of inquiry interweaves dispositions and practice. Strands in this intricate braid include our organizational systems and policies; our approach to teaching and learning; the network of relationships among children, teachers, families, and administrators. This weaving supports all of us to be curious, attentive, collaborative, fluent in the languages of value and vision, interested in perspectives other than our own and willing to be changed by the ideas and experiences we encounter.

In this context, professional learning is not about getting individual teachers up to speed with discreet aspects of their work, nor is it about ensuring that the whole staff is on board with the latest developments in the Quality Rating System.

• • • • • • Professional learning is focused on bringing teachers, children, families, and administrators together as a research collective—as a community that learns.

Professional learning strengthens the identity of an early childhood program: its touchstone considerations are "Who are we as a community?" and "How will we live into our vision?" When we commit to pedagogical practice as professional learning, we take up the work of collaborative research and study; that work, in turn, strengthens our capacity for collaborative research and study. We grow into being teacher researchers, rather than waiting to give teacher research a try until we feel we've figured it out. We learn who we are as we live into the community we seek to be. In this way, we create community that is not an aggregate of individuals, but a community of shared intent and collective practice.

Organizational theorist Meg Wheatley writes about community in the context of living systems as understood by natural science.[1] She draws parallels between the ways in which living systems and thriving human systems (like schools and child care programs) organize themselves, pointing to three domains that sustain flourishing life. An organization begins with *identity*: a shared purpose and intention, "a belief that something more is possible now that the group is together," a conviction about who we will be together. As an organization encounters *information and ideas,* things can get shaken up; disequilibrium enters the picture. Members of the community work together to move through disequilibrium, arriving at new, expanded understandings; *relationships* sustain an organization's evolution.

Using Wheatley's conceptualization, we can think of pedagogical practice as the on-going effort to energize both relationships and identity. A community becomes increasingly adept at taking in and making meaning of information in ways that expand its capacity to live into purpose and intention. It becomes a healthier and more vibrant living system.

Taking the Long View

In early childhood education, in-service learning and professional development typically take the form of one-time workshops and stand-alone trainings. We may attend a workshop on literacy activities one month, followed the next month by an in-service training about classroom environments, followed a month later by a local mini-conference addressing the latest developments in the region's Quality Rating Scale. Educator Wendy Cividanes has coined the term "drive-through training" to describe this approach to fast-and-ready-to-serve workshops, conference offerings, and web-based instructional seminars.[2] These, she says, are like picking up fast food at a drive-through: convenient, familiar, and quick, an easy way to take care of the requirements for on-going training.

But we know that fast food is not nourishing. It doesn't offer much substance or sustenance, and the satiation it provides quickly dissipates, leaving us hungry again too soon after eating. What would unfold if we abandoned the drive-through and, instead, embraced Slow Food as a model for our professional learning?

The Slow Food movement emphasizes local, seasonal, fresh foods, produced in ways that preserve biodiversity, celebrate food traditions, and respect the people who work with food from field to fork. Slow Food was launched "to counter the disappearance of local food traditions and people's dwindling interest in the food they eat and where it comes from."[3] This model serves us vastly better than the fast food approach to professional development.

We can anchor our learning in the authentic and particular: the questions sparked by our daily experiences with children, by the challenge and stretch of our teaching. We can call forward the knowledge and insight that families and teachers and children collectively hold. We can seek to understand our inherited lineage as teachers of young children—the thinking about teaching and learning that has shaped our field, from Piaget and Dewey and Wright Edelman to The National Black Child Development Institute, the Worthy Wage Campaign, and the movement towards shared movement. We can re-localize our learning, re-invigorate our study, so that we are re-connected to each other and to the immediate liveliness of our work.

Slow Food—and meaningful professional learning—prioritizes abundant time over efficient time: time to linger and puzzle and talk together; time for a question to reverberate and fill the space; time for a thought to take shape, be spoken, be heard, be considered. Professional learning as pedagogical practice is anchored in sustained study of substantive ideas over a long stretch of time. It is emergent and responsive, an on-going exploration of ideas shaped by our observations of children and by self-reflective examination of our teaching, by study of foundational and innovative texts in our field, and by challenges to habitual thinking and doing.

When professional learning is pedagogical practice, there is continual interplay between the direction we set for our study and the questions that offer themselves for exploration along the way. Curiosity and conversation, research and reflection, musing and meaning-making saturate our days together. It is an integrating practice, through which we learn our core values as we live them, and live our core values as a way to learn them. It is the practice of research and study which strengthens and sustains the practice of research and study.

Professional learning as pedagogical practice is on-going and every day. When we shape professional learning as pedagogical practice, we commit to the long haul and take the long view of time. We calibrate professional learning to the scale of years rather than weeks or months. Our aim is to grow into a community that learns, to shape a culture of inquiry; this take spacious time and is far from efficient—but it is soul-nourishing and deeply sustaining for intellect and heart.

Leadership for Culture-Making

What are the leadership implications when we conceptualize professional learning as the work of culture-making?

A pedagogical leader holds the space for generativity. Her focus is on the thinking and learning process; she's not outcome- or results-driven, but invites reflection on values and vision and the ways in which they are expressed in practice. She orients the community towards experimentation, improvisation, imagination, and seeks substantive and provocative questions for the community to engage.

A pedagogical leader cultivates in herself and in the community an appreciation for and aptitude with complexity. She welcomes disequilibrium and aims to unsettle the community's thinking. Rather than settling into the easy, if dull, terrain of pre-formulated learning activities, a pedagogical leader stirs the community to journey together into the complex landscape of teacher research, of collective inquiry, and the puzzlements and intellectual challenge that lives there.

A pedagogical leader seeks to increase the diversity of perspectives that contribute to a conversation, understanding that many stories can be true at the same time. Systems consultant Tenneson Woolf reminds us that the essential capacity for engaging a multiplicity of stories is curiosity rather than certainty.[4] A pedagogical leader calls forward this capacity to slow down and ask questions, to dance with contradiction, to stay humble and self-reflective and tentative about making conclusions.

A pedagogical leader develops intellectual discipline in the community, the discipline that is necessary for collaborative study and intentional action. This discipline takes the form of a shared commitment to protocols for teacher research, dynamic approaches to collaboration across divergent perspectives, and thorough examination of daily routines and inherited practices like circle time, naptime, and mealtime.

A pedagogical leader links theory and practice in a continual conversation. She guides the community to reflect on teaching practices, which leads to the development of pedagogical understandings. And she offers theoretical frameworks to examine in relationship to the community's experiences. This braiding together of theory and practice is at the heart of collectively constructed knowledge; it carries the community into an always-stronger culture of inquiry.

A pedagogical leader tells the stories of the community— stories about children, stories about educators, stories about families. She understands that stories affirm a community's sense of identity, serving as a mirror in which we see who we have been, who we are now, and who we are becoming.

In these ways, a pedagogical leader orients her work towards culture-making rather than maintaining efficiencies and compliance. She serves as a catalyst for individual teachers, families, and children to grow together into a community that learns, innovates, imagines, and inspires.

A Community of Shared Intent and Practice

Margie Carter

When I work with administrators who want to improve quality in their programs, I offer a challenge to expand their thinking. "Beyond getting accredited or improving scores in a rating system, what do you want to be known for?" Sometimes I get push-back: "Do you mean, what do I think is possible?" I make a gentle correction: "What would you like to imagine is possible?" This exploration is one of those dances that Ann speaks about. How do we define and chart a course for ourselves, pursuing the question of who we really want to be, while others impose a more constrained accountability system?

The contrast of "drive-through training" with the Slow Food movement offers some important clarity. Many of us feel a sense of urgency for the early childhood education field. When our passions flow deep and we see quality compromised, we are tempted to shout, in Director Luz Casio's words, "We are wasting these precious years of children's brain development!" Luz is a gentle, fierce warrior on behalf of the children, staff, and families of her bilingual program serving low-income children. But she tries to catch her breath, slow down, recognize, and recalibrate: "I want to build the dispositions and brain muscles of reflective practice."

Wise woman, Luz, moving beyond the role of a supervisor focused on the urgent demands of the day, and offering us a window into a daily mantra of a pedagogical leader. In our urgency about making sure children learn what they need to know in order to be successful in school, we can easily shortchange an educator's right to think and mull, study and seek wider perspectives for their work. The frenetic energy that shapes the program called "Race to the Top" too often finds a parallel expression in overlooking that this is a lifelong learning journey both for children and their educators.

Ann suggests choreography for a difficult dance Luz must undertake, especially in a program with funding streams tethered to tight timelines and a more restricted view of outcomes.

When we shape professional learning as pedagogical practice, we commit to the long haul and take the long view of time. We calibrate professional learning to the scale of years rather than weeks or months.

How do we find a rhythm and partners for a dance of this scale? I coach pedagogical leaders to conceptualize and choreograph their moves in three time blocks:

1. What could I start doing next week? (It doesn't cost a penny to shift your own disposition and vision, and your view of what children, families, and staff deserve.)

2. What could I potentially shift by the end of a year? (Perhaps revamp staff hiring and orientation practices, re-make the focus of staff meetings, and issue a call for educators to join and share the results of a collaboratively developed research project.)

3. What systems do I want to have in place within five years? (The journey to align values with organizational culture and practices.)

Of course, most new dances require a learning curve, ample practice, and a good sense of humor over missteps. It helps to engage in reconnaissance, both on and off the dance floor. Perhaps you'll seek out a pedagogical coach, take a leadership class, or attend a study tour to dance with the stars. Any of these could be part of a strategic plan to help you undertake the work of defining and living your values as a leadership team of an early childhood program.

Sustained Study of Substantive Ideas

Luz Casio offers inspiration as a pedagogical leader who, in Ann's words, works with "a conviction of who we will be together." Luz honed her knowledge and skills by pursuing the roles of coach, student, administrator, and part-time adjunct faculty at a community college. Luz learned English as a second language as an adult. She amassed and read, in English, a large professional library, and guides her staff in their focused study of these books, bringing to life what Ann calls "the intellectual discipline that is necessary for collaborative study and intentional action." Despite demands on her time to adhere to her multiple funding accountability systems, Luz stays focused on the outcomes that *she* values and wants to collect evidence for:

Outcomes for children:
- Growing in trust and confidence from being in a culturally safe, joyful place.
- Being curious and loving to learn.
- Developing a strong identity as a learner and as a member of a culture and community.
- Going to kindergarten with a photo book about their strengths and 'funds of knowledge' so they are seen and known right away by their new teachers.

Outcomes for teachers:
- Seeing children's strengths and competencies rather than deficits.
- Having a new sense of curiosity and purpose in their role as teacher.
- Gaining confidence in using observations and writing meaningful learning stories.
- Finding their own voice and leadership style.
- Enjoying their work and imagining a career in early childhood education.
- Becoming an advocate.[5]

These outcomes, articulated as her organization's primary commitments, serve as touchpoints as Luz plans professional learning. They guide her decision-making as she designs educator meetings and in-service days, and commits funds to provide opportunities for her teachers to take classes, attend study tours, or develop presentations for conferences. Luz holds tight to these resonant outcomes, especially in the time-crunch flood of other demands that she demonstrate accountability for more narrowly conceived outcomes linked to school readiness and achievement.

Ann braids words that reflect complex, stirring ideas for us. I must read some of her sentences over and over:

> Professional learning strengthens the identity of an early childhood program: its touchstone considerations are 'Who are we as a community? How will we live into our vision?' When we commit to pedagogical practice as professional learning, we take up the work of collaborative research and study; that work, in turn, strengthens our capacity for collaborative research and study. We grow into being teacher researchers, rather than waiting to give teacher research a try until we feel we've figured it out. We learn who we are as we live into the community we seek to be. In this way, we create community that is not an aggregate of individuals, but a community of shared intent and collective practice.

As I read, Luz comes to mind and I can picture this braiding process as she brings values and vision to life in her program. When I revisit Ann's list of practices for pedagogical leaders, I can see traces of Luz in each one. She reminds me that yes, yes, yes, I've seen versions of this in centers where directors develop themselves as pedagogical leaders and understand professional learning as the work of culture-making.

• •

What do you understand as the elements of a learning culture in an organization?

• •

Using these elements, how would you assess the learning culture for adults in your current work?

• •

E.L. Doctorow once said that 'writing a novel is like driving a car at night. You can see only as far as your headlights, but you can make the whole trip that way.' You don't have to see where you're going, you don't have to see your destination or everything you will pass along the way. You just have to see two or three feet ahead of you. This is right up there with the best advice about writing, or life, I have ever heard.

—Anne Lamott[8]

6

A Principle *for* Reimagining Our Work:
Engage with Educators as you Hope They Will Engage with Children

Lilian Katz offers a strong challenge to those of us whose work is primarily with educators in the context of professional learning. She says:

> Some in-service educators are especially intent on getting something accomplished for the children, and seem to construe the situation as 'getting to the kids through the teachers.' If we want to help children (and no doubt we do), then we should do so directly instead of trying to 'use' teachers. The focus should be on helping the teachers as persons worthy of our concern and caring in their own right. Define [your] role as someone who helps and works with teachers for their own sakes. When we do that wholeheartedly and well, the children will surely benefit also.[1]

Katz asks us to bring to educators the same deep regard that we hope educators bring to children, the same devoted concern for their well-being, the same commitment to support their growth and joy. I read this as a call to align our convictions about educators with our convictions about children, giving coherence to our leadership.

What we believe about children's rights and capacities informs how we craft professional learning. If we believe that children are capable of inquiry and are active constructors of knowledge, then we create opportunities for exploration that grow from and speak into children's passions and pursuits and their developmental unfolding. And we provide educators with support for reflective, responsive planning. Educators, in turn, engage children with curiosity and attention, with the dispositions of researchers, seeing children as the source of curriculum.

If, however, we believe that children are more capable of accumulating and memorizing information than of constructing knowledge, we line their days with skill-and-drill, scripted curriculum. And we train educators to be technicians, lead them through workshops full of how-to activities, lesson plans, and protocols for assessment that give them scripts for what to do and say in the classroom. Educators, then, look to activity books as sources for curriculum, and focus most of their attention on managing behavior issues and discipline challenges. Here's how I hope that educators engage with children:

- I hope that educators hold children in the highest regard.

- I hope that educators invite children to stretch even as they affirm children's competence and knowledge.

- I hope that educators honor heart and spirit as well as mind.

- I hope that educators plan responsively and with curiosity, with clearly articulated values and pedagogical commitments.

- I hope that educators make children's learning visible to them, as well as their questions and misunderstandings, in a way that invites further questioning and learning.

- I hope that educators engage children in the pursuit of an idea over long stretches of time.

- I hope that educators are willing to be changed by what they learn from and with children.

And here's how I hope that pedagogical leaders engage with educators:

- I hope that we hold educators in the highest regard.

- I hope that we invite educators to stretch even as we affirm their competence and knowledge.

- I hope that we honor heart and spirit as well as mind.

- I hope that we plan for professional learning responsively and with curiosity, with clearly articulated values and pedagogical commitments.

- I hope that we make educators' learning visible to them, as well as their questions and misunderstandings, in a way that invites further questioning and learning.

- I hope that we engage educators in the pursuit of an idea over long stretches of time.

- I hope that we are willing to be changed by what we learn from and with educators.

When we engage educators as we hope they engage children, we see them as capable participants in the project of inquiry, rather than as instructors whose job is to transmit content knowledge and academic skills to children. We see them as innovators, rather than technicians, as creators rather than consumers— people who generate questions and insights and new knowledge.

Listen to how Louise Boyd Cadwell describes the dispositions of educators:

> We want to know what the children think, feel, and wonder. We believe that the children will have things to tell each other and us that we have never heard before. We are always listening for a surprise and the birth of a new idea. This practice supports a mutual quest for understanding.[2]

Pedagogical leaders hold this same mindset about educators. We're curious to know what educators think, feel, and wonder. We expect to learn from them, as well as with them. We anticipate that educators will give birth to new ideas—not just new to them, but new to us. We join educators on a mutual quest for understanding, just as they join children on such a quest.

Embodying a Commitment to Congruity

This understanding that we ought to engage with educators as we hope they engage with children has been called "the principle of congruity" by Lilian Katz—"a kind of consistency, harmony, or concordance between the way we teach teachers and the way we want them to teach."[3] Pedagogical leadership supports the process of inquiry with educators, so that they, in turn, can support the process of inquiry with children.

It's easy to stumble here. We can be seduced into thinking that what we have to offer is the top priority for educators' learning, believing that our perspectives and experience, our knowledge of teaching strategies, our understandings of child development and behavior issues ought to have a primary position in our interactions with educators. We fall back on traditional models of adult education, typically drawn from our experiences in high school and college courses. But we'd wince if children's teachers carried this approach into their classrooms, foregrounding their ideas, their experiences, their voices.

The notion of congruity asks that we recognize that our ideas and experiences have a place in the conversation, but not the dominant place. Our goal as pedagogical leaders is to cultivate a community that learns, a community that walks together—a community of thinkers, discovering questions and constructing knowledge together. Our contribution to this community is not instructional, but investigative, exploratory, experimental—improvisational rather than prescriptive.

An invigorating idea! But what does this look like, in practice? How do we embody a commitment to congruity? We can begin with our organizational systems and policies:

- How might we structure our welcome and orientation for new staff, so that it parallels how we hope educators welcome and orient children and their families?

- How might we organize staff meetings and professional learning days, so that they parallel the rigorous discussions of substantive ideas that we hope educators have with children?

- How might we organize consistent and substantive reflection time for educators, so that it parallels how we hope educators offer children unhurried time for meaning-making, both on their own and in collaboration with each other?

- How might we structure staff evaluations, so that the process parallels how we hope educators invite children to reflect on their learning?

Let's play with one of these areas, tease it open a bit ...

Consider staff meetings and professional learning days. In the annual cycle of many early childhood programs, these hold a rotation of topics—health and safety practices, literacy activities, holiday planning, sensory play—familiar content, discrete bits and bobs that touch on a range of considerations.

Similarly, in many early childhood classrooms, educators offer a rotation of activities aligned with academic or developmental goals, seasonal holidays, or trivial pursuits—enjoyable and innocuous at best, tedious at times, never too long-lasting.

But what about intellectual vitality? What about the life of the mind—questioning, analyzing, inventing? What about heart, aesthetics, culture?

• • • • • • If we hope that educators configure their classrooms as lively homes for significant undertakings, for in-depth investigations, for energizing experimentation, for encountering and negotiating different perspectives, then we ought to re-make our staff meetings and professional learning days in the spirit of congruity.

We can take up a year-long (or longer!) professional learning focus, exploring one big idea from a range of vantages, over the course of the year's staff meetings and in-service days. Our professional learning can become a year-long graduate seminar, choosing one question to study, a question that reverberates: What is learning? What is social justice teaching in our center? What is teacher research? What is documentation? What is school readiness? What is authentic collaboration with parents?

We can dive deep into these sorts of questions, not moving towards predetermined answers or outcomes, but towards an always-stronger identity as a community that learns. Rather than trying to "cover" all the content that educators might master, we can offer intellectually, spiritually, emotionally invigorating learning that strengthens the dispositions at the heart of a community committed to inquiry—dispositions to think, wonder, question, take risks, and listen beyond assumptions.

Carrying a Commitment to Congruity into the Life of the Community

Organizational systems and culture set the tone for other expressions of congruity:

What are the many ways that we can build substantive, challenging collaboration into the community? Opportunities for children and adults to cross-pollinate ideas, to be challenged and stretched by encountering startling perspectives, to disagree, to wrestle with their differing understandings and approaches?

How do we invite adults and children to linger in generative space? How can we build spaciousness into our thinking and doing, so that ideas can stay unfinished for awhile, so that we have time to ponder, to follow the thread of an idea to see where it leads us? Time to revisit and revise our earlier thinking? How do we embrace mistakes, and invite examination of mistakes, looking for the seeds of new understandings? How do we allow ourselves to meander into unexpected places?

How do we invite and honor cultural knowledge into our center? Children's cultural knowledge, educators' cultural knowledge, families' cultural knowledge? And, hand-in-hand with this, how do we welcome expertise, insight, and wisdom from arenas beyond teaching and learning—poetry, for example, and athletics, and natural history?

In what ways do we make visible the learning and questioning of the community? When we consider documentation as public inquiry, how do our stories change? Are we including multiple perspectives, questions, and uncertainties in our documentation and display? Are we using documentation as a way to strengthen our identity as a community that learns?

The work of educators is to support children to be as human as they can be. When we embody a commitment to congruity, our work as pedagogical leaders is clear: to support educators to be as human as they can be, engaged whole-heartedly and with the fullness of their intellect in the unfolding, unpredictable, perplexing, delighting life we share with children and families.

Engage with Educators as you Hope They Will Engage with Children

· 131 ·

Lingering in Generative Space

Margie Carter

It seems to me that, in this chapter, Ann adds to our understanding of the Golden Rule, a call to the ethics of reciprocity found in nearly every religious tradition. It ought to be obvious that our beliefs about children inform how we structure professional learning experiences for educators—that notion of congruity that Lilian Katz signals. So, for example, if we envision that educators will offer children in-depth investigation projects, then the educators need the experience of those sorts of projects as part of their own learning. When I've suggested this to administrators, they've called out all sorts of barriers: Time for off-the-floor paid professional learning is so limited, and must address annual required trainings. They want their teachers to deepen their understandings of learning domain content such as math and science, language and literacy. And, they argue, shouldn't my educators have the chance to benefit from immediate consideration of applied cutting-edge research, such as brain science which illuminates approaches to helping children with neurological differences, childhood trauma, second language learning, and self-regulation?

We've worked around these barriers in a range of ways. One powerful approach has been to re-conceptualize and re-structure the use of staff meetings and professional learning days; we acknowledge the challenges of losing momentum because of staff turnover and we establish a course of reflection and study for the staff that offers multiple entry points. It does no good to rush through any learning you want to offer your educators. Any knowledge that will benefit their practice has to be made their own and explored in a variety of ways over time. Perhaps the exception to this are those required trainings that must be repeated every year on topics such as safe food handling, and emergency preparedness.

My suggestion is that you handle required trainings in a way that keeps the review lively, rather than deadly, by transforming the content into games, the same way you can get children ready for school culture by playing "the kindergarten game" just before they leave your program. One center I've worked with made a mandated training on blood-born pathogens into a new game every year—from Pictionary to charades, crossword puzzles to the radio quiz show "Wait, Wait, Don't Tell Me" to "Two truths and a lie." Important content and updates were reviewed, but equally important, the dispositions of playfulness were continually renewed.

Places to Flourish

What comes to mind when you hear Ann's term "lingering in generative space?" If you, like me, are a person who enjoys poking around the internet for examples of ideas, you'll appreciate what you uncover about generative spaces. Initially coined as a term with regard to designing a health care environment as "a place to flourish," the concept is explored on education sites as well. Ann offers us a captivating picture of how a generative environment helps adults and children flourish in their collective identity as a learning community.

Pedagogical leaders understand that they have an active role in cultivating the conditions necessary for a generative environment—conditions that include building trusting relationships; nurturing a desire to contribute ideas; creating opportunities to grow as professionals. For conversations to generate new ideas, it's important to keep core values in the spotlight in tandem with specific agreements about supporting each other's learning.[4] Some may call this setting ground rules, but I think of it more like digging and fertilizing the soil to establish healthy roots. To create brave spaces, in which people take risks, open themselves with vulnerability, and avoid defensiveness and judgment, it's necessary to uncover and articulate what respect and trust look and sound like. That can happen through establishing group agreements.

In our book, *Reflecting in Communities of Practice*, my co-authors and I describe group agreements like this:

Setting agreements for group processes is [a] key element in establishing trust and productive reflection between members. Agreements help establish expectations for group participation and remind members to consider others' learning needs. They help curb unproductive behaviors and serve as a 'grounding' place if discussions get heated. Your agreements set the tone for your group's collaborative culture …

However you develop your agreements, keep the list short, focused on essentials, and stated as commitments to act or behave in certain ways rather than as more general beliefs. For instance, rather than saying 'we will show each other respect,' say what respect might look like. 'We will show each other respect by listening thoughtfully and not interrupting.'[5]

Ann Hatherly reminds us that, "Culture in the organizational sense is the unique combination of values, assumptions and beliefs that builds over time when people work together. It is a set of informal expectations which shapes the way people think, feel and act."[6] In setting a course towards becoming a community that learns, an early and essential protocol is to reflect on how people in the community learn best, so that this can be honored as the community thinks and reflects together.

Creating agreements about how you want to be together unleashes a willingness to take risks and offer innovative ideas. With a set of agreements, work conversations will become more honest, productive, and creative. People will be willing to risk suggesting an idea that is off the beaten path. They will listen more carefully to each other and find connections between their ideas.

Done well, this practice mirrors what educators aim for with children: not lists of rules posted on the wall and used for behavior management, but a way to make visible the culture that the community will strive to create together, by how they behave with each other.

Setting the stage with agreements allows us to go deeper and wider in our conversations. Building on the foundation of agreements, a group could take up any of the four questions Ann offers at the end of this chapter to begin lingering in generative space.

· ·

What are the many ways that we can build substantive, challenging collaboration into the community?

· ·

How do we invite adults and children to linger in generative space?

· ·

How do we invite and honor cultural knowledge into our center?

· ·

In what ways do we make visible the learning and questioning of the community?

· ·

I urge you to be teachers so that you can join with children as the co-collaborators in a plot to build a little place of ecstasy and poetry and gentle joy.

—Jonathan Kozol[9]

7

A Principle *for* Reimagining Our Work:

Come Together with Families as Collaborators, Colleagues, and Critical Friends

Families are central characters in every child care program, but often they are two-dimensional characters. They exist primarily as adjuncts to their children: they're the people who drop off the children, pick up the children, and manage the home front. And—they exist as irritants to educators: they don't read our documentation, they're late picking up their children, they send their children to child care when they're sick, they pack unhealthy lunches, they ask us to pay unreasonable attention to their children's sleep schedules.

These are the ways we typically talk about parents, yes? In our field, we've fallen into the habit of dismissing parents' concerns as exasperating distractions from the work we value: "They want us to get their children ready for school; they don't see that play is children's work!" We diminish parents' humanity, we belittle their concerns in our staff room conversations, we try to "educate" them about their children's growth.

We claim our classrooms as our turf, and we have a lot of power there. Even in classrooms which emphasize parent engagement, as with Head Start, the program takes the lead on fundamental planning. Program staff establish the classroom aesthetic and the rituals and the daily rhythms. Typically, teachers or administrators set the rules for behavior and the expectations for participation. They determine the curriculum, choose the books and materials, and lead the conversations. And, typically, program staff post sign-in sheets and family message boards at classroom doorways, and, so, mark the boundary between home and child care, between family life and life in early childhood centers.

In many ways, we're stuck in a model of relationships derived from elementary and middle school, in which roles are more tightly—or succinctly— defined. Teachers teach, they're the experts in education. Parents ensure their children's attendance, stay informed about what's happening at school, support the professionals, and do their part at home. They may even volunteer or work as aides at school—but under the direction of educators.

But we're not teaching school. Our arena is child care and early education, and that's a whole different context. The people we spend our days with, most intimately, are babies and young, young children—people who have been alive on this planet for only a few years, people who are new to the world, people who deserve great tenderness and care. In our context, parents are absolutely responsible for ensuring that children are cared for according to their values and hopes, and we educators and caregivers are responsible for offering our fullest attention and mindfulness. If we narrow the relationship between parents and educators to sharing information, we fail to acknowledge the potent and staggering honor of caring for children's well-being that we share.

And it is a staggering honor: families entrust their children to our care often before they know us. Likely, they've met the director, and probably they've toured the center, but, if they've encountered us at all, it's usually with a wave and a smile, or a quick and superficial exchange. On their children's first day in our care, parents leave their children with strangers, and that flies in the face of everything they're wired to do: to keep their children safe; to know, in particular and intimate detail, about their children's moment-to-moment lives; to play a primary role in each unfolding day and each wakeful night. Such trust, to leave their children in the care of others! Imagine the additional weight of trust that immigrant families feel, knowing that if they were swept up in an immigration raid, their children would be left with us until emergency plans could be launched.

We should be brought to our knees with humility in the face of parents' high trust, brought to our knees with the weight of responsibility. When we look through this lens of humility and responsibility, we know the essential role of genuine relationships between families and early childhood educators, but, too often, we're not looking through this lens, but through the lens of habit and convenience, and what we see, looking through that lens, are borders between us and families.

Building Invisible Borders

We manifest borders—intentionally or not—when we ask families to "volunteer" to do what we want them to do: to drive us around on field trips, to do the classroom's laundry and cleaning, to build playground equipment and run bake sales.

Borders are manifest when we ask families to attend parent conferences in which we control the conversation, dispensing information about their children and asking parents to share personal information with us.

Borders are manifest when we expect families to come to family meetings whose agendas are long lists of our rules and expectations.

We inherit these borders from a model of school that doesn't fit our circumstance, and we create these borders by our beliefs and attitudes.

I know. I'm speaking from long personal experience …

———

For sixteen years, I worked in a full-day child care center in Seattle which served families privileged by race, class, and education. The parents were architects and software designers, doctors and attorneys and financial consultants. When I began teaching at Hilltop, I felt "less than" the families: I saw a great distance between their affluent lives and my low-income, low-status identity as a child care teacher. I felt awkward with them, and self-protective.

I claimed the classroom as my own. I was warm and thoughtful in my conversations with families and in the written documentation that I crafted for them—and I was clear about what I hoped the families would bring to the classroom, which wasn't much. I was "the educator" and they were "the parents," and I had the classroom well in hand.

But when the children and I began to take on social justice activism, building from the anti-bias goals for teaching and learning[1], the nicely-manicured borders that I'd constructed between myself and the families became tangled and entangling, and, soon enough, were in the way. To take up issues of fairness and unfairness with the children, I had to have real conversations with families, conversations that had an edge of vulnerability and self-disclosure. Parents and I shared our experiences of injustice and privilege, we talked about our values and beliefs, about what we hoped children would know—and not know—about issues of race, and disability, and militarism, and lesbian and gay rights. And as we had these real conversations, I began to see the parents as real people, more dynamic and multi-dimensional than "working parents" or "affluent parents." They became real people, with lives and stories that reached beyond their parenting. And I began to offer myself as a real person, with a life and stories that reached beyond my teaching.

And the borders that I'd so carefully tended gradually became irrelevant and foolish.

———

When we live separated by borders, it's easy to lose sight of the essential humanity of the people on the other side. I did that, when I reduced the parents at Hilltop to two dimensions: their role as parents and their affluence. I had to take myself in hand, set myself on a course to a new way of seeing and being with parents. I learned from the educators at Chicago Commons, a publicly-funded program serving low-income families—a setting wildly different than the program where I worked. The educators at Commons challenged themselves to remake their image of parents living with the insecurity and viciousness of poverty and racism, seeing them, not as incapacitated by their circumstances, but as insightful, rich in internal resources, and eloquent about their dreams for and commitments to their children. The educators at Commons taught me the necessary value of seeing families in three dimensions, with a lens that illuminated their humanity.

Parents are too busy, we say, explaining the borders we've put in place. They're stressed out, they're crunched for time, and so we shouldn't ask much of them, or, when we do, we shouldn't be surprised when they disappoint us. Or we spin in a different direction: parents are *over-involved*, *too demanding*, have *unrealistic expectations* for their children or for us, they're *helicopter parents*, and so we should be wary of their requests, ready to fend them off. We should keep a tight rein on what we're willing to accommodate. Or—another storyline that we follow— parents aren't very good at parenting: they're inattentive, harsh with their children, they let them eat junk food, and allow too much screen time. These simplistic caricatures of parents allow us educators to live comfortably on our side of the border, not tending particularly closely to the people on the other side.

Crossing the Border

A simple, powerful act of curiosity can carry us across the border: who are the people who live on the other side? Border crossing begins when we consider parents' perspectives as human beings, complex and with wide-ranging lives. How would parents like us to think of them? What do parents want us to understand about their lives, their strengths, their longings? Several years ago, to anchor a staff conversation about our relationships with parents, I asked families at Hilltop: What do you want our staff to know about your life? Listen to their answers:

> "I feel some vulnerability as a parent—I see my parenting flaws and I see how skillful teachers are, and I feel self-conscious sometimes. I need teachers to create a safe climate for me."

> "We need you to understand and support that there are many reasons that parents work and that it does not necessarily indicate less interest or concern in child rearing."

> "We are concerned about balancing our lives and our children's lives— play/work, explore/teach, goof off/be responsible."

"My career is important to me and I hope I am a good role model for my kids, working in a field I'm passionate about, doing work that I believe is important."

I asked another question: What are your strengths as parents? What a gorgeous list they created! Compassion for children's issues; a strong focus on children; openness, warmth, acceptance; perseverance; recognition of my shortcomings; patience and flexibility; consistency; a sense of humor.

• • • • • Borders begin to dissolve when we consciously shift our ways of thinking about parents, focusing, not on their stresses and failings, but on their strengths, the emotional and psychic resources that parents offer, their tenderness, full-heartedness, complexity.

Whether our programs serve families who grapple daily with the violence of poverty and racism or families wrapped in the comforts of privilege, we can change our thinking, and see parents as strong: eager to understand, grow, discover, investigate; curious to discover both the power and fragility of their children; powerful in their bonds with their children, which makes them active, responsible partners in the growth of their children; eager to reflect on and rethink their experiences; and able to act on behalf of their own children and all children.

This way of understanding parents moves us from a deficit orientation to an orientation anchored by regard, and curiosity, and humility. It carries us across the border that divides "parents" from "educators" and into the possibility for human relationship, person to person.

Listen to this strong offering by Paola Cagliari, a leader in the schools of Reggio Emilia, Italy:

An essential motivation which leads each of us to communication is the perception that the other is willing to listen, is interested, respectful and acknowledges your capacities and competencies. Communicating means exposing yourself. Who of us would choose to expose herself or himself in a context that is indifferent, prejudicial, unappreciative, judgmental or even hostile?

When a school denies parents the right to participation, it commits an act of violence.

If parents seem not to be interested in our program, there's a reason, and if we believe them not to be interested, what is our reason? And what will we do? Are we prepared to have competent parents in our school? To let go of our absolute control?[2]

Competent parents: competent to understand the intricacies of classroom life; competent to engage in dialogue across differences; competent to challenge our teaching practices; competent to shape the culture of our child care centers; competent to share, with us, the creative work of making community.

To see parents as competent requires that we loosen our grip on our classrooms and our centers, that we step away from the belief that educators ought to have the final, determinative voice in making essential decisions about the nature and shape of life in our programs. Paola Cagliari frames the possibilities for relationships like this: "In the alliances between parents and teachers, we have the opportunity to be close to the children."[3]

That's a powerful word, *alliance*. It's defined in Webster's dictionary as an association of groups, or people, or nations who share a common aim. It comes from the Old French word for a *relative, a kinsman*, a word that means *unite, bind to*.

Alliances: binding together as kin, sharing a common aim.

Alliances don't have boundaries; they don't have carefully protected turf. Alliances are family relationships, messy, full of surprise and delight, deeply emotional, intimate, challenging. Alliances are adventures, long and complex journeys undertaken with commitment and curiosity.

Our alliances with families hold the promise of open-hearted relationships in which we move beyond the formal roles of "educator" and "parent" and open our lives to each other as passionate, foolish, tenderhearted people. Parents will do things that irritate us, of course; that's the nature of relationships, and we'll irritate the parents right back. But we can keep our focus on building alliances with parents rather than getting snared by our self-protectiveness, fear, and annoyance.

Alliances connote mutual participation, shared effort and engagement. We educators can expect to learn from families, to be changed by our relationships with families. We offer ourselves as real people to families, sharing our lives beyond our teaching. And we involve families in the work of constructing our programs.

Alliances with families create the context in which children can be best supported. Children feel securely held when key adults in their lives stand in a close and caring circle around them, and, securely held, they are easy in their lives and able to give themselves over to their emotional, intellectual, physical, and spiritual developmental work.

So, how do we create new possibilities for relationships with families—relationships that work as bridges that link allies, rather than borders that keep us separate?

We can begin with our language.

A cornerstone role that a pedagogical leader plays in an early childhood program is to call the community into self-examination, holding up the mirror of values and vision. She asks questions that shine bright light into shadowed corners, directing our attention at the habits we've formed in our conversations and our practice, habits that accrue to shape the culture of our community. "Who are we as a community?" a pedagogical leader asks. "Does our way of talking about families express the vision we hold for ourselves? Does it align with the values that we seek to embody?"

At Hilltop, we used to talk about "parent participation." We meant a passive, teacher-directed role for parents. It was more about delegation than active, substantive, influential involvement by parents. Then our pedagogical leader introduced us to the writing of Jim Greenman, who says: "Full partnership between a family and the child care center means that a family will have significant influence over their child's experience at the center: his or her care and education. ... Partnerships are about power and shared decision-making."[4]

From *participation* to *partnership*: from *borders* to *alliances*: a change of language, suggested our pedagogical leader, could help us consider our behavior with families. How might we live into *alliances*, our pedagogical leader asked. How might we share power and decision-making with parents?

Sharing Power

Our pedagogical leader suggested that we turn first to our classroom environments. We asked families to bring in family photos and to create pages for a family book, to share images and stories from their weekends. We held gatherings during which families painted tea cups for their children, or decorated pillow cases for their children's nap pillows, or designed special treasure boxes for each child. These sorts of invitations were lovely, and warm, and heart-felt, and parents were glad to jump in with us, to offer something of themselves into the classroom, as a way to keep their arms around their children while they're apart. These family artifacts were beloved by children, and were held in honor by us.

This was a good beginning. But offerings of photos, of music, of foods that speak to families' identities are not "sharing power," are not "alliances." The invitation to families to bring things to the classroom that make their family lives visible was important—and wasn't enough. It marked the beginning of the journey toward relationship, not the end.

And so, our pedagogical leader challenged us to take up another question, one that carried us beyond environmental changes. How could we invite families into shared decision-making, into shaping the daily life and the curriculum of the classroom?

We considered where we tended to have our most substantial, formal interactions with families: at parent conferences and family meetings. Our pedagogical leader turned our attention to those gatherings, and asked: What does our approach to family meetings and parent conferences communicate about what we believe the relationship between parents and teachers ought to be?

We were unsettled by our answer. We organized our family meetings around presentations by us educators about program logistics, our expectations for families, our teaching practices and curriculum plans. They communicated that we saw parents as people who ought to follow the rules that we set about how things happened at our center.

Hand-in-hand with this approach to family meetings, we took a traditional approach to parent conferences: one teacher, one family, a developmental assessment disguised as a lovely hand-made book with a personally written narrative, but still, an evaluative document. Our conferences communicated that we believed that families were passive recipients of our expert opinions about their children.

But we *said* that we valued meaningful collaboration with families, and that we were eager for shared reflection and meaning-making with families. We *said* that we believed that learning happens in relationship.

And so, we worked with our pedagogical leader to re-make our family meetings and parent conferences to bring us into better alignment with what we valued.

Family Meetings with Relationship at the Center

We looked at the long lists of logistics and classroom details that typically filled the family meetings, and worked with the pedagogical leader to gather them into an in-depth orientation package to give families when they enrolled. Now, the family meetings were wide open for us to use in service of relationships.

We decided to center our family meetings around a focused conversation about a specific question. Each classroom teaching team chose a question that genuinely interested them, an idea they were curious to explore over the course of the year with families, questions like: What are the rights of children? What does "school readiness" mean? How do relationships become our curriculum? How might we articulate a "mission statement" for our classroom?

The teaching team prepared for the meeting by talking with the children to learn how they thought about the big question. They shared the children's ideas with families ahead of the conference. The children's insightful perspectives strongly contributed to the depth of conversation during the family meetings.

There was no big intention for a particular outcome or conclusion to the conversation; we imagined it as the beginning of a year-long collaboration in thinking. We did take notes during the meetings and sent those notes to families, and we created display panels that reflected the experiences we shared together during the meetings. Sometimes, there was momentum towards a more formal expression of the shared thinking at these meetings; one year, the families and educators in my classroom crafted a value statement for our year together:

We want children to feel rock-solid safe. We celebrate their uniqueness and want them to be affirmed in their individuality and encouraged to pursue their passions and interests and to cultivate their gifts. Hand in hand with this, we want children to experience community and relationship, to be at ease with a range of people and to deepen their compassion for others. We want there to be room for children's emotions, for exuberant play, for conflict and collaboration, and for quiet introspection. We want the children to learn to act for fairness. We want children to see their lives reflected and affirmed in many ways, so that they develop a sense of their history as thinkers, players, and friends.

Our family meetings included an exchange of gifts. Before the meeting, the children and educators created gifts to welcome families to the meeting and during the meeting, the parents created gifts to leave in the classroom for their children: a mural of self-portraits by the children, for example, which inspired their families to create a mural of their homes laid out along a street; close-up photos of children's hands displayed throughout the classroom, with an invitation to families to find their children's hands (during the meeting, we took photos of parents' hands and added them to the bulletin boards, and, in the days that followed, invited the children to find their parents' hands).

The shift in the focus of our family meetings sparked potent transformation in the relationships among educators and families. The conversations that unfolded during the meetings were lively and immediate, unscripted and collaborative. These conversations continued through the year, as families and educators, together, continued to poke at the questions and ideas that we'd taken up during the meeting: we became thinkers together, constructing new understandings together. During the meetings, we were real with each other, and playful, and generous with our hearts. These first gatherings asked us to see each other in the fullness of our human selves, and the relationships that grew from this transcended narrow "teacher-parent" dynamics.

Collaborative Conferences

Working with our pedagogical leader, we also changed our parent conferences, with a commitment to share power and decision-making with competent parents. We used to do developmental assessments and meet with families to share those assessments. But we *said* we believed that learning happens in relationship, and that we sought to learn from and with families. So, we crafted a new approach to conferences that we called "collaborative conferences."

At Hilltop, children came together in small groups for long-term investigations; we built our collaborative conferences around those long-term investigations, inviting parents to come together with educators to study the children's thinking. We did this while an investigation was in process, not waiting until it was done to "report" on it, but jumping in with families so that we could, together, shape the course of the investigation.

We started a conference by taking up the big idea that the children were wrestling with in their investigation—genuinely, as adults, not role-playing or being disingenuous, but getting our minds around the work that the children were doing. Then we studied traces of children's work—a transcription, a video clip, children's sketches or constructions—to tease out the children's theories and cognitive knots, places where we might lean in for deeper study. We considered each child's contribution to the investigation, and how that reflected her or his developmental trajectory, and where she or he could benefit from more challenge or stretch. Together, teachers and parents planned our next offering to the children's investigation group: families would write to the children with a provocation or with encouragement, or would leave something in the classroom for the children to encounter as part of their on-going work.

Changing the way we offered family conferences reverberated through other aspects of our relationships with families. We were learning to genuinely listen to families, in a powerful and transformative way—to listen in the way that Carla Rinaldi describes: "This courage to listen ... is to say 'I hope to be different when I leave, not necessarily because I agree with you but because your thoughts caused me to think differently.' ... If you believe that others are a source of your learning, your identity, and your knowledge, you have opened an important door to the joy of being together."[5]

Our commitment to collaborative conferences set us on a course towards living into this notion that "others are a source of your learning, your identity, and your knowledge." We developed new ways of understanding what it means to be an educator, seeing ourselves, not as experts delivering assessments, but as people thinking carefully and with no small astonishment and occasional consternation about children's learning, and doing that thinking in collegial and committed relationships with families. We moved from *talking to* families about their children to *thinking with* families about teaching and learning. We moved from hoping that families would be different because of our expert offerings to hoping that we would be different because of our collaborations with families.

Collaboration—partnership—contains disagreement, negotiation, and compromise, for sure, and it also opens into new understandings, warm intimacy, and shared pride. It promises to disrupt our well-established routines and send us, at least temporarily, into uncomfortable disequilibrium. It requires listening with humility and courage, patience, and good humor. We have to re-think our assumptions and reconsider our teaching practices, we have to share the power and decision-making.

Making Ourselves Visible

There's another way in which we can build alliances with families, can become "kin," known to each other human to human. We can offer ourselves to families in real and significant ways, just as we ask families to offer themselves to us. The traditional practice in early education, informed by that misalignment with formal schooling, is a one-way intimacy: educators know a lot of personal information about families' lives, sometimes vulnerable information: divorce, job loss, financial insecurity, illness, challenging family dynamics. But educators are known only as educators, with maybe a few carefully-revealed personal details. We can re-make that culture, so that it's a two-way intimacy.

When we meet with families to learn from them about their children (sometimes visiting their homes), we can ask parents what they'd like to know about us, personally as well as professionally, and we can offer personal stories, not waiting for questions. We could even invite families to visit our homes, instead of going to their homes. That'd sure give us a taste of the personal offering that families experience!

I was nervous when I set myself the challenge of offering myself personally: What would parents ask about me? Typically, they asked things like: Where did I grow up? How did I make my way to Seattle? Where else have I lived? How did I come to be a teacher? What bugs me about my work? If I wasn't a teacher, what would my work be? What do I do on the weekends? Was I married? Did I have children? Were my parents alive? Do I have brothers or sisters? Parents asked the sorts of questions that people might ask each other at a dinner party in the home of a mutual friend, or at a wedding reception, those sorts of social gatherings where some shared connection is assumed as a starting point, and where, often, lovely and genuine exchange happens, human to human.

In addition to these informal ways of making ourselves visible to families, we can commit to a practice of written documentation that is human to human. We can move beyond checklists and learning outcomes, beyond making a report about our assessment of children's learning, and offer stories, real stories, about children's play. We make ourselves visible in those stories that we tell—in what we choose to tell stories about, what we see as important and intriguing and tender. We make ourselves visible with the language we use to tell those stories, and the descriptions we offer of how the children's play touched our hearts, or left us curious, or sparked new understandings. We make ourselves visible when we share our questions and musings about the meaning of the children's play. Our documentation can be a way of being present as a full human being, not just as an evaluator assessing children's learning in a list of benchmarks or outcomes

We can think of our documentation as a conversation rather than as a report. If our documentation is printed on paper, we can suggest that families take their children's journals or portfolios home so that they can linger with them at times that work best for them, after the children are tucked into bed, with a cup of tea, or in the morning over coffee. If our documentation is in digital form, we can be sure that families have a way of accessing it from home. And we can invite families to respond to what we've written about the children's play and about our thinking—ask them to write about what catches their attention, what strikes them as significant, what touches them, what ideas they have for how we might extend or challenge the children's thinking.

• • • • • Documentation can be a dialogue, a sharing of stories and musings, an exchange among partners and allies—among people made kin by their shared commitment to children.

We can approach our use of social media in this way, as well, exchanging notes and photos that invite stories and insight, rather than just a quick chuckle and a "Like."

Using the physical space of our classrooms to make families visible; changing our practices so that we share power and decision-making with families; offering ourselves as full human beings, tender-hearted and curious and uncertain and eager; engaging in conversations rather than lectures or reports: the alliances we build with families create new possibilities for deep engagement with our work, an engagement of mind, heart, and spirit.

Believing that parents are a source of our learning, our identity, our knowledge—and acting on that belief—opens "an important door to the joy of being together."[6]

Margie Carter

The Courage to Listen

So much of what Ann accounts here is a testament to what Brené Brown calls the power of vulnerability. Brown reminds us, as Ann describes so poignantly, "When we shut ourselves off from vulnerability, we distance ourselves from the experiences that bring purpose and meaning to our lives."[7] It's no coincidence that many of our important writers regularly reference courage as an essential quality required for living fully in a fear-filled world. Again, Brown highlights:

> The root of the word *courage* is *cor*—the Latin word for *heart*. In one of its earliest forms, the word *courage* had a very different definition than it does today. Courage originally meant 'To speak one's mind by telling all one's heart.' Over time, this definition has changed, and, today, courage is more synonymous with being heroic.[8]

I see humility, not heroics, in Ann's story, and a potent question: "Are we prepared to have competent parents in our school?" Willing, maybe; curious, perhaps; eager, possibly; but prepared? Ann suggests we have some soul searching to do, as well as some dispositions and skills to develop. Rinaldi mentions the courage to listen.

> This courage to listen … is to say 'I hope to be different when I leave, not necessarily because I agree with you but because your thoughts caused me to think differently.' … If you believe that others are a source of your learning, your identity, and your knowledge, you have opened an important door to the joy of being together.[9]

Imagine hoping to be different as a result of an encounter with listening! Pedagogical leaders can coax along this kind of courage by suggesting that educators "listen for new perspectives you can embrace from parents, just as you listen for them with children." In describing her experience at Hilltop, Ann identifies some serious transformation in their educators:

We moved from *talking to* families about their children to *thinking with* families about teaching and learning. We moved from hoping that families would be different because of our expert offerings to hoping that we would be different because of our collaborations with families.

When educators shift from talking to children to thinking with them, we hope they're changed by their relationships with children. Likewise, we hope this happens in educators' relationships with families. The changer and the changed.

Preparing Ourselves for Competent Listening

Listening for parent perspectives requires not only our ears, but our eyes and hearts. We learn to tune in to the beat of our hearts. This isn't always daisies and sunshine; there can be some painful reckoning for us to do. We may notice in ourselves unexamined assumptions that muffle our understanding of other voices. Ann describes discovering how her attitudes about entitled families placed a border around her heart and restrained her relationships with parents. This is often the case when educators' lives are economically or culturally different than the families we work with. We must tune in to our role in the dynamics of how power is exercised, overtly and covertly. Families may hold us in high esteem, because of their cultural values about educators; or, they may view us as less esteemed employees of their family. Given the legacy of racism, white privilege, and economic disparity, we may be unprepared for a mutually respectful partnership. In what Ann describes as crossing the borders of vulnerability, we may not recognize the micro-aggressions in our talk and actions, ways in which we subtly, without awareness, express prejudiced or privileged attitudes. We may fail to recognize what Norma Gonzalez and her colleagues call "funds of knowledge"—the cultural and experiential wisdom that families hold—because our lens is overly clouded with expected norms or because we neglected to examine our assumptions.[10]

Relationships of trust grow from sharpening our listening and cultural competency. We create the possibility of being changed as we encounter other ways of knowing and living in the world.

Gonzalez outlines areas for deeper awareness and respect as educators listen, do home visits, and come to know children and families, especially with cultures and communities they are not part of and may have blinders about. She suggests that educators and family service workers carefully listen to families with a curious mind and sensitive heart. What they learn will deepen their respect, ground their relationships, and expand their ability to partner well on behalf of children.

- What do you understand about norms or sense-making in households that are different from yours? For example, a family may use a family bed, so when children are put on a solo cot for naptime in your program, they can't find comfort.

- What can you learn about how a family's current home feels in comparison to their sense of place? If they have been in transit for a while, how are they creating something familiar and safe?

- How will you learn their hopes and dreams for their children? And how will you learn the ways in which they want you to support those dreams?

In a conversation with Smart Start's Community Engagement Specialist Mary Jo Deck, I learned of another tool for uncovering funds of knowledge: "PhotoVoice," a qualitative research method designed to capture the voices, contexts, and concerns of individuals through photographs they take.[11] In North Carolina, Deck's organization used a PhotoVoice project to learn from parents about the real issues in their lives that Deck's agency might address. I wonder how this might be adapted for use in early childhood centers to deepen understandings and partnerships with families. We document life in our centers, but what if we offered questions for families to answer with photos from their lives? Could this bring us together in new ways?

Imagine the new appreciations and respect that might emerge when we see photos that capture families' answers to questions like: "What challenges do you face trying to get your child to our center each day?" "Who are heroes and sheroes in your family that help shape how you go about your life?" Deck says the PhotoVoice process at her agency led to deep listening and changed relationships:

> The PhotoVoice process, with the camera or without, offers an open-ended opportunity for parents to talk openly about their lives, share with one another and educate us. What participants choose to photograph not only brings a theme and detail of a story to the group but then frames the conversations and questions that result, offering a clear guide to additional issues that the group has in common.
>
> As the conversations weave in and out of stories and feelings, parents will share what they need, what works and what doesn't. We laugh and share common experiences. For instance, one of the elements highlighted was a series of photos of routine household responsibilities. There are laundry pictures, baskets, both woven fiber and plastic, overflowing; socks and shirts hanging out of dresser drawers and sinks piled with dirty dishes. This was totally spontaneous and four of the six women recorded it.
>
> There were times when each of us held our breath as one individual mom talked about a particularly painful experience and we didn't really know how to respond except to listen. And nod. And know that all we had to offer was the sense of shared understanding. Issues of racial prejudice and economic disparities are powerful negatives that were brought into the conversations. When this happened, suddenly your own biases about these realities were exposed and your preconceptions become empathetic awareness. Then there were other moments when both individuals and the group laughed aloud for long moments when we recognized ourselves in the situation.[12]

PhotoVoice projects sound so relevant to our principle of coming together with families in new ways. Educators study the photos as documentation families bring us. We learn to hear and see differently, becoming changed and more competent in the process.

What are you inspired to try?

Where do you feel vulnerable?

How will you mobilize your courage?

Listen to one another by breathing in the speaker's voice. You breathe in and take the speaker into your lungs and ears and heart.

*—**Maxine Hong Kingston***[10]

8

Pedagogical Practice: The Thinking Lens as a Research Tool

The primary commitment for pedagogical leaders is to shift an organization's focus from regulations, outcomes, and assessments to investigation, experimentation, and reflection. They make this shift by working with the principles that we've been considering, and by putting into place teaching practices that carry a community from instruction to inquiry—practices that cultivate a community that learns.

It can be unnerving for educators to let go of predetermined curriculum and lay down the activity books. Left with nothing to hold onto for guidance when they're asked to "do inquiry," educators can flounder, falling back on tried and familiar lesson plans about topical themes and reaching into their resource boxes full of felt board stories and community helper puppets.

Educators need something to hold onto, something to steady themselves as they step off deeply familiar ground into new terrain. Laying down the lens of checklists and learning activities, educators need a new lens through which to examine their days with children, colleagues, and families. They need a lens for inquiry, a lens for thinking, a lens for research.

Here's a description of teacher research, from Daniel Meier and Barbara Henderson's book, *Learning from Young Children in the Classroom*:

> Teacher research is systematic, critical inquiry made public. As an approach, teacher research provides a habit of mind and a set of tools that help teachers to stop reacting, and begin to see that by just looking, and then telling others what they see, they begin to deepen and clarify their role as early childhood educators.[1]

Meier and Henderson go on to say that teacher research means "framing one's professional life as a set of questions."[2]

This is a potent reconceptualization of what it means to be an educator. We've been seduced by the mindset that our competence as educators is best demonstrated by our success in instruction—by how well we help children develop broad topical knowledge and measurable academic skill. "Teachers *teach*," we think, and so we double down on the learning activities we offer, determined to prove our worth, our right to be called educators. Meier and Henderson provoke us to reconfigure this understanding of our role, emphasizing our capacity to engage questions rather than deliver answers, our ability to look closely and reflect deeply with colleagues, our aptitude as researchers, thinkers, generators of knowledge—people who take up systematic, critical inquiry together.

What does it mean, to be a teacher researcher? Meier and Henderson call forward three core elements: *a habit of mind*: the dispositions of improvisational artists—attentiveness and curiosity, an openness to what offers itself, imaginative engagement with the here-and-now, non-attachment to outcome; *disciplined reflection anchored by a set of tools*; *documentation practices* that emphasize educators' thinking and questioning about the children's thinking and questioning.

We've considered dispositions for teacher research in earlier chapters. Let's hone in, now, on the second element of teacher research. What might be a useful set of tools for teacher research?

Protocols for Inquiry

Neither curriculum books brimming with activities nor detailed assessment checklists cultivate the practice of research. We don't need scripts or lesson plans, but protocols for disciplined and reflective study—protocols for inquiry—research protocols.

A protocol is a process that an organization adopts to put its values and commitments into action. A thinking protocol formalizes an early childhood program's commitment to pedagogical practice, creating shared language and a process for inquiry. It's a way of establishing that "This is how we think together." A protocol carries a program from one year to another, anchoring a community that learns even as there is turnover in staff and administration. Unlike a script, a thinking protocol doesn't direct educators' behavior; rather, it's a tool for improvisation, with a strong emphasis on self-awareness, attentive presence, and appreciation for questions and not-knowing.

A thinking protocol arises from the conviction that "the kind of talking needed to educate ourselves cannot rise spontaneously and unaided from *just* talking. It needs to be carefully planned and scaffolded."[3] A protocol provides a structure for conversations—a structure that a community commits to following in every conversation. It transforms "just talking" into pedagogical discussion.

The Thinking Lens for Learning Together with Children is the thinking protocol that I've used in my teaching practice.[4] It was seeded years ago, when the staff at the child care center where I taught committed to changing our teaching practice, bringing it into alignment with our vision and values about learning and questioning, about collaboration and co-construction of understanding.

For many years, we built our curriculum around folktales. Each month, the director brought to our staff meeting a picture book that told the story of a classic folktale. We'd spend the meeting creating a web of activities inspired by the book that would touch on typical domains like literacy and numeracy, fine and gross motor development, science and art. Each educator would take the web back to her or his classroom, post it on the bulletin board, and launch into carrying out the wide-ranging activities over the course of the month—until we met again the following month to consider another folktale and craft another web.

That practice began to change when we encountered the pedagogical practices in Reggio Emilia. One month, during a staff meeting, we cut short our web building to watch the video, *To Make a Portrait of a Lion*, an imagistic and lyrical offering that traces an investigation of the large marble lions in the city square by the children and educators at La Villetta preschool in Reggio Emilia.[5] I didn't see the whole film; I left the room to cry in the hallway, my tears an upwelling of the longing I felt for the reverberant interplay of mind and heart, spirit and body that the film captured.

Braided into the poetry and visual beauty of the study of lions was potent intellectual engagement with the epistemological study of learning and knowing, full-hearted honoring of fear and courage, invitation into embodied encounters with story and idea. I saw, in that film, a new way to be an educator—and so did other people on the staff. Several of us sought out the mentorship of our staff coach, committing ourselves to living into the ideas offered by the film, living into new possibilities for our work, living into inquiry.

Over the next years, we developed practices and tools to support our commitment. We worked with the Board of Directors to free up money in the budget for a pedagogical leader position (a role that moved from a few hours a week to full time, over a period of ten years). And with the pedagogical leader, we crafted a protocol for critical thinking and reflective practice. Our intention was to give ourselves sturdy guidance to be researchers. We didn't want scripts for what to do, or new lesson plans to replace the old ones. We wanted support for reflective, responsive teaching and learning, for a pedagogical approach to our work. We created the first iteration of what is now the Thinking Lens to formalize our shared commitment to growing a culture of inquiry by giving us shared language and a shared process.

The Thinking Lens begins with observation. We watch and listen to children as they move through their days, curious about and attentive to the shape and texture of their pursuits. Something catches our attention, and we take up the Thinking Lens:

Know yourself. Open your heart to this moment. Be self-aware. Be conscious of the lenses through which we watch and listen to children: our values, beliefs, cultural identities, hopes, irritations, expectations, and institutional pressures. We seek to stay mindful of our perspectives, even as we're curious to understand the children's perspectives.

Take the children's points of view. Crawl into this moment that we're observing and inhabit it as the children inhabit it, seeking to better perceive their understandings and misunderstandings, their questions and theories, their passions and pursuits.

Examine the environment. Consider the influence of the physical space, materials, and use of time on this moment and the possibilities it holds—or stifles—for children. The environment gives us useful information that helps us understand the nuances of this moment; studying the details of the environment informs our meaning-making.

Collaborate with others to expand perspectives. Strive to learn from families about how they understand this moment for their children in light of their values and their vision for their children's learning and growing. Come together with colleagues, each with our unique ways of seeing and thinking, in a dialogue to understand the meaning of this moment for the children. Seek out the perspectives offered by child development and schema theories, by social justice and anti-bias activism, by leading thinkers in our field and in other fields: not just brain development, but dance; not just play research, but poetry.

Reflect and take action. The Thinking Lens asks us to plan and enact one offering to make to children in response to the meaning of this moment that we've observed. Then, we create written documentation that tells the story of this cycle of observation, study, planning, and offering. And we observe and listen again, and move through another cycle of inquiry anchored by the Thinking Lens.

Joining Our Attention to the Children's Attention

When we use the Thinking Lens, we set ourselves in motion as researchers and learners. The process of self-reflection, meaning-making, and responsive planning helps us "stop reacting," it creates open space—breathing space, thinking space—in which we can consider the meaning of the children's play instead of leaping into (re)action. A colleague, Keran Elgie, describes the Thinking Lens as a series of little stop signs reminding educators to pause for reflection. And in those spaces created by the Thinking Lens, we join our attention to the children's attention, as Carrie Melsom suggests, rather than rushing in to ask the children to join their attention to what we think has merit in this moment of their play.[6]

Consider the notion of attention. In *The World Beyond Your Head*, philosopher Matthew Crawford writes: "Attention is the thing that is most one's own: in the normal course of things, we choose what to pay attention to, and in a very real sense this determines what is real for us; what is actually present to our consciousness. Appropriations of our attention are then an especially intimate matter."[7]

How often we appropriate children's attention! We seize children's play, their musings, their conversations to serve the learning goals that have our attention.

• • • • • • When we grab hold of children's play to wrestle it into a "teachable moment," we dishonor their sovereignty as thinkers.

Crawford reminds us: we disrupt the questions, investigations, discoveries, and exchanges that are real to children, substituting in their place the lessons and skills that are real to us.[8] This is instruction for us to be cautious about appropriating children's attention. We must protect children's right to investigative, inventive, relational thought—their right to pursue what has their attention. The Thinking Lens slows us down, holds us back from subverting children's attention to our own purposes—at least, not without thoughtful consideration of what has the children's attention and what our purposes might be.

In an interview with Krista Tippet on the public radio broadcast, "On Being," poet Mary Oliver described the value of "listening convivially."[9] She said, "Attention without feeling is just reporting. Empathy is what transforms it."[10] Convivial listening, empathetic attention: this is the sort of presence we are called into by the Thinking Lens. We witness children's lives with self-awareness (*know yourself; open your heart to this moment*), with generous curiosity (*take the children's points of view*), with humility and openness (*collaborate with others to expand perspectives*). And then, only after this mindful witness and far-reaching consideration, do we take action. This is teacher research, moving beyond quick action and reaction to "just looking"—convivially, empathetically—and digging into what we see, and wonder, and feel, and are confounded by, and intrigued about, and pulled

The Thinking Lens© for Learning Together with Children

· ·

Know yourself. Open your heart to this moment.

What is your immediate response to the children's play and conversation? What feelings stir in you? What touches your heart as you watch and listen? What in your background and values is influencing your response to this situation? What adult perspectives, i.e. standards, health and safety, time, goals are on your mind? What leaves you curious, eager to engage?

· ·

Take the children's points of view.

What are the children trying to figure out? What theories are they testing? What questions are they asking with their play? What understandings and misunderstandings and experiences are the children drawing on? Are there patterns in their inquiry that reveal a trajectory of thought? Are there inconsistencies in their thinking, any contradictions to explore further? How are the children building on each other's ideas, perspectives, and contributions?

· ·

©Margie Carter, Deb Curtis, Ann Pelo

Examine the environment.

How are the organization and the use of the physical space and materials impacting this situation? How are schedules and routines influencing this experience?

Collaborate with others to expand perspectives.

How do your colleagues understand the meaning of the children's play? What insights do the children's families have? How does this play reflect or challenge their beliefs, values, or practices? What child development or early learning theories might you consider? What other arenas of knowledge and insight might you consult?

Reflect and take action.

What values and intentions do you want to influence your response? What action might you take to help the children see their own and each other's ideas? What might you do to invite the children to take a different perspective? How will you invite collaboration? What might you do to deepen children's relationships with each other, their families, the Earth, and/or the community? How will you continue to seek out the children's points of view? How will you collaborate with families?

towards. It is teacher research undertaken in the spirit of what Albert Einstein called "many-sided thinking."[11]

There are two simultaneous courses of study for us, as teacher researchers. We consider *what* the children are thinking about, and we consider *how* the children are thinking. We explore ideas of substance alongside the children, and we seek to understand children's thinking.

We engage this study by moving between a receptive role—listening, watching—and an active role—offering, initiating. We move from observation (receptive) to self-reflection and study (active) to listening to a range of perspectives (receptive) to making an offering to children (active) to observing and listening some more (receptive). We can think of our work as a dialogue with children, colleagues, and families: sometimes we're listening, curious to understand what's being offered, and sometimes we're speaking, adding our thoughts and wonderings into the conversation. Or we can understand our work as a dance, in which we trade turns as the leader and the follower. Or we can see our work as a game of catch: we catch a ball tossed by the children, hold it to get its measure, and then toss the ball back, watching for what the children will do with it. These are all metaphors to get at what it is to be a teacher researcher: we're not constantly acting (or reacting), but moving at a considered pace, attentive to the reverberations of our actions, and willing to have our thinking changed by what we see and hear. The Thinking Lens slows us down to this tempo of reflection and response, so that the action we (eventually) take is infused with intention.

In its fluid cycle of self-awareness, consideration of multiple perspectives, and intentional, value-dense action, the Thinking Lens acknowledges our inescapable subjectivity. We don't strive to be detached or "objective," understanding the impossibility of untethering ourselves from all that influences and informs our thinking. Instead, we allow ourselves to be full-hearted, empathetic, and self-conscious. We seek to stay awake to what's influencing our feeling and thinking, and to accept responsibility for our beliefs, values, and histories. As teacher researchers, we observe and ask questions and interpret and converse and plan from a distinct point of view—our *own* point of view, which is always subjective, born in experience, culture, conviction. "A researching [educator] recognizes her part in the processes being researched," says Peter Moss.[12] And Tom Hunter reminds us to be "as human as we can be."[13] The Thinking Lens invites us to work mindfully within our subjectivity, as we co-construct meaning and action.

Pedagogical Documentation Brought to Life

The Thinking Lens is a protocol for teacher research, and teacher research is an expression of pedagogical documentation, "a process for making pedagogical work visible and subject to interpretation, dialogue, confrontation (argumentation) and understanding."[14] This breaks open our singular and isolated perspectives to create collective understandings. It changes our focus from talking about individual children and their behavior or learning, to talking about ourselves and our thinking about children's thinking process. Our conversations become tentative and introspective rather than certain and proscriptive, vehicles for our exploration and experimentation and learning.

This sounds belabored, drawn out, and ill-suited to the rhythms of life in an early childhood classroom, with a feel of slow deliberation rather than fluid responsivity. But once internalized, the Thinking Lens becomes instinctive and flowing.

A story from a toddler classroom helps illustrate the Thinking Lens in motion ...

———

Serving as a pedagogical companion, I spent a morning with Mandie, an early childhood educator, in her classroom of two-year-olds, as part of a project about mentoring and pedagogical leadership. Mandie and I met over lunch to reflect on our morning with the children; Mandie shared a story that has stayed with me because of her willing vulnerability in self-examination. Here's my retelling of what Mandie shared with me:

During the full-tilt hullabaloo of play this morning, I looked across the room and saw Austin standing on a table. My heart raced; I was agitated, I wanted him off the table, I wanted him to know it's not okay to stand on tables in the classroom. I wanted him to settle down: he's constantly in motion, squirreling around the room, getting into mischief, like this morning, when he climbed up on the table. And I was embarrassed, with you in the classroom; I wanted you to think well of me, as an educator. All this was my first rush of feeling, and before I could stop myself, I got [assistant teacher] Amy's attention and gestured to her to get Austin off the table.

But as I waited for Amy to lift Austin down, I slowed down enough to get curious. I wondered why Austin was standing on the table. So I looked more closely at him: he wasn't jumping around or goofing off, he was looking at something on the wall, something that was just out of reach above him.

I moved so that I could see what Austin was looking at: it was a photo taped onto the wall. I realized that Austin was trying to get a better look at this photo that we'd hung at our adult eye level, too high for the children to see clearly from the floor.

By now, Amy had Austin in her arms. I called across the room, "It's the picture! Give him the picture!"

Amy pulled the photo off the wall and handed it to Austin. He grinned, took the photo and scampered across the room with it to Cathy (another teacher). He pulled a chair up next to Cathy. He held the photo tight in his small hands, and gazed from the photo to Cathy, back and forth, smiling at her and at the photo. It was a photograph of Cathy, and Austin had brought it to her.

I was stunned. I didn't know that Austin had that tenderness in him, or that he was so aware and thoughtful. I definitely had my thinking shaken up today.

Mandie beautifully captures the process of meaning-making articulated in the Thinking Lens. **Know yourself:** *that racing heart, that instinct that Austin should not be on the table, the edge of irritation that he's squirreling around, again—and also, curiosity.* **Take the child's point of view:** *Why is Austin on the table? What is he looking at?* **Examine the environment:** *The photo is hung too* *high for the children, and the only way for Austin to access it is by climbing up on the table. **Reflect and take action:** "Give Austin the photo!" And, then, watch, humbled and curious, to see what Austin will do with the photo. Mandie joined her attention to what had Austin's attention, thinking about Austin's thinking and feeling: his desire for and capacity to create connection.*

These few moments held a transformation of experience for Mandie. She shifted from classroom cop to curious observer. She advocated for Austin's goodness rather than admonishing him as naughty. She got a glimpse of another person's humanness, and got to act on behalf of that humanness.

And these few moments held a transformation of experience for Austin. Rather than being chastised as "the squirrely kid" breaking a classroom rule, he was seen as and supported to be a generous, warm-hearted companion, attentive to what is around him and to the possibilities for connection.

Mandie reminds us to slow down, to pause for a few seconds—even for just three breaths—before leaping into action. This whole cycle of observation, self-examination, meaning-making, and action took maybe two minutes, probably less: it was not an eye-catching long-term investigation with full-color display panels. But it was impactful for Mandie's continuing development as a teacher researcher, and for her capacity to join her attention to the children's attention and, so, become their ally and comrade. Mandie demonstrates the shift from reaction to research that's possible by "just looking, and then telling others" what we see. There is time for this in every classroom, every day.

———

Teacher research can unfold over more time and space than these few moments that Mandie and Austin shared. Pedagogical leaders can support educators to use the Thinking Lens to make meaning of and plan responsively from their observations, and so, grow investigations that take shape over days or months.

Using the Thinking Lens as a Pedagogical Leader

Whether in a few fleeting moments in a morning with toddlers or during a planning meeting of educators and a pedagogical leader, the great gift of the Thinking Lens is that it cultivates the mindset and skill set of teacher research by doing teacher research. It strengthens the capacity for pedagogical practice through enacting pedagogical practice. We don't have to work towards or wait for anything to be in place first, there is no prerequisite knowledge needed in order for us to step into the practice of teacher research. We learn how to use the Thinking Lens as a protocol for teacher research by using the Thinking Lens as a protocol for teacher research.

But—a caution. The Thinking Lens is not something simply to hand to educators, one more requirement or expectation for them to shoulder. It's a tool for growing a culture of inquiry through its deliberate use by a pedagogical leader in a community of practice. Educators meet with the pedagogical leader for regular meetings, in which educators offer stories of moments with children that have caught their attention. The pedagogical leader facilitates a conversation anchored by the Thinking Lens aimed at unpacking those stories, and, so, deepening the possibilities for responsive action. Thinking protocols need facilitation that promotes participation, invites and honors diverging viewpoints, and builds trust that allows educators to offer their experiences, questions, insights, and challenges.[15] With the facilitation of a pedagogical leader, a protocol can be the anchor point for a community of practice.

This likely means some reworking of how a teaching team uses planning meetings. At Hilltop, for many years, our weekly meetings of each teaching team were all about housekeeping details, classroom logistics, and discussions of children's behavior. They gave educators a chance to be together, away from the children, but all too easily became gripe sessions; they were mundane and repetitive and remarkably unstimulating. When we committed to pursuing a new course for our teaching, and crafted the first iteration of the Thinking Lens to use as a protocol for teacher research, we reconfigured our weekly team meetings.

We agreed to spend the first 45 minutes of each meeting studying observation notes, using the Thinking Lens to guide our meaning-making and planning. We saved the last 15 minutes for discussion of classroom housekeeping and behavior, but, over time, even that fell away, and we used the full meeting for the practice of teacher research. Our meetings energized us, and left us with clear plans for how we'd move through the days ahead, until our next team meeting the following week.

The observation notes that we studied during team meetings were just that: notes about a moment of children's play that intrigued or compelled us, jotted on a scrap of paper—nothing polished and carefully curated, but raw, fresh, the paint still drying on our thinking. With each observation, the pedagogical leader piloted us through the Thinking Lens, from self-examination to meaning-making to planning. The teaching team and the pedagogical leader worked together on each observation, and, so, we learned tremendously about each other as thinkers.

The pedagogical leader held us to the Thinking Lens, gently calling us back to each step when our conversation strayed or when we too quickly leaped into generating a list of activities that we could do related to the surface appearance of an observation. By the meeting's end, we each had an offering to make to children, anchored in intention. Meeting by meeting, we strengthened our pedagogical muscle. Meeting by meeting, we grew the culture that we valued, the culture at the core of our vision to be a community of joyful, collaborative inquiry.

One value of using a research protocol like the Thinking Lens is that it creates shared access to a way of thinking and being. It articulates and formalizes the process of reflection, meaning-making, planning, and documenting that is at the heart of pedagogical practice. With the Thinking Lens, we have shared language and shared process, and all the participants in the community own the inquiry. The protocol, captured on paper, represents the internalized identity of a community that learns. It both reflects and strengthens the dispositions necessary to a culture of inquiry, dispositions to listen, to wonder, to be surprised and moved; to be willing to be challenged and changed by our experiences with children, families, and each other; to pay more attention to creating possibilities than to pursuing pre-defined goals; to embrace complexity and its companion, uncertainty.

An essential element of a culture of inquiry is steady attention to issues of social justice teaching and learning. The Thinking Lens focuses our seeing and thinking in ways necessary to such attention. We're called to consider the values and beliefs, the experiences and understandings and cultural lenses that influence what we notice. We're challenged to take the children's points of view and to consider the perspectives of colleagues and families, to take up the current thinking in the professional literature. We're instructed to take action with awareness of our values and intentions.

When we inhabit the Thinking Lens in these full and substantive ways, we will surely be carried into consideration of culture and its ramifications for justice and injustice. As we dive into exploration of the Thinking Lens in the next chapters, we'll look closely at the ways in which responsive pedagogical practice and social justice thinking and action are bound together.

Teacher research, say Meier and Henderson, means "framing one's professional life as a set of questions."[16]

Questions. Not answers. Not expertise. Questions, which are the beating heart of research. "I wonder why?" "What if?" "Who else?" The Thinking Lens carries us into the arena of research by asking us to lay down the activity guides and lesson plans that are weighted with answers, and, instead, to take hold of questions. They will spool us always forward, sure guides in the project of becoming a community that learns.

Margie Carter

Infused with Attention and Intention

I want to poke away at a few of the concepts Ann offers here because perhaps they initially appear paradoxical.

Protocols can be seen as a tool for improvisation

Most protocols are viewed as a code of behavior, set of rules or strict procedures to follow for things like hand washing, emergency drills, scientific experiments, or approaching a royal family. These protocols are intended to become ingrained, step-by-step procedures, to be undertaken without a second thought. For educators, the National School Reform Initiative (SRI) has developed a number of valuable protocols to use for studying children's work, getting help with dilemmas, and making meaning of equity issues.[17] Aimed at analytical thinking with the support of critical friends, these protocols are also to be carefully adhered to, using a suggested timeframe within each component.

How then can a protocol be seen as a tool for improvisation?

If we revisit the qualities of improvisation Ann outlines in Chapter 2, her intent is about laying down scripts that prescribe behavior in favor of cultivating dispositions that support the culture of inquiry. We're reminded:

Improvisation asks that we are fully present.

Improvisation is unscripted, but participants can rehearse.

As improvisational players, we join our attention to the children's attention, and together, we set off on a journey into new terrain, creating the map as we go.

The Thinking Lens protocol asks us to make meaning of the journey, to be *attentive* to details, *intentional* in seeking out other perspectives, *attentive* to preconceived notions, *intentional* about unpacking the "why" of our assumptions, and on and on, so that we are rarely on auto-pilot in our days with children, nor squandering the precious time that we have off the floor to meet with colleagues. As a tool for improvisation, protocols such as the Thinking Lens are structures for openness, infused with attention and intention.

Work mindfully within our subjectivity

In the presence of colleagues from other countries, I'm often somewhat embarrassed to explain that most teacher education in the United States continues to emphasize the need to be objective, an idea that postmodern thinking dismantled some time ago. With U.S. educators, I emphasize the importance of not conflating the idea of fairness with objectivity. In fact, we can only approach the notion of fairness or objectivity by becoming intimately aware of and acknowledging our inescapable subjectivity.

Rather than pretending that we are objective, I suggest that we strive to fall in love with every kid within our reach. Approach each child and their family with a search light to capture what delights you about who they are, what you see as their competencies, uniqueness, and beautiful humanity. Keep Mandie in mind as a role model. She spotted Austin standing on the table, simultaneously spotted her knee-jerk assumptions, and nimbly moved into improvisation, bringing full recognition to Austin's delight in an important relationship. You can be mindful in your intention to reinforce each child's identity as an affable, resilient, kind, and remarkable human being. Look for the intelligence in those babies' cries, those toddlers' arms and legs, and preschoolers' declaration, "You can't come to my birthday." With the Thinking Lens as your tool, you can spotlight what stirs memories, makes your heart flutter, provokes your thinking, and desire for a deeper dive.

Steady attention to issues of social justice

When using the Thinking Lens to make meaning of what you are seeing, you become more aware of possibilities you might have otherwise overlooked. Always probing for what you know about your predispositions, preferences, and hot buttons, your subjectivity becomes more recognizable. You replace judgment with curiosity and begin to see how issues of race, class, culture, and gender go beyond personal circumstance and reflect a historically built system of privileging some over others, sometimes disguised by carefully perpetuated norms.

Regular inquiry guided by the Thinking Lens makes you smarter, more humble, and courageous. You become situated in questions that move you away from passivity, eager for wider perspectives and deeper knowledge. With this protocol, Ann affirms:

> We're called to consider the values and beliefs, the experiences and understandings and cultural lenses that influence what we notice. We're challenged to take the children's points of view and to consider the perspectives of colleagues and families, to take up the current thinking in the professional literature. We're instructed to take action with awareness of our values and intentions.

When you give steady attention to issues of social justice you are extending rights to children, recognizing where your passions for equity can be pursued, offering possibilities, and renewing hope for our fragile lives.

. . . .

What is your experience with using thinking protocols for your work?

. . . .

When you consider the Thinking Lens protocol, which of the areas for reflection seems like a good starting place in your work context?

. . . .

Which of the areas for reflection seems especially challenging in your work context? Why?

. . . .

*I have no answer for anything really ... I teach my students how to ask questions. In the word **question**, there is a beautiful word— **quest**. I love that word. We are all partners in a quest ... The essential questions have no answers. You are my question, and I am yours—and then there is dialogue. The moment we have answers, there is no dialogue. Questions unite people, answers divide them.*

—*Elie Wiesel*[11]

9

The Thinking Lens: Know Yourself

Inquiry begins with observation that sparks reflection.

But observation of what? To what should we give our attention?

In the context of teacher research, observation is not the clinical sort of evaluative stance that has come to dominate its meaning in our field. Rather, observation simply means giving our attention to what has the children's attention—being wide awake and curious and aware of what the children are up to, not in a corrective way, nor in an instructional way, but as a companion to children in the project of understanding.

Observation doesn't require a pre-established list of skills or knowledge that we're watching for. What we do when we observe is notice, with open hearts and curious minds, what the children are doing during the ordinary, everyday moments of our time together. These moments hold riches for our learning about children's learning, when we pay attention.

Every moment that we share with a child has a story worth exploring. Through our attention and curiosity, our stance of delighted intrigue, our offering ourselves wholly, we find those stories. In the bathroom, two children chat about why they don't like to flush the toilet. At lunch, a child observes that "the color of food gets on your tongue when you chew." These seemingly most unremarkable moments hold depths to plumb, when we lean forward and really listen.

Our starting place as observers is not *what* we observe but *how* we observe: with curiosity ("What's the story in this moment?"), with self-awareness ("What touches my heart in this moment?"), with delight ("How does this moment embody the joyful marvel of children?"). What we learn about children's thinking, and about our own thinking, is more nuanced and evocative than any checklist.

In education, observation is often characterized as clinical and detached, directed towards assessment and carried out by "neutral" evaluators who strive towards some "objective" measure of a child's learning or skill. As teacher researchers, though, our aim is not evaluation but understanding of and joining with children's pursuits. We recognize that we are neither neutral nor objective, but fully present as our full human selves. We're not detached; we're absolutely involved, beginning with what we choose to pay attention to, with what we notice and don't notice in the play we're observing. Our aim is not to detach ourselves, which is impossible, but to be aware of the lenses through which we observe, and to work with those intelligently.

We can learn from The National Quality Standard of Australia, which acknowledges that educators bring "a unique collection of beliefs, values, interests, knowledge, experience and perspectives to planning, practice and relationships."[1] Another way to say this: educators operate with subjectivity, and there's no avoiding that. Subjectivity: the perceptions, experiences, cultural understandings, convictions, personal histories, and family stories that make us who we are. The opposite of subjectivity is objectivity, detachment, dispassion, impartiality, neutrality.

We don't want to be dispassionate and detached—even if we could be, which is pretty much impossible. We want to bring our full human selves to our community, with self-awareness. We want to observe, and reflect, and plan, and engage with children as ourselves, consciously and intelligently.

"Skillful educators," Australia's National Quality Standard goes on to say, "are aware of their beliefs and knowledge and the theoretical perspectives from which they come. This is important because it helps us to understand why we decide on: content for our curriculum—what to teach, planned experiences and learning; approaches for managing behavior; how we set up the environment; what resources we choose; particular programs or methods; which teaching strategies to use; how we will relate to people; how we assess."[2]

Conscious Self-Reflection

The Thinking Lens begins by recognizing our subjectivity: *Know yourself; open your heart to this moment.* Our inclination and training as educators is to talk about the children and their learning, erasing ourselves from the story. But the first gesture of the Thinking Lens acknowledges our place in the story as people with insights and memories, feelings and values, and hopes and concerns which influence what we see and hear. When we don't acknowledge and talk about our perspectives, and, instead, jump to discussion of the children, we might *think* that we're talking about the children, objectively. But without conscious self-reflection, we're *really* talking about ourselves and our default way of seeing and understanding. We may as well address our subjectivity at the get-go, so that we're seeing clearly: we explore our perspective as one point of view among many to consider.

The first step of the Thinking Lens invites this self-awareness, and offers us guidance as we seek to become more skillful in our observation and meaning-making:

Know yourself. Open your heart to this moment.
- What is your immediate response to the children's play and conversation? What feelings stir in you? What touches your heart as you watch and listen?
- What in your background and values is influencing your response to this situation?
- What adult perspectives, i.e. standards, health and safety, time, goals are on your mind?
- What leaves you curious, eager to engage?

I dreamed my way into an understanding of how to look at ourselves looking at children. In my dream, I arrived for a visit to a school for young children to find the staff in the process of hanging a sign in their entryway, a beautifully crafted ironworks art piece that said, simply, *Hyperoppery.* I asked one of the educators what the sign meant, and she told me that it was there to remind them about observation: "We've had the bad habit of looking superficially at children's play, and of waiting and watching for something unusual, instead of paying attention to everyday moments and their revelations. We're putting up this sign to remind us to look closely and constantly."

The morning after that dream, I spent time with a dictionary, trying to unearth the meaning of that dream-word, *hyperoppery*. *Opia*, I learned, denotes sight, and is derived from Greek: *view, look, see.* And *hyper*, also from Greek, connotes *above, beyond, exceedingly, over.* And, so, a definition for *hyperoppery*: To look beyond the surface; to view exceedingly closely; to see over and through expectations and assumptions, into the depths of meaning available in each moment.

We employ hyperoppery when we engage the Thinking Lens as a protocol for self-examination and study. It is a directive to look closely at ourselves, as we engage with children, and to look beyond the surface of children's play into the complexities of thought and feeling. It challenges us to look into and through our expectations about what children ought to be learning and beyond our assumptions about what we know.

• • • • • • Hyperoppery asks that we see ourselves seeing.

A story about hyperoppery ...

————

A few years ago at Hilltop, a group of white three-year-olds instituted a game about putting people in jail, a game that spun out over several days, repeated with increasing finesse and quickly becoming part of the group's shared culture. The two educators in the group, Alison and Alice, kept an eye on the game and helped children navigate the scuffles that surfaced. About a week into the jail play, they got a call from Gail, Sophie's mom. Sophie had begun to complain at home about the jail game; she was afraid of being captured and put into jail, afraid of being locked away from her parents, afraid of the darkness she imagined in jail, and the isolation. Gail was concerned, and asked that the educators take action on Sophie's behalf by putting an end to the jail game.

Alison was stung by Gail's call, not wanting her—or Sophie—to be upset. She wanted to stop the children's jail play right away, and put an end to the concern. I was the mentor teacher, in the role of pedagogical leader; I suggested that the educators hold off on banning the play, and, instead, watch the game up-close for a day or two, make notes about what the children did and said, and bring those notes to the weekly teaching team meeting for us to study together to better understand this play that so dramatically compelled the children's attention.

And that's what we did. Alice and Alison captured on paper the key phrases and gestures and motifs of the jail game, and brought their notes to the team meeting. We read through the notes, and then took up the Thinking Lens to guide our discussion about the play and how we ought to respond to it.

Practicing hyperoppery, we began with the first step of the Thinking Lens: **Know yourself; open your heart to this moment.**

Alison, abashed to think that she'd failed Sophie, described her difficulty in watching the play with clear eyes. "I was looking for frightening or fierce aspects," she said. "I watched with an awareness of Sophie's fear."

Alice jumped in. "I was aware of Gail's concern, too, and it pushed me to be a little defensive about the play, and about us, as educators. I didn't watch for what was frightening in the game, but for the ways in which it wasn't all that scary."

"I like the boldness of the play," I said. "I'm drawn to big play, and to the movement and loudness and tempo of play like this jail game. I'm less patient with timidity than I ought to be, and pretty tolerant of hullabaloo."

Alison remembered playing jail as a child. "We played during recess; I was in kindergarten, or maybe first grade. Our game was like tag, but if you got caught, you had to go to jail under a large metal slide. I remember the thrill of danger that made the ordinary game of tag more interesting. But I believed that kids don't go to jail in real life, and so I wasn't scared, not completely."

Our conversation certainly reflected our cultural lenses as white women, and was situated in the context of the children's lives as white, middle-class kids not subjected to the disproportional jailing experienced by communities of color. The children's jail play seemed to fall within reasonable bounds. But we were concerned for Sophie.

"I remember what it felt like to be scared, when I was a kid," Alice said. "For kids, fear is more like terror than 'being frightened.' You feel out of control, at the mercy of the thing that scares you. I can pull that feeling right to the surface, even now."

Alison was quick to agree. "I feel for Sophie. I hate thinking that she feels that terror in our classroom. But, at the same time, I want her to toughen up a little bit. I want her to stand on her own two feet and not need her mom to intervene for her."

"I was irritated at first, when Gail called," Alice confessed. "I thought, 'Trust us. We're aware of the jail game and we're coaching kids about setting limits on how they want to play or not play.'"

"But Sophie, bless her, is turning to her mom because she's scared of the game and hasn't been able to tell us that in a way that we could hear," I said. "We have a bunch of threads to follow here: Sophie's right to feel safe, and our goal that she develop the capacity to act on her own behalf; Gail's concern for Sophie's experience; and the resonance of the jail game for the children who play it, as well as for those who try to avoid it, like Sophie."

From here, our conversation turned to the next steps of the Thinking Lens, as we sought to understand the jail game from the children's perspectives, and from families' perspectives, and through the lenses of schema theory and social justice goals, child development understandings and myth and story. Each step asks that we employ hyperoppery, looking beneath the surface to see into the meanings and resonances and dissonances of the play.

———

Hyperoppery expands our intellectual ways of seeing to include emotional and embodied ways of wondering and knowing. It turns our gaze inward, where we see our compassion for a child's fear, our memory of terror, our exhilaration at danger, our defensiveness in the face of a parent's challenge, our desire to be known as competent, our pull towards bold play, our impatience with caution, our hope for a child's increasing capacities. With hyperoppery, we see *how* we're seeing: the ways in which we're looking especially for the frightening aspects of a game, or looking away from them. We use phrases like: *I feel*; *I remember when I was a child*; *I value*; *I want.* The first step of the Thinking Lens invites this hyperoppery, and, so, ensures that we are aware of the "beliefs, values, interests, knowledge, experience, and perspectives" that influence our observation and what we do in response to what we observe.

The invitation to articulate our experiences, emotions, values, and questions communicates that all the people in the conversation have something necessary to contribute to our effort to understand children's play and learning. Rather than seeking expertise in some external source, the Thinking Lens begins with the significant insight, wisdom, and knowledge that educators bring to the conversation, and the ways that our varied and divergent perspectives, taken together, illuminate the moment under consideration.

The Thinking Lens asks us to focus on ourselves first, acknowledges our place in the story as people with insights and memories, feelings and reactions, values and hopes and concerns. And the Thinking Lens asks us to be responsible with our perspectives, aware of the ways in which they influence what we see and hear and how we behave. It is essential that we acknowledge our gut-level, instinctive responses, in order to be clean and clear as we seek the children's perspectives; if we don't, we overlay our "stuff" onto the meaning we make of children's experiences.

· · · · · · · · If we don't pause to notice our responses, we react. But when we stop to feel what we feel, we can spin forward into inquiry, inventiveness, and intentionality in our teaching.

The first gestures of the Thinking Lens are invitations to pay attention: What touches your heart, stirs your curiosity, captures your attention? Why? How do you see the children's competence and confidence? What gets in the way of your clear seeing?

Considering Culture

Hyperoppery: To look beyond the surface; to see through assumptions. When we practice hyperoppery, we are awake to our cultural embeddedness—the ways in which *who we are* shapes *what we see* and *how we understand.* We can expand the questions in the first step of the Thinking Lens to include attention to our cultural selves: What is your first reaction or judgment? What experiences in your life are called forward? What values come to the surface for you? Can you trace those values to their cultural roots? What adult perspectives about race, class, gender, sexual identity, and other aspects of identity are on your mind—or about which might you be unaware?

We come to our interactions with children, families, and each other loaded up with our cultural perspectives: I write this as a white woman, formally educated, raised in a Christian family but no longer participating in a religious community, straight and with a male partner, enthusiastically athletic, hovering on the edges of middle class. All this leaves me with particular ways of seeing and being seen in the world; I pay attention to certain things and don't notice other things. I'm excited by some kinds of play and I try to squelch other kinds of play. I respond to children's behavior based on my multi-faceted cultural point of view.

The self-awareness to which the Thinking Lens holds us accountable includes awareness of our cultural lenses. Lisa Delpit writes, "We do not really see through our eyes or hear through our ears, but through our beliefs."[3] When we observe children, we observe them through our beliefs, our expectations and blind spots, our life experiences, the meanings we've assigned to race, gender, class, sexual orientation, body shape and size, age. The Thinking Lens doesn't ask us to strip away these lenses—which would be impossible—but to be conscious of them, to know that they exist, and to work mindfully with them. We are the educators that we are because we are the people that we are. We don't want to cease existing as ourselves; we want to be as human as we can be, with self-awareness.

In our field, we tend to focus on children's cultural identities—their race, gender, sexual orientation, socio-economic class—but we don't talk much about our own cultural identities. In "mixed company," there is often quick discomfort when we call attention to our own and our colleagues' cultural lenses and so we mostly avoid this socially impolite subject, and are clumsy and awkward when we take it up.

There's a dominant societal myth that we make our lives as individuals, and that emphasizing group membership can hold us back or set up unfair advantages. This myth holds up a system of inequity across many lines. Those in privileged groups (such as white, straight, middle class, formally educated, physically heathy people) are perceived as the norm, and when we start talking about cultural identity, we come face to face with privilege and oppression, with belonging and not belonging, creating a dissonance that we often want to side step.

When people outside this normative class raise issues of culture, they're chastised as complainers, or perceived as "having a chip on their shoulder," or shut down as trying to create problems. We are well-practiced at avoiding conversations which draw attention to culture.

The Thinking Lens asks us to trade that avoidance for hyperoppery, and acknowledge the role of culture in our teaching, beginning where good teaching begins, in observation.

An example of what it looks like to use the Thinking Lens to call forward our cultural selves ...

———

An educator at Hilltop, Kirstin, brought this observation to the weekly meeting that she and her co-teacher, Lisa, had with me, the pedagogical leader:

Five-year-old Jack and three-year-old Lacey have been playing this game most mornings for the last week ... When Lacey arrives, Jack runs eagerly to her, calling out, "Let's play baby and dad!" Lacey jumps right in with him, and Jack picks her up and carries her to the drama area. He sets her down and she lies on the ground, waiting for Jack's direction. "Now cry, baby." "Now go to sleep." "Now eat, baby." Lacey does what Jack suggests, and Jack responds to her, comforting her when she cries, rocking her to sleep, feeding her. He pretends to change her diaper, and he picks her up and sets her down and plays peek-a-boo with her. He's playing the role of dad to the hilt, and Lacey's completely squared away as the baby—she doesn't move her body on her own, but waits for Jack to instruct her or move her.

As Kirsten finished describing this game, she added, "This game bugs me, and I'm not sure why."

Her co-teacher, Lisa, had an emphatic response: "Each time I see this game, I put a stop to it. I tell Lacey that she's a powerful girl, that she can move her own body. And I tell Jack to let Lacey walk, that he's not to carry her anymore."

The two teachers began talking about Jack and Lacey and the dynamics of this game. The game was fairly innocuous in the context of our program; we tend to be quite comfortable with children's physicality and with affectionate, informal touch between children. Lisa and Kirsten considered the age difference between Jack and Lacey, and the social learning that occupied each child: Jack's work to develop flexibility in his play and leave room for other children to contribute to it, Lacey's work to find her voice to shape collaborative play. As they talked, we realized that it was a stretch to configure the game itself as problematic. And we recognized that it was a tender and fluid way for these two children to connect across significant differences, together knitting a story about a caring relationship.

We backtracked to the first step of the Thinking Lens, which we'd skipped right past as we tried to understand why the game got under Kirsten and Lisa's skin. And there we found our answer.

Know yourself.

- *What is your first reaction or judgment?*
- *What experiences in your life are called forward?*
- *What values come to the surface for you? Can you trace those values to their cultural roots?*
- *What adult perspectives about race, class, gender, sexual identity, and other aspects of identity are on your mind?*

Lisa offered, "When I see Jack telling Lacey what to do and even moving her body for her, all my protectiveness for Lacey as a sixteen-year-old girl on a date comes out. I want Lacey to tell Jack 'No!' and I want Jack to hear it!"

Kirsten concurred. "That's just it, isn't it! As a woman, I hate seeing a girl being so passive. I want Lacey to be strong and independent, in control of what happens to her physically."

"Yes!" said Lisa. "And I want Jack to be sensitive to and careful about girls' rights to make decisions about their bodies."

And there it was, culture spilled out on the table as part of the conversation about this baby and dad game. Once we'd named it, we could work with it intelligently. Kirsten and Lisa decided that, in fact, they'd back away from Jack and Lacey's game, not swooping in with directives, but offering a simple check-in with each of the children: reminding Jack to ask Lacey if he could pick her up, and nudging Lacey to let Jack know if she wanted to walk. They'd ask the children what would happen for the dad and the baby when the baby learned to crawl, and let that be provocation for bringing a new complexity into the roles. Acknowledging the reverberations of their cultural identities as feminist women allowed Kirsten and Lisa to think more spaciously about Jack and Lacey's game, and to move from a place of self-awareness and thoughtfulness rather than reactivity.

———

Educators don't consider children's play only as "educators." We come together in community as straight women and men, and lesbians, and gay men, and transgender people. We're feminists. We're socially conservative. We're people from working class backgrounds or from wealthy backgrounds. We're white people and people of color, insiders and outsiders, people who feel they belong and people who feel they don't belong. We're *people*, with deeply held values and beliefs, informed by our many-faceted cultural and social identities— not generic or anonymous "teachers," but real people living alongside children and families and colleagues. The Thinking Lens asks us to bring our full selves to our work, to know ourselves and open our hearts to the moments we share with children.

Margie Carter

Being Responsible with Our Perspectives

Ann's offerings in this chapter remind me that what we call "professional development" should focus on learning about ourselves, not just on how children learn and develop. Professional development as self-awareness. This is essential if we are to work with deep intention and be responsible with our perspectives. Once we face our inescapable subjectivity, we have to be responsible with it. This is part of the guidance that a pedagogical leader offers, and Ann's dreamed-up term, hyperoppery, reminds us that the foundation of our responsibility is to look beyond the surface. We employ hyperoppery not only in giving attention to what has children's attention, but in constantly examining the sources of our own points of view. Maybe we should take our cue from Ann's dream and hang a banner to remind us:

> *Hyperoppery*: To look beyond the surface; to see through assumptions. When we practice hyperoppery, we are awake to our cultural embeddedness— the ways in which *who we are* shapes *what we see* and *how we understand*.

Ann gives us two examples of how a pedagogical leader walks beside educators, helping them find what's underneath their feelings about children's activities. She joins Alice and Alison to study notes that the teachers take about the "jail game" in light of the report from Sophie's mom that Sophie is afraid of this play. Then, she uses the Thinking Lens to probe for deeper understandings, starting with how Alice and Alison see things:

> The first gesture of the Thinking Lens acknowledges our place in the story as people with insights and memories, feelings and values and hopes and concerns which influence what we see and hear.

As we read about Alice, Alison, and Ann's conversation, it's helpful to know that all the players in this story are wrapped in white skin. A "jail game" would likely have a far deeper source of anxiety if these were dark skinned or new immigrant families. While a pedagogical leader helps educators uncover their own, as well as the children and families' perspectives, she can also point out, beyond the surface, the cultural embeddedness of our perspectives on this story. Using a social justice lens, we can interrogate systems of oppression and exclusion. Would our responses change if we knew that any of these children had a family member in jail or were absorbing the reality of police shootings of Black males?

In predominantly white settings, pedagogical leaders have the opportunity to deepen the community's thinking about the ways that systems of privilege and racism impact children and families, asking questions like "How might we understand the term 'school to prison pipeline' if we imagine the jail game unfolding in a different child care setting? How would our thinking change if Sophie were Black?" In communities of color, pedagogical leaders can mobilize thinking about keeping children emotionally and physically safe while the airwaves are filled with fear.

In the baby and dad story, Ann brings alive how the Thinking Lens can help us notice how our perspectives on gender influence what we see and hear. As a pedagogical leader, Ann guides these deeper reflections so that the teachers respond with intention, not in a knee-jerk reaction. Race, gender, social class, physical ability, language, sexual identity: culture always informs how and what we see in children's play, and the meaning we make of it.

Protocols such as the Thinking Lens help us give attention to values and goals, gain clarity on the perspectives of the children and of the adults, and allow us to spin forward into inquiry before we jump into action. I'm reminded again of the earlier quote offered from William Ayers, which seems so pertinent here:

> Reflection is more than thinking, although thinking and thoughtfulness are essential to begin. Reflection is thinking rigorously, critically, and systematically about practices and problems of importance to further growth ... Reflection is a disciplined way of assessing situations, imagining a future different from today, and preparing to act.[4]

. . . .

When you think about taking up the Thinking Lens for your work, what excites you? Does anything stand in the way?

. . . .

How could you begin to cultivate the role of a pedagogical leader who draws on the Thinking Lens in your work?

. . . .

The most practical thing we can achieve in our teaching is insight into what is happening inside us as we teach.

—*Parker Palmer*[12]

The Thinking Lens: Making Meaning

Participation in a community that learns—a community of researchers and thinkers bound together by the shared project of inquiry—calls forward and strengthens in us the capacity to be in discourse with all sorts of perspectives. Perspectives that challenge us and perspectives that expand our thinking. Perspectives that rub us the wrong way and perspectives that move us. Perspectives that confound us and perspectives that tickle us. In community with colleagues, families, and children, all of us striving to be (and to support each other to be) as human as we can be, we are guaranteed the experience of disequilibrium.

Author and environmental activist Rick Bass writes in *The Wild Marsh*: "What is community? I submit that it is not people of similar intent and goals, or even values, but rather, a far rarer thing, a place and time where against the scattering forces of the world people can stand together in the midst of their differences, sometimes the most intense differences, and still feel affection for, and a commitment to, one another."[1]

This is what we're about in our work: creating community with children, families, and each other, knowing that we won't always see things the same way or agree with each other, knowing that our engagement with each other entails complexity and contradictions and will likely unsettle us and leave us changed.

Our communities are the coming-together of multiple perspectives in continuous negotiation, and our role as pedagogical leaders is to amplify this.

We've learned to value the essential role of disequilibrium in learning, and we strive to build it into our offerings to children. When we commit to participation in a community that learns, we set our adult selves on a course towards frequent disequilibrium, as our ways of thinking and understanding bump up against other people's ways of thinking and understanding. Often, what we think we know doesn't fit with what we discover in other people's perspectives, and that leaves us off-balance, seeking steady footing. Our work as pedagogical leaders is to reframe disequilibrium from something uncomfortable that's best avoided to an experience that we willingly seek out. Disequilibrium is home ground for a community that learns, and it is a lively place to make camp.

Standing together in the midst of our differences, we practice holding those differences with affection for and commitment to each other. We practice the art of "both/and" instead of "either/or." This doesn't mean we're lazy or mushy in our thinking or conversations, in the sloppy spirit of "anything goes" or "it's all good." It does mean holding the dynamic tension as dynamic—an energizing force, a source of change and growth, a manifestation of ability and power. We consider our perspectives alongside the perspectives of other people in our community, and our thinking expands, changes, grows more nuanced, becomes more complex. Our default perspective becomes one of many perspectives to consider, rather than the obvious or only way to think.

When we step away from our habitual ways of seeing and understanding, we find new details in familiar storylines, we discover connections in what had seemed unrelated, we re-contextualize the long-known. When we change perspective, stale assumptions vanish and new possibilities are revealed.

This shift in seeing both requires and reinforces in us the qualities of imagination and curiosity: the willingness to reconsider what we'd thought to be true, and the ability to set aside our customary points of reference and ways of thinking. It calls for hyperoppery, asking us to look beyond our usual sight lines and past our expectations and assumptions. To take another person's perspective—to step outside our particularities to consider another person's particularities—asks of us flexibility in our thinking, humility, non-attachment and tentativeness, a willingness to reconsider and re-examine our assumptions, a commitment to resist the rigidity of ego and absolutism. This is how we stay engaged and alive, awake and leaning into life.

In early education, we value perspective-taking; it's part and parcel of our everyday lives. We ask children to take other perspectives when we coach them about resolving conflicts and when we seek to foster empathy and generosity of spirit in them. We ask families to take other perspectives when we offer them our understandings of their children. And we use the Thinking Lens to ask educators to take other perspectives. It asks us to:

- Take the children's points of view.
- Examine the environment.
- Collaborate with others to expand our perspectives.

The Thinking Lens asks us to keep our thinking fluid and expansive rather than habitual and static, and, so, to enlarge our understandings and add to our questions. It asks us to open our thinking, to invite other perspectives into our effort to make meaning of children's play. Building on principles of constructivism, the pedagogical practice embodied in the Thinking Lens guides us to come together as teacher researchers with humility and curiosity and attentiveness, taking the children's points of view, examining the environment, seeking out the thinking and questioning of other people, and consulting the understandings offered by developmental theories, social justice frameworks, and other arenas of knowledge.

Take the Children's Points of View

For many educators, habitual practice is to leap from seeing to doing: we notice a child digging in the sand, or stacking blocks, or rolling playdough into balls, and we jump in with a comment or question or a prop or a directive. We're eager to teach, and teaching, we think, means us doing something to or for a child.

The practice of teacher research asks us to pause before we act—to notice what we see and consider what it signifies about a child's trajectory of thought, feeling, and experience. To be a teacher researcher is to look below the surface of a child's play, unwilling to be satisfied with our immediate assumptions about the appearance of the play and its topical focus. We want to understand the meaning inside the play—the reverberant question, the search for understanding, the pursuit of knowledge at the heart of a child's play. As teacher researchers, we brake our instinct to react, and, instead, we study children's play to develop hypotheses about what the play is really about. This allows us to respond to children in the fullest, most useful ways possible, joining our attention to their attention and, so, supporting their true learning, not by teaching, but by honoring their study with our attentive care.

Carla Rinaldi, a pedagogical leader in the schools of Reggio Emilia, Italy, writes that "The young child is the first great researcher. Children are born searching for the meaning of life, the meaning of the self in relation to others and to the world, the meaning of their existence, the meaning of conventions and customs, and of the rules and the answers we provide."[2] Inside the dinosaur drama play, underneath the game about a family of kittens, and inside the deep hole in the sandpit, children are researching questions that compel them. The energizing challenge of teacher research is to look past the surface of these games, not reaching for the dinosaur theme box or the picture book about kitties, not quizzing the children about how deep their hole is. Instead, we wonder: Why dinosaurs? Why a family of cats? Why the hole?

We reach for the children's purpose, for what Pam Oken-Wright and Marty Gravett call "intent."[3] They ask, "What is the child saying with her words, play, representation, or even with body language? We may hear and understand the words she is using, but what thinking is behind it? What is the child's image of the idea at hand? What does she know, what ignites her passion, what confuses her, what throws her into disequilibrium about the topic she is considering?"[4] These questions direct our attention beneath the immediate and apparent, and, often, beyond a child's conscious awareness of what she's doing. Oken-Wright and Gravett distinguish between explicit and imbedded intent.[5] *Explicit intent* is a child's articulation, verbally or physically, of her intention: "I'm building a tall tower as high as the ceiling." *Imbedded intent* is the purpose inside the play which a child may not be able to articulate, and may not, herself, recognize: why build so tall—what does that signify to this child? It's the imbedded intent that we seek to understand with the second step of the Thinking Lens:

Take the children's points of view:

- What are the children trying to figure out? What theories are they testing? What questions are they asking with their play?
- What understandings and misunderstandings and experiences are the children drawing on? Are there patterns in their inquiry that reveal a trajectory of thought? Are there inconsistencies in their thinking, any contradictions to explore further?
- How are the children building on each other's ideas, perspectives, and contributions?

We don't find the child's perspective by asking her what she's doing. She may have some thoughts about her explicit intent, but awareness of and language for imbedded intent is not a young child's strong suit. It's not a child's job to tell us what she's pursuing, inside her play; it's our job to uncover the meaning inside her play.

To do this, we set ourselves on parallel courses of study: we consider what the children are thinking about, and we consider how the children are thinking about it. We explore ideas of substance alongside the children, and we seek to understand their way of questioning, testing, working with contradiction, wrestling with and through disequilibrium. We join the lineage of researchers, like Jean Piaget, intrigued by children's thinking. Piaget began developing his theories of children's cognition because his curiosity was caught by the reasons that children gave for their wrong answers on tests, which seemed to him to reveal important defining qualities about how children think. This can be our stance, as well. Believing that children have a unique and invigorating way of thinking, we join our attention to their attention in order to learn from and with and about them. We listen and watch from a stance of humility and tentativeness, expecting to be changed by what we experience.

Considering Family and Culture

Taking the children's points of view means more than thinking about their thinking, though. We seek to understand children's rootedness in family and culture that is both context and content for their play.

Often in our field, our conversations emphasize children's individual pursuits, passions, and dispositions, the things they do well and the things they struggle with. This tendency is given extra weight by the current froth about learning assessments, which focus on children's individual learning. This orientation can narrow the lens of our seeing. The second step of the Thinking Lens directs us to consider children's familial, cultural, and community frameworks, reference points, and understandings, locating children in the reverberant contexts of their lives. It's not just "children" who play, but white children and children of color, children born into their families and children adopted into their families, children with one mom or two moms or no mom, boys and girls, children whose families use food stamps at the grocery store, and children who spend weekends at a second home away from the city.

• • • • • • Children are embedded in family, culture, and community, and to take their points of view means to see them in those contexts.

Their thinking and playing and wondering and inventing are influenced by what they understand about who belongs and who doesn't belong, about the worth of people who belong and who don't belong, about the ways in which belonging is measured, about the consequences of belonging and not-belonging, about how a person moves from belonging to not-belonging and vice versa. They hold internalized social, cultural, and family beliefs about what it means to ask questions and to receive answers, about what it means to be a learner and go to school, about what a teacher ought to do and how a teacher ought to be treated. They hold enculturated values about the use and care of toys and tools and play spaces, about the worth of the world out-of-doors. They have understandings about gesture and tenderness, about the physicality of expression, about how loud is too loud and how rough is too rough. On and on, this familial and cultural knowledge is bound into their cells and it shows up in their points of view.

To decipher the meaning inside a child's pursuits, to read their intent, we try to locate ourselves in their familial and cultural points of view. Read the questions in the second step of the Thinking Lens again, with all this in mind, and notice their deeper implications for understanding:

Take the children's points of view.

- What are the children trying to figure out? What theories are they testing? What questions are they asking with their play?
- What understandings and misunderstandings and experiences are the children drawing on? Are there patterns in their inquiry that reveal a trajectory of thought? Are there inconsistencies in their thinking, any contradictions to explore further?
- How are the children building on each other's ideas, perspectives, and contributions?

The second step of the Thinking Lens asks that we listen to children with humility, not assuming that we already know what they're doing, not taking charge of their play in order to direct it towards outcomes we've already established, but listening with openness to what the children have to offer us. Staying flexible in our thinking, willing to hold off on drawing conclusions about what the children are up to and what they need from us—or what we can do to move towards a pre-determined outcome for a child's learning—we seek to follow a child's trajectory of thought and we hope it leads us to our own disequilibrium, unsettling what we assumed to be true. *That's* a good day at work.

Diving Below the Surface
Listen to a child who speaks without words. This is instruction for how to engage the second step of the Thinking Lens …

———

An eighteen month old boy, Jamie, sits at a tub of water alone. The tub is filled with lukewarm soapy, sudsy water, a washcloth and a sponge. It's a classic set up, something we'd expect to find in most toddler classrooms, and, so, something we might think we've seen a million times, something we know and understand well. But watch Jamie—really watch him.

He lifts the sponge and studies it, dips it into the water, squeezes it, watches the suds froth and drip. He runs the sponge along his arms. He holds it out and blows on it.

Jamie drops the sponge into the tub and picks up the washcloth. He studies it, dips it into the water, squeezes it, watches the suds froth and drip. He runs the washcloth along his arms. He holds it out and blows on it—the same sequence that he followed with the sponge.

And then! Jamie drops the washcloth and blows on the suds on his hands. He picks up the washcloth again and touches it to his face. New maneuvers, layered onto the twice-repeated sequence. And then another new gesture: Jamie drops the cloth and brings suds to his face with his hands.

He spends a thoughtful, silent fifteen minutes at the tub of water. There's plenty of activity around Jamie: across the room, toddlers stack and knock over big cardboard blocks; right next to Jamie, at another tub of water, an educator and a child splash and talk. But Jamie looks up from his tub only once, startling at an especially loud crash of blocks and an eruption of tears; his attention jumps towards the commotion and he watches as the children begin to sort themselves out, and then he turns his attention back to the water and suds, and continues his play.

After we move through the first step of the Thinking Lens, taking time to notice and consider the roots of our immediate responses to Jamie at the tub of water, we begin to consider Jamie's point of view, seeking to understand his intent. We move beyond the general and anonymous: "Jamie's a kid, he likes to play in water." We dive beneath the superficial: "Jamie is engaged in sensory play." We seek the particular and personal: What is Jamie's purpose at the tub of water?

As we seek to make meaning of Jamie's play, bodies of educational knowledge about schema theory and brain development serve as general guideposts. Our meaning-making, though, is deeper and more intimate than the broad summaries that developmental overviews and learning goals offer. We begin to understand what has the children's attention when we ask ourselves questions like:

- What is Jamie trying to figure out? What theories is he testing? What questions is he asking?
- What understandings and experiences might he be drawing on and enacting?
- Are there rhythms or patterns in his inquiry that reveal a trajectory of thought or wondering or remembering or imagining?

What has Jamie's attention? He's not "doing sensory play": that's reductionist and dismissive and disrespectful. He's immersed in a pursuit that involves suds and water and the similar yet distinct materials of sponge and cloth.

As we begin to tease out possible understandings of Jamie's play, we offer ideas tentatively, acknowledging that we don't really know the content of Jamie's heart and mind: *"I wonder if … " "Maybe … "* We use the language of hypothesis anchored in observation: *"I think that Jamie is _____ and the reason I think that is _____."* And, moving thoughtfully and humbly, we begin to lay out an array of possible meanings:

Maybe Jamie's play is about creation—suds from water, bubbles from suds. *The evidence for this hypothesis*: Jamie squeezes the washcloth and sponge, making suds that are thick and slow-moving: does he see these as something made by the sponge and cloth, or by his squeeze? He blows on the suds, which animates them: does he see the bubbles as an extension of or as something different from the suds floating in the tub?

Maybe Jamie's play is about sensual pleasure—the warmth of water on cool bare skin, the touch of hand to cheek, the movement of breath to bubble. *The evidence for this hypothesis*: The dreamy look in Jamie's eyes, his far-away gaze: these betoken an inwardness of experience, a giving-over to texture and touch. They may be evidence of an embodied experience rather than considered experimentation. How does Jamie open his senses to the world? How does he engage sensory invitations?

Maybe Jamie's play is about relationship—bath time at home and the tender time with a caregiver. *The evidence for this hypothesis*: Jamie uses the cloth and the sponge in gestures that echo those of bath time washing, moving up his arms and onto his cheeks. Maybe this is a way to recapture a sweet experience that he's shared with someone dear to him; who does Jamie live with and what are their bathing rituals? Or maybe this is a way for Jamie to experiment with taking care of himself: might he be trying out the sort of washing that he typically experiences as the recipient of someone else's care?

These hypotheses are vastly more interesting and respectful than the dismissive label of "sensory play." As we articulate them, we recognize the nuance and complexity of Jamie's play, and see his deep capacities of heart, mind, and body. We see Jamie more fully. And we become more fully present ourselves, attention sharpened, and learning invigorated.

Alert and curious, we let these hypotheses reverberate with their possibilities, and we turn to other perspectives to gather in the insights they offer to help in our consideration of these hypotheses.

Examine the Environment

The third step of the Thinking Lens directs us to pay attention to the structural and environmental influences that are shaping the moment that we're seeking to understand. Does the environment offer any information that helps us understand what's going on?

- How are the organization and use of the physical space and materials impacting this situation?
- How are schedules and routines influencing this experience?

As we seek to understand Jamie's fifteen minutes with the water and suds, we consider elements of the environment and time, and see how they speak to our hypotheses. We wonder about the impact of offering a tub of water rather than a full-on water table: how did that shape Jamie's experience? The tub was set up with the sponge and washcloth already in it, seeming to offer a suggestion about how to engage the water: how did that shape Jamie's experience? Jamie chose to play in the tub of water; he wasn't directed there by a teacher. And he had abundant time there without interruptions either intentional or unplanned: no other child tried to join him, no teacher stepped in to talk to or to coach Jamie or to rotate him into another learning station. How was Jamie's experience impacted by the length of time he spent, and by his solitude?

These questions aren't aimed at evaluating the environment and routines in the manner of environmental rating scales like the ECERS and ITERS. Instead, the intention of this step of the Thinking Lens is to help us notice the way the physical environment and the use of time shape children's experiences so that we can better understand children's play and so that we become more savvy about how we configure space, materials, and time.

Collaborate with Others to Expand Our Perspectives

The fourth step of the Thinking Lens directs us to turn towards colleagues and families, asking their perspectives about the play we're trying to understand.

- How do your colleagues understand the meaning of the children's play?
- What insights do the children's families have? How does this play reflect or challenge their beliefs, values, or practices?

These questions call for the practice of hyperoppery: looking beyond our familiar ways of seeing and thinking, looking past our habitual expectations and quick assumptions, into new vistas and intricate details glimpsed in perspectives other than our own. It can be unsettling, for sure, this expanding of our perspectives: it's startling to see that what seems an obvious conclusion to us is not at all the obvious conclusion for a co-teacher, startling to have our eyes opened to something that hadn't occurred to us at all until it was thrust into our consciousness by a child's parent. It's disquieting to have our assumptions flung back at us as only assumptions, not the one truth or the preferred truth or the desirable truth.

Remember the skunk in the heater vent, in Chapter One, and the children's letters to her, and the chasm between Tim's and my ideas about how we ought to respond? Tim's considerations were nowhere on my radar, would never have entered my mind; I'd have gone happily forward with my playful plan to write back to the children in the persona of the skunk if Tim and I hadn't talked, our perspectives bumping up against each other with force enough to slow me down. A correspondence with the skunk might have been a fine course to take, laden with rich jewels of experience for the children. But I'd have lost out, even as I got to follow my own trajectory: my thinking would have been shallower, my understandings less complex, my questions less searching. From the heart of this experience, I raise a toast to the disequilibrium sparked by the contact of diverging perspectives.

Our work with this step of the Thinking Lens is to stay curious and humble, to ask ourselves: What can I learn from my colleagues? How can their ways of thinking about this moment help me think better? What have I overlooked? Where have I been lazy in my thinking? We seek to shake ourselves up, to be called out on our assumptions. Carla Rinaldi reminds us that "If you believe that others are a source of your learning, your identity, and your knowledge, you have opened a very important door to the joy of being together. We are not separated by our differences but connected by our difference. It is because of my difference that I am useful to you because I offer another perspective."[6]

A nuance to consider when we seek the perspectives of colleagues and children's families:

• • • • • We tend to assume that we share the same understandings of big constructs like race and racism, gender and sexism, and other aspects of cultural identity and context. But, in fact, we don't.

We have to ask, again and again: How have we each experienced the meaning and impact of these elements in our lives? How have we each been shaped by societal structures which privilege some of us and disenfranchise others? What do each of us know about these arenas? Where does our knowing overlap and where does it conflict? How are our perspectives about children's play influenced by our cultural knowing and not-knowing?

When Lisa and Kirsten and I began to talk about the daddy and baby game (the story is in Chapter Nine), it was an important and necessary first step to speak as women—remember Kirsten's exclamation that "This game bugs me!" and her realization that "As a woman, I hate seeing a girl being so passive." But from there, our work was to unpack our perspectives as women—how we each understood and experienced what it is to be a woman and whether and when we'd be comfortable being traditionally taken care of as women or when, by contrast, we'd claim the moniker of "feminist." Our cultural perspectives intersected in some ways, but, also, were particular and distinct. When we seek the perspectives of our colleagues and of the children's families, we step into consideration of cultural ways of seeing. That's likely to make us squirm, but that's okay, it's worth the discomfort to expand our awareness and sensitivity.

We're not seeking other perspectives in order to confirm what we already think, but, rather, in order to be challenged, unsettled, cast into disequilibrium. With families, particularly, this means that we don't ask the obvious and easy questions, but real questions about children's play. And we invite families' perspectives not to be polite or go through the motions, but genuinely to learn, to have our thinking challenged and changed. We ask not only about their children, but about our teaching, and about the environment and the use of time:

- What do you think is meaningful about this play for your child? Does anything about this play surprise you or puzzle you? Anything about it confirm or expand who you know your child to be?
- What do you think is meaningful about this play for the other children? Anything about it confirm or expand who you know these children to be?
- Where do you see intersections and divergences between your child and the other children in this game?
- How does this play reflect or challenge your family's beliefs, values, or practices?
- What do you think of how I stepped in (or didn't step in) during this play? Does my action fit with what you hope for your child? For the other children?
- How would you like me to proceed, in relation to this play?

These sorts of questions dismantle the carefully-tended border separating teachers and families, carry us across the line of demarcation into the terrain of shared meaning-making and the co-construction of knowledge. We're not asking "Have you seen your child play this game before?" and leaving it at that. We're asking to have our thinking expanded, challenged, and changed by families' insights and questions, by their values and commitments. We're seeking to expand our perspectives.

Broadening Our Horizons

The Thinking Lens points us towards theoretical frameworks and their perspectives about thinking and learning. What child development or early learning theories might you consider?

This question asks us to consider theories about how children learn and grow, how they become who they are; theories about teaching; theories about how culture is transmitted and enacted; theories about brain development and how thinking happens. In our field, many of us have adopted the language we learn from the educators in Reggio Emilia to reference our theoretical perspectives: what is our image of the child, our image of the educator, our image of the family?

When we seek to make meaning of children's play, we can turn to these sorts of theoretical perspectives to locate our study in a broadening context: the particulars of this moment, these children, this environment, these educators and parents, set into a larger narrative. *The Early Years Learning Framework for Australia* offers some useful questions to turn us toward consideration of the bodies of knowledge that inform our meaning-making:

- What theories, philosophies, and understandings shape and assist my work?
- Who is advantaged when I work in this way? Who is disadvantaged?
- What aspects of my work are not helped by the theories and guidance that I usually draw on to make sense of what I do?
- Are there other theories or knowledge that could help me to understand better what I have observed or experienced? What are they? How might those theories and that knowledge affect my practice?[7]

As teacher researchers, we can draw on the research and theories generated by other thinkers to stretch and shake up our thinking. And we can draw on other arenas of thinking and wondering, like literature, ecology, history, theater, the sciences. The Thinking Lens asks: What other arenas of knowledge and insight might you consult?

I taught for several happy years with John Benner, who held an advanced black belt in Aikido. He frequently brought his knowledge from Aikido into our study of children's play, offering insights about the interplay of body and mind, the weaving of action and intention, and about the use and flow of energy between people. Into our lively conversations, I'd offer a poem that I'd read recently, or an idea from my study of ecology and natural history. All of this expanded our conversations beyond the borders of typical child development and sparked new insights and new puzzlements for us. It wasn't simply that we were each more present as our full selves to the conversation, though that was sure true. It was that the scope of our thinking was both broader and more complex, versatile and spacious.

A Spin through Perspectives

The Thinking Lens invites us to move beyond our singular or prescribed avenues of consideration and interrogate a more wide-ranging body of knowledge and experience. It asks us to set our assumptions and quick conclusions aside, letting go of the easy confidence of certainty that characterizes instruction and embracing the humility of uncertainty that describes inquiry. When we do this, we surely expand our perspectives.

We observe a simple, everyday moment of play, and begin our spin through perspectives ...

———

A sunny, cool autumn morning. A group of three-year-olds in the sand box. A scattering of yard toys. A few children begin stacking the sand toys, and then a few more children join them, and, then, in a rush of momentum, all the children in the yard come together to pile the toys into a corner of the sand box. One child, Luke, calls out, "It's a castle!" and other children take up the charge: "A castle! A castle!" "Build the castle!"

Balls, sieves, shovels, rain gutters, buckets: the pile of toys grows tall.

———

Know yourself. Open your heart to this moment.
Consider your perspective. You might feel tickled by the children's zeal, or intrigued about what the children are up to. You might be delighted by the children's spirit of shared adventure.

You might feel irritated by the way the children are piling up the toys, worried that toys will be broken or that a child might be hurt.

You might be concerned about how your supervisor or a parent might see this play, and how they'd view your choice, for now, to watch instead of stepping in to teach the children something—better care for the toys? How to build a castle? You might be thinking about safety: the children are moving fast and in close proximity to each other, with lots of implements in their hands. You might wonder if you ought to re-direct this play.

Take the children's points of view.
Some considerations, as you crawl inside this moment and try to see it as the children see it:

Everyone is involved: The children take this on as a collective effort, and they all contribute to this shared endeavor. It seems both to reflect and to amplify their sense of connection to each other, of belonging in a group together.

It's a really tall stack: It's evocative of the way that toddlers stack up blocks and knock them down, but this seems to have a different intention: it's all about up.

What about *castles? The stack is significantly big*: it has a grandness to it, heft and height. For young and small children, it's potent to work on such a scale. Maybe "castle" is the nearest language for representing the grandness of the piled toys.

Examine the environment.

The toys were initially scattered in the yard, left randomly where they'd been used (or not used). There was no suggestion of a castle at first, at least not to your eye. The toys are familiar to the children, buckets and shovels, ramps, sieves; they've used them often and in various ways—though in this play, none of the toys is used in their usual way or in the way that they're "meant" to be used.

The children's activity is sort of like a big clean-up project. Their energy has some of that clean-up spirit, everyone working in a rush and a swoop.

Collaborate with others to expand perspectives.

How do your colleagues and children's families think about children stacking toys above their heads? About children using toys in ways that are different than their intended uses? About collectivity and collaboration? About the urgent energy of three-year-olds on a mission? How do your colleagues and children's families see this stacking of toys: mess or clean-up—and how do they feel about mess and clean-up? What insights and questions and challenges do your colleagues and children's families have to offer that you've not considered?

What can you learn from child development and learning theories? One thread to pursue, among many: the play, we've said, is evocative of the way that toddlers stack up blocks and knock them down. What does schema theory have to teach us about that play? In schema theory, this is an example of trajectory play, with the trajectory being upwards.[8] And this vertical trajectory play speaks to the physics of balance and imbalance, of height and vertical distance, of linear structures.

This considered reflection is a far cry from the immediacy of reaction that is tempting in a moment like this—a quick caution about safety, an injunction to use the toys properly, a re-direction to a digging project or a ramp project that would put the toys to use "more constructively." And, slowing us down, this perspective-taking asks us to look beyond the immediate appearance of the play—the children's explicit intent to build "a castle"—and resist the urge to offer coaching about and props for castle design or sand castle construction.

When we look at this sandbox moment from a range of perspectives, our meaning-making becomes complex and nuanced and insightful, and the possible offerings that we might make to children become resonant and provocative, rather than superficial and restrictive. We come to see this play not as an outbreak of toddler chaos, but as a delighting and engaging expression by the children of the potency of collaboration in pursuing a bold project in physics, something to marvel at and honor by a thoughtful response. When we engage the multiplicity of perspectives that are at play in every moment, we see more clearly, we see anew. We move beyond habits of thinking and assumptions, and new possibilities offer themselves—possibilities for children, and for ourselves.

Disequilibrium is a Place to Make Camp

Margie Carter

For many years, I wanted to run from uncertainty, not make camp there. Uncertain plans, directions, or landscapes left me feeling anxious and out of sorts, an unsettledness that no doubt stemmed from a childhood spent in the upheavals of divorce, a new blended family, and the steadily encroaching alcoholism of my father. And looking at my thesaurus just now, I find some synonyms for disequilibrium that aren't very inviting—*instability, imbalance,* and *volatility*. Over time, I've recognized that the other synonyms mentioned—*uncertainty* and *flux*—are easier to imagine as a destination to camp out. Going camping means leaving home, heading out to encounter unpredictable wildlife, weather, and facilities. Not for everyone, but I bought a tent and sleeping bag and began to take more risks, not only in the natural world, but in social and work settings.

Ann's characterization of disequilibrium lifts me with inspiration, and I'm acutely aware of the extensive practice it takes to live in this place with grace. What kind of practice helps? Trust walks and team building activities work well for some. I took some theater improvisation workshops and began to incorporate some of those dispositions in my life. I took up a yoga practice where I learned more about physical balance, being mindful and open, but not attached to outcomes.

To help teachers move past the search for "the right way" or "right answer" into deeper thinking with an experience of "constructing their own knowledge," Deb Curtis and I invented interactive strategies for our coaching and college teaching, which ultimately became our first book, *Training Teachers: A Harvest of Theory and Practice.*[9] For instance, in a workshop to consider how an environment fosters or defeats a sense of belonging, we'd send educators on a scavenger hunt around the building to find something that represents each of the following:

- Something that sparks a favorite childhood memory;
- Something you don't understand;
- Something that makes you feel respected;
- Something that insults your intelligence;

- Something you would take to a deserted island; and
- Something that has at least three uses other than the obvious.

The objects the group came back with helped us get to know each other in new ways, and provided a new look at our work and learning environments. We'd end by brainstorming a list of changes we'd like to bring about in our work environments.

More recently, I watched Ann and a colleague, Ijumaa Jordan, bring wobbly exercise balance discs to a professional learning day to give educators the physical experience of finding balance; educators were quick to make metaphorical connections between their physical play and the effort to move through disequilibrium. Brilliant!

These sorts of interactive strategies invite educators to feel comfortable with disequilibrium by recognizing the value of "structures for openness" in place of a scripted teaching methodology. This firsthand experience helps educators recognize the many possibilities for creating a teaching practice that is responsive to the unpredictable time of life called childhood. We want teachers to find their balance as they trust their relationships with children and families in the context of following the children's lead, rather than following the instruction of experts about the best methods to reach mandated learning outcomes. And, in turn, we want teacher education coaches and colleagues to gain confidence in inventing their work with teachers in a way that parallels how they hope educators will invent learning experiences for children.

Multiple Perspectives in Constant Negotiation

Making camp in the disequilibrium of letting other perspectives change you suggests risk, vulnerability, and self-forgiveness when you goof up. For white educators and pedagogical leaders working cross-culturally, it's so important to remember what those exercise balance discs reveal about the exhilaration of staying in tune with yourself and not falling flat on your face. Seeking to maintain a sense of balance and poise, we worry at questions like: What if I unintentionally offend someone? What if they think I'm a racist? What if I start crying? It's useful to notice these worries, but rather than make them the focus of our interactions, our work is to replace those concerns with questions that genuinely seek to understand another perspective. We wonder, "How is my colleague experiencing this conversation?" And then check that out. "Can you offer me any thinking from your perspective?" Here's how pedagogical leader, Kelly Mathews describes what she's learned as a white woman working cross culturally:

> Taking a risk is determined by an internal alarm. Something dings or rings or screams and says, this isn't comfortable; this is beyond my skill set; I can't do this—or I shouldn't do this—or some other message that says, CAUTION.

> I've been delivering professional development sessions for years now—there is no internal alarm as I reach a stage and address hundreds of people for a keynote. There's excitement and energy, for sure, but it doesn't feel risky. But recently, I've had the opportunity to work with another professional development facilitator, Ijumaa Jordan, an African American woman, who has invited me to work with her to write articles and create and deliver professional development sessions that explore play equity issues, the racial identity development of young children, and the negative impact of the 'colorblind' approach. Let me be clear, working with Ijumaa is *not* a risk as she is a thoughtful, supportive, intentional friend and mentor—but the content can feel risky to me, as a white woman who has been surrounded by privilege. Exploring these ideas out loud and for publication in early childhood journals feels risky. It feels risky but it also feels right. It feels right because, as I deepen my understanding of the impacts of systemic racism, I realize that people of color take risks nearly every moment and white people need to understand that and not always play it safe. It feels right even though I know my risk is not the same risk Ijumaa takes when she talks about them. And even as it feels right, I worry that even in writing this, the focus is on my feelings about the work, rather than decentralizing white experience in anti-racism work. It feels hard and complicated

and there are times where I feel ill-equipped but *my comfort is not more important than young children's healthy and supported racial identity development.* So I take a deep breath, and I dig in—to the ideas, the questions, the pain, the beauty, the impact. I embrace the risk because the word 'ally' can't just be a noun and I (and we) have work to do.[10]

When Ann says, "Standing together in the midst of our differences, we practice holding those differences with affection for and commitment to each other," I picture Kelly and Ijumaa standing together as they work their way through their different inheritances from the pernicious disease of racism. They face into how they each feel, how people perceive and treat them differently. They've become critical friends with affection for and commitment to each other. Kelly and Ijumaa exemplify the Rev. Dr. Martin Luther King's idea of "beloved community," which bell hooks describes like this: "Beloved community is formed not by the eradication of difference but by its affirmation, by each of us claiming the identities and cultural legacies that shape who we are and how we live in the world."[11]

Unwilling to be Satisfied by Our Immediate Assumptions

I'm provoked to ask, "In your work, what do you resign yourself to settle for, though a deeper hunger lingers within you?" Sometimes our experiences are so far from our real desires that we just settle for what we get, which in turn, starts to dampen hopes for any other possibility. So much of what is offered to educators and administrators to improve quality has very little to do with what we value or what we sense would make our work better. We're taunted with unsatisfying promises: one-minute management tips, 10 easy steps, 101 curriculum activities—as if these would engage our interest, let alone our talents. Ann offers a different notion: that we should be unwilling to be satisfied until we've asked deeper questions and explored other likelihoods. And she suggests enticing outcomes: "Stale assumptions vanish and new possibilities are revealed." These stale assumptions could be about what's possible in relationships with children and families, with people whose lives are very different from ours, with the potential for our work to be deeply satisfying. Ann paints the bold strokes of how this might feel:

> Staying flexible in our thinking, willing to hold off on drawing conclusions about what the children are up to and what they need from us—or what we can do to move towards a pre-determined outcome for a child's learning—we seek to follow a child's trajectory of thought and we hope it leads us to our own disequilibrium, unsettling what we assumed to be true. *That's* a good day at work.

Bodies of Knowledge that Inform Our Meaning-Making

The Thinking Lens asks us to consider multiple perspectives. We can't always do this in face-to-face conversations. Educators seek different perspectives for exploring the significance of daily observations, drawing on the skills of forensic detectives: looking for traces, witnesses, connections, and previous records in an effort to piece together an understanding of why something happened, what could be explored next. The Thinking Lens offers questions to help us move beyond the superficial and the familiar in this detective work.

We recognize children as imbedded in family and culture, and we acknowledge the need to locate ourselves in those points of views and funds of knowledge. Our understandings can also be informed by theories, research, and professional literature within and outside the educational arena; by animals, birds, rocks, mountains, rivers, and trees; by TED talks, fables, poems, music, science, and the arts.

Meaning-making is an ongoing reflection process, always tentative; as time moves along and you encounter more perspectives, it can be disconcerting to discover what you've overlooked and not questioned. I want to recall an example from my own professional learning of a time when I began to understand some perplexing observations in light of new knowledge and theories about culturally relevant teaching. I'll share reflections on highlights of my journey within the structure of the questions that Ann offers us from *The Early Years Learning Framework for Australia.*[12]

My dilemma in my early years of coaching work: As a believer in learner-centered, progressive education for all children and educators, I was dismayed to repeatedly see dedicated, progressive, well-meaning white teachers failing to meet up with the hearts and minds of children of color, especially young Black boys.

What theories, philosophies and understandings shape and assist my work? In Chapter Two, I described the ways in which Paulo Freire and Myles Horton influenced my thinking, especially their call to replace the banking method of education with one of problem-posing education. This, and the philosophies of John Dewey and the theories of Jean Piaget, shaped my early embrace of progressive education. I strongly believed that children have to construct their own knowledge, and that their learning should be shaped by a natural progression through developmental stages, not directed by teachers.

Who is advantaged when I work in this way? Who is disadvantaged? The way that this philosophy was applied in early childhood classrooms served white children and white teachers well, but often left children of color unengaged, and eventually getting into "trouble." I didn't understand, for a long while, why this was, but young Black boys, particularly, seemed unsure how to understand what they were supposed to do. Their active minds and bodies rarely found a focus or resting place. This left them excluded from solid relationships and successful learning. Furthermore, they got a reputation as "the bad kids" among their white peers, which surely meant they were internalizing an identity of "not being good enough." I think the whole group of children and the teachers became disadvantaged of a productive, enjoyable learning experience together. I began to recognize that I really needed to do more reflecting to understand blind spots in my thinking and working theories, because I do believe that children and teachers of all cultures can benefit from the ideas of progressive education.

Ijumaa Jordan helped me articulate that the problem is not the Black children, but white teachers teaching from their cultural perspectives within an educational system steeped in white privilege. All children deserve education that is centered around their racial and socio-cultural identity—a commitment which is at the heart of progressive education. As Jordan says, "an identity of 'not being good enough' is part of the harm that can be done by not decentering whiteness, by failing to offer a culturally responsive educational experience." These many years later, I've come to understand that when classrooms are designed for those already benefiting from the white culture of power, children of color will suffer, if not fail.

What aspects of my work are not helped by the theories and guidance that I usually draw on to make sense of what I do? In those early days, my effectiveness as a coach suffered because it took a while for me to spot that my assumptions about the best way to teach weren't translating into useful practices and were undermining my commitment to social justice. I re-read Piaget as my bible, trying to better understand the development of young Black boys while continuing to emphasize to all teachers the importance of children constructing their own knowledge. Now I see that I hadn't yet grasped the core understandings and orientations embedded in "I," or individual-oriented cultures, and "we" cultures which emphasized collective identity. Nor had I yet explored the implications of the cognitive learning styles that often accompany these cultural differences: "field-independent" (oriented toward independent processing) and "field-dependent" (a more social and interpersonal orientation). I needed to study these bodies of knowledge to enhance meaning-making in my coaching.

Are there other theories or knowledge that could help me to understand better what I have observed or experienced? What are they? How might those theories and that knowledge affect my practice? Graduate school at Pacific Oaks College expanded my thinking beyond Piaget and "anti-bias education" to include "culturally relevant practices." I began to understand that teachers need to recognize deeper issues of culture and to adjust their teaching styles with individual learners. My thinking about a teacher's role in setting the stage for different learning styles and cultures began to shift as I was exposed to the theories of Vygotsky and the ideas of social constructivism and scaffolding children's learning. Lisa Delpit's formulation about how issues of power are enacted in classrooms helped me see the limits of my own perspectives and approach.[13] Delpit poignantly describes how white people have shaped the culture of power with codes or rules (often absorbed and unspoken) that guide participation in that power; this, in turn, shapes teachers and schools. She says:

> If you are not already a participant in the culture of power, being told explicitly the rules of that culture makes acquiring power easier. In my work within and between diverse cultures, I have come to conclude that members of any culture transmit information implicitly to co-members. However, when implicit codes are attempted across cultures, communication frequently breaks down. Each cultural group is left saying, 'Why don't those people say what they mean?' As well as 'What's wrong with them, why don't they understand?'[14]

So, I came to recognize that I was promoting an implicit way of talking and interacting that had roots in the culture of power. I was encouraging free-flowing classroom environments and teacher talk that communicated that "Everyone is free to move around the room and find something interesting to play with," which was far too confusing for children of color whose home cultures have cultural codes where stronger adult direction is a value. If children of color were to benefit from the approach/philosophy/theories my coaching aimed for, they needed more scaffolding. In some cases, it might work better for an educator to take the hand of an African American child and say, "Let's walk around the room and see what you could play with that would be fun and help you learn things that are useful to know. I'll show you each of the choices; you may come up with something else, and that's okay."

Jordan reminds me, "There's no one prescriptive approach for all African American children, and white teachers, especially, have to be diligent not to generalize, stereotype, or offer a surface understanding of children's culture." Delpit's writing expressed concern that some educators misunderstood the implications of her theories, which weren't advocating drill and skill teaching for children of color, but, rather, more explicit teacher talk that provides a stronger structure. This is, of course, quite a different pedagogy than teachers directing the children's every move. Again, structures for openness that serves diversity, creativity, and problem solving.

I started watching more closely the ways in which skilled African American child-centered educators interacted with children, and this further illuminated my understanding of culturally relevant practices and Delpit's idea of helping children of color learn the rules of the culture of power. Delpit challenges educators to help children of color value their own family, culture, and language, recognizing, for instance, that in addition to "school English" there is also Black English or African American Vernacular (AAV): "How we talk at home is different, not wrong, from how we talk in school." Again, Jordan cautions me to understand that helping children of color with "school talk" will make them more palatable to the white world, but undoing racist systems that uphold inequality is the real goal, not assimilation. Delpit advocates for teaching that helps children critique the dominant culture power structures; this resonates with Freire's pedagogical approach, which directs us to learn to "read the word to read the world."

One fond memory from this period of tremendous growth for me was my experience helping a white teacher rethink what she was seeing when she described three Black boys who "always flailed around and disrupted circle time," who were "always on the move during open-ended play time." I videoed these boys during the morning, and then, during naptime, Carol and I watched the scene with the sound off, looking closely for details to describe. Then we played it again, this time concurrently playing the soundtrack of a song I had discovered on a children's album by Sweet Honey in the Rock.[15] Introducing the song *"Juba This and Juba That,"* Sweet Honey offered an explanation of its origins in history during slave times, a rhythmic way to send codes which eventually evolved into the song and dance genre of rhythmic hand clapping and dance.

Eureka! Instead of pathologizing these Black boys, Carol could now marvel at their talent and self-awareness that their bodies had so much to communicate.

(Today, we would understand they were building important brain pathways, aware that active play is a critical part of sensory motor development and actually builds neural pathways necessary for children to focus, self-regulate, and carry out a task.) With this new insight, she began changing how she used her circle time, alternating more active call and response rhythm activities with quiet sitting and listening. She slowly reconfigured her environment to provide more space for children's bodies to move as they worked. For instance, she arranged some tables with chairs, and others without chairs. Carol had a loft built for the classroom that incorporated a mini-obstacle course in its design. We began to see flaws in our assumptions that "allowing" big body movement inside would lead to chaos and behavior disruptions. Being able to move more, in fact, helped the children focus; today's neuroscience underscores that observation of ours.

A final point worth making: Because I lived in a predominantly white world, I recognized the importance of diversifying my social life, my reading, shopping, and range of cultural events, so that I would be changed, and become a more effective ally, coach, and social justice advocate. Finally, a place to make camp in my disequilibrium with insights nudging changes in my thinking about pedagogy and my coaching practices.

As my mind pulls away from these reflections, I'm immediately reminded of another example of coming to these understandings, shared by my colleague Deb Curtis. In her very child-focused and child-directed preschool class, a child in an Asian family said to her, "I really like coming to preschool and all of the things we play with here, but when are you going to teach me something?" Priya's question provoked Deb to begin exploring how she could be more explicit with the children about the learning opportunities she offered them. So, for instance, she'd say, "When I ask you to draw your block structure, it's because that will help you think more about how you made it balance. The more thinking you do about how you learn when you play, the smarter you get." "When you work with me to make 'an instruction book' for how kids can build towers with bridges that don't fall down, you'll realize how much you've learned about jobs called structural engineering and architectural design, and you can inspire others to learn about that, too." Eventually, we summarized Deb's teacher research about how educators can explicitly describe "how to learn more when you play" into a set of principles for coaching children to learn about learning, published as a chapter in our book, *Learning Together with Young Children.*[16]

As an individual or group of educators, could you choose a dilemma you face and practice using the questions from the Australian framework to uncover new possibilities? As I tried this, I found it enormously helpful to recognize what ideas were influencing my practice and then consider what assumptions and theories weren't proving useful in supporting children's learning, especially in cross cultural contexts. Most teacher education in the United States fails to help educators specifically consider the theoretical frameworks influencing their practice. When you try analyzing a dilemma with the Australian questions, notice how easy or hard it is for you to name any philosophy or theories that guide your work. This will help you become more intentional in applying the theories and philosophies you want to guide your teaching.

* *

How grounded in theoretical and philosophical perspectives do you think your work is?

* *

Consider whether it would it be helpful for you to reflect on these questions from our Australian colleagues:

- *What theories, philosophies, and understandings shape and assist my work?*

- *Who is advantaged when I work in this way? Who is disadvantaged?*

- *What aspects of my work are not helped by the theories and guidance that I usually draw on to make sense of what I do?*

- *Are there other theories or knowledge that could help me to understand better what I have observed or experienced? What are they? How might those theories and that knowledge affect my practice?*

A nun I know … speaks of a certain mood of 'unexamined receptivity,' which does not mean, she says, merely the willingness to listen carefully or patiently. 'It has to do with quieting your state of mind as you prepare to listen. It means not pressing on too fast to get to something that you think you 'need to get to' as the 'purpose' or 'objective' of the conversation … There's a difference between 'getting' and 'receiving' … ' There's something about silence and not being in a hurry and not being in an overly convivial or overly determinative state of mind, or one that's loaded with too much intentionality that seem to give a message about receptivity.

I also think that children need some reason to believe that what they say will not be heard too clinically, or journalistically, or put 'to use' too rapidly, and that the gift they give us will be taken into hands that will not seize too fast upon their confidence, or grasp too firmly, or attempt to push an idea to completion when it needs to be left open, incomplete, and tentative a while.

—*Jonathan Kozol*[13]

The Thinking Lens: Planning

Planning: a word that carries decades of meaning in our field. Educators plan curriculum and activities. Educators use charts to create lesson plans to teach content and academic skills. To help them plan, educators reference lists of age- and grade-linked goals that lay out what children are expected to learn. This is the long-standing and time-worn concept of planning, and it's anchored in specific stories about teaching and learning: educators are accountable for delivering knowledge and children are accountable for mastering that knowledge. For this to come together most effectively and efficiently, educators organize content into discreet arenas and design incremental steps towards proficiency. They plan.

In the pedagogical practice embodied in the Thinking Lens, this conceptualization of planning is turned on its head. Rather than planning in order to lead a child to a particular revelation, or to direct a child's thinking towards content knowledge that we've determined has merit, we plan in ways that are useful for the child's course of exploration—which is to say, for the child's development as a thinker.

The goal of our planning is to honor and support the children's imbedded intent—the purpose inside their play. We aim to sustain children's course of exploration: the theories they're testing, the questions they're pursuing, the understandings and misunderstandings with which they're wrestling. We consider *what* the children are thinking about, and we consider *how* the children are thinking about it. And we plan opportunities for children to engage their thinking more deeply, or from a new angle, or with a new complexity, to strengthen their identity as hungry and able thinkers and learners.

With the Thinking Lens, learning is not teacher-directed—following the model in which educators plan learning activities with the goal that children will achieve measurable outcomes. Nor is it child-directed—following the model in which educators organize the environment and then step back, not structuring children's play or offering direction for their pursuits. Instead, it's a co-created project of investigation, questioning, and understanding, in which children pursue ideas of meaning and substance with educators' companionship and mentorship, and educators strive to understand and strengthen children's thinking about their pursuits.

Guided by the Thinking Lens, educators listen to and watch children's play with self-awareness and curiosity. We seek to make meaning of their play by consulting a range of perspectives, and we plan responsive offerings to children aimed at honoring the intellectual, emotional, and relational meaning embedded in their play. We move between receptive and active roles, between listening and speaking. This makes for a lively spirit of immediacy, and calls for the strong muscle of intellect and intention. It's harder work than either a teacher-directed or a child-directed approach to planning, and it's more sustaining, more invigorating. We're present to what children offer us, and we're thoughtful about those offerings, listening for their reverberant meanings; we're inventive and humble in our reciprocal offerings.

We plan in the way that researchers plan. We don't simply watch and wait and measure, nor do we try to force an outcome by sheer effort and will. We have an active role, but not a directive role: an exploratory role, the role of experimentation and inquiry. We form hypotheses and we test them. We add to our knowledge even as we support children adding to their knowledge. We participate in the project of learning, alongside the children. We seek to increase the complexity of our thinking about children's thinking, as we join our attention to the children's attention, and move from a stance of tentativeness and curiosity.

The Thinking Lens is a planning tool for co-constructing learning. The last part of the Thinking Lens swings us from reflective study to intentional action:

Reflect and take action.

- What values and intentions do you want to influence your response?
- What action might you take to help the children see their own and each other's ideas? What might you do to invite the children to take a different perspective?
- How will you invite collaboration? What might you do to deepen children's relationships with each other, their families, the Earth, and/or the community?
- How will you continue to seek out the children's points of view? How will you collaborate with families?

Planning to Act from Values and Intention

Our planned offerings speak volumes about our beliefs about the purpose of education and how to realize that purpose. Traditional approaches to planning grow from values that foreground the mastery of content knowledge and academic skills. The approach to planning articulated in the Thinking Lens holds intentions for and values about collaboration, questioning, complexity, critical and inventive thinking. It holds values for inquiry, the children's and our own: inquiry about questions that matter, questions of substance, questions that puzzle and intrigue: real questions, which Bob Strachota defines as questions that engage "the teacher and the learner in exploring the mysteries of the universe, rather than [questions] which engage the learner in exploring the mysteries of what the teacher wants her to say or know or do."[1] Values for questions inform the sorts of offerings that we make to children—invitations to explore why and how and what if.

Our values about social justice teaching and learning inform our planning: values about interrogating assumptions about belonging and not-belonging, about identity and worth; values for empathy and solidarity. We hold values about ecology, values about connection, values about intellectual striving and about physical expression and spiritual exploration. The last step of the Thinking Lens asks us to call forward the values and intentions that we want to shape our planning, and use them as references as we decide what we'll offer to the children.

Planning to Deepen Children's Thinking

Remember Carrie Melsom's declaration that "educators ought to join our attention to the children's attention, rather than asking the children to join their attention to what we think they ought to pay attention to, or to the learning goals and content knowledge that has our attention"?[2] We join our attention to the children's attention by planning offerings that speak to the questions the children are holding, the ideas they're exploring—not on the surface, but the deep thinking and exploring held inside children's play. Our planning is spacious, flexible, and imaginative: we follow a child's trajectory of thinking and wondering—her imbedded intent—rather than striding towards a pre-determined outcome in content knowledge. Our offerings are invitations to dig deeper, to follow a line of inquiry, to seek new questions:

- What action might you take to help the children see their own and each other's ideas?
- What might you do to invite the children to take a different perspective?
- How will you invite collaboration? What might you do to deepen children's relationships with each other, their families, the Earth, and/or the community?

These questions are aimed at keeping us connected to the children's thinking—and keeping children connected to their thinking.

Planning to Deepen Our Understandings

The Thinking Lens asks us to plan for our own continuing learning: How will you continue to seek out the child's point of view? This simple question undergirds our role as teacher researchers. We plan offerings based on our hypotheses about what has the children's attention—the questions and considerations inside their play. How the children take up (or don't take up) our offerings helps us sharpen our hypotheses, gives us feedback about whether we're on the right track, informs our research as we swing through another cycle of observation, meaning making, and planning.

When we plan as teacher researchers, we stay humble and curious, flexible and non-attached. We plan only one next offering, not weeks down the road, because we know that how the children make use of each offering will shape our next offering.

• • • • • • • • Our plans are not all-encompassing gestures of omnipotence, but queries: "Am I understanding what has your attention?" "Is this useful for your pursuit?" "What else can you show me about what you're thinking about?" Step by step, our research carries us into expanded and deepened understandings.

Planning to Learn with Families

How will you collaborate with families? asks the last step of the Thinking Lens—because we come together with children's families to construct understandings and unearth new questions. The Thinking Lens doesn't ask how we'll *inform* families about our plans, or how we'll *report* the children's undertakings to them, or when we'll give them our *assessment* of their children's learning. It asks us to collaborate with them: sharing our observations of children's play for continued study together, generating hypotheses and considering action that we might take, all of us researchers, joining our attention to the children's attention, expanding our understandings with the range and scope of our diverse perspectives.

Moving from Meaning-Making to Action

The planning process follows a rhythm of expansion and contraction, expansion and contraction. It begins with the meaning-making held by the first steps of the Thinking Lens, which expands the possibilities for understanding by consulting a range of perspectives and articulating hypotheses about the meaning of children's play. From there, a contraction: we choose one hypothesis to pursue—and then we expand our thinking, again, considering all sorts of offerings that we might make in relation to that hypothesis. Then, another contraction: we choose one offering, and plan with precision for how we'll make that offering.

Generative and invigorating, this approach contrasts with other ways of planning both in intention and practice. Rather than a monthly or seasonal rotation of activities on topical themes, or learning stations set up to teach for outcomes, or discrete games and projects linked on a curriculum web, planning with the Thinking Lens unfolds one step at a time, with detours and meanders and unexpected course changes always possible—in fact, hoped for, as new questions offer themselves and new puzzlements and problems arise, both for the children and for us.

What this planning process looks like: Consider this game that we'd see in all sorts of programs …

Three children are tucked into the drama area: one child is the mommy cat and the other two children are her baby kittens, and together, this kitty family moves through the rhythms of family life. The mommy makes supper and the kittens gulp and swig and burp and laugh. The mommy puts her kittens to bed, tucking them in lovingly and firmly. But the kittens don't stay in bed—they get up in the night and goof around in their bedroom, playfully wrestling and pulling the covers off the bed and throwing their stuffed animals around. The mommy swoops into their room and scolds them back into bed, tucking them in with their stuffed animals and bedclothes back in place. As soon as she's gone, the kittens leap up again and sneak out of the room, out of the house, out of the yard—they're run-away kittens! It's a lark, at first, until they become lost and frightened, and then they call out for their mommy, mewing plaintively. The mommy hurries to her kittens, and comforts them, and ushers them home. She makes a meal for the children, and they read a book together, then she puts them to bed, and the cycle repeats itself ... On and on, through the morning in the drama area, these three children enact this spinning story, mommy and kittens together.

———

Before we step into planning, we move through the first few steps of the Thinking Lens. We open our hearts to this moment, feeling its full reverberation. Then we take the children's points of view, and examine the environment, and seek other perspectives to help us understand the play inside this play. And then we begin to braid these considerations into hypotheses about the meaning of this play—hypotheses that will carry us into taking action.

Homing in on a Hypothesis

It's a good bet that the children's kitty play doesn't mean the children are interested in learning about cats. Diving below the surface of their play, we seek to find its potent resonance. In conversation with colleagues and families, we generate a list of possible meanings. The children's kitty play may be about:

- the roles of mommies and children;
- being good and misbehaving;
- following and breaking rules;
- the daily rhythms of family life;
- being separated and being re-united.

These hypotheses keep us from chasing off after cute activities related to the surface appearance of the children's play—cat families, or the intricacies of cat care. We lay our hypotheses alongside insights from children's families and our co-teachers, information from child development and schema theory, and wisdom about being human offered by myths and age-old stories that echo with the themes in the children's play, and we look for reasons to choose one hypothesis over another as the hypothesis we'll follow when we make our first responsive offering to the children.

How *do* we choose? How do we know which hypothesis to take up?

Some considerations to guide our choosing: The Thinking Lens directs us to articulate the values and intentions that we want to foreground—our hopes for children's learning and the beliefs and commitments that undergird those hopes. We study our list of hypotheses and ask: What values and intentions would be in play if we pursue the roles of mommies and children? Being good and misbehaving? What values and intentions would we prioritize if we take up the thread of following and breaking rules, or the daily rhythms of family life, or being separated and being re-united?

• • • • • • This examination of values and intentions keeps us aware and clear as we choose a direction to explore. We aim to move consciously from awareness of our values, cultural perspectives, and beliefs, rather than being unconsciously swept forward by them.

What makes us more interested in one hypothesis and less interested in another? What makes us foreground one possible trajectory and background another? We can invite the values and intentions of the children's families into this evaluation of possibilities. Do their values and intentions give us reason to lean one way or another?

Another way of looking at the possible hypotheses is to consider which seems most immediately resonant in light of who these children are, individually and collectively. When we study the hypotheses about the kitty game through this lens, we ask questions like: What other play have we and their families seen the children engage? Do any of the themes from the hypotheses show up in other play? What's the social and emotional culture of this particular cohort of children? What do these children care about and wonder about? What big ideas have been spilling into children's play? What big ideas have we been intentionally spotlighting?

If, after these lines of examination, we're still uncertain about which way to go, concerned about choosing the right hypothesis to explore, here's the good news: there's no way to go wrong with our intentional action. What we offer the children may engage them fully, with reverberations that sing out wonderfully through the weeks ahead. Or it may not land for them at all, it may fizzle or flop. It may spark in a direction that we don't anticipate, a direction that seems completely unrelated to our intention. No harm, no foul. We're going to learn something, no matter what; as teacher researchers, we watch what comes of our offering with openness and curiosity, with non-attachment, and what we see teaches us about what has the children's attention—and what doesn't. We're in service of inquiry, of thinking, of following the threads of questions. When our offering captures the children's minds and hearts, it creates an exhilarating buzz of energy that carries us all forward. When our offering lands flat, it's disappointing, but it's not no-good.

Loris Malaguzzi, one of the founders of the schools in Reggio Emilia, Italy, suggested that we ought to think of a hundred possibilities for the meaning and direction of children's play, so that, when the children offer us the hundred-and-first, we're warmed up and ready to go.[3] And the great writer Flannery O'Connor said, "Sometimes I work for months and have to throw everything away, but I don't think any of that time was wasted. Something goes on that makes it easier when it does come well. And the fact is if you don't sit there every day, the day it would come well you won't be sitting there."[4] We become teacher researchers by doing research; our muscle and skill are only strengthened by our thoughtful offerings, intentionally made, and by our careful study of what comes of them, exhilarating or disappointing.

So—we choose a hypothesis that we'll explore with an offering to the children. And then we consider what action we'll take in relation to that hypothesis.

Looking at our list of possible meanings for the children's kitty game, let's play with the hypothesis that the game is about being good and misbehaving.

Setting a Course for Action

We don't, now, set off on a weeks-long course of activities related to being good and misbehaving or intended to teach the children about standards and consequences for good and bad behavior. We're in a conversation, not a monologue, and it's our turn to contribute an idea, and then listen some more.

We consider what we might offer that will support the children's dispositional learning, the development of mind and heart rather than the acquisition of topical knowledge. We strive to strengthen dispositions like self-awareness, capacity for collaboration, eagerness to contribute, curiosity about diverse perspectives, persistence, and keen communication.

What might we offer children that will fortify these dispositions even as it invites further engagement with the big idea they're pursuing? Some arenas of action to consider:

What could we offer that would invite children's self-awareness?

- about their thinking;
- about their feeling;
- about their wondering;
- about their knowing.

How could we help children see their own and each other's ideas? How can we make their thinking visible?

- the theories and questions embedded in children's play;
- the patterns that reveal a trajectory of thought;
- loosely formed ideas that need further exploration; contradictions or inconsistencies;
- understandings and misunderstandings at the heart of children's thinking.

What could we offer that would invite collaboration and contribution?

What could we offer that would deepen children's relationships?

- with each other;
- with their families;
- with the natural world;
- with the community.

What could we offer that would invite children to take a different perspective?
- being inside, being outside;
- being small, being big;
- being another person or creature.

How might we call forward children's emotional and spiritual ways of knowing and relating?
- their perspective-taking and curiosity, empathy and compassionate action;
- their reverence, awe, awareness of mystery;
- the full spectrum of feeling, from grief to joy, anger to tenderness, fear to confidence, self-doubt to pride.

How could we invite children's physical engagement?
- with their senses;
- with strength and muscle;
- their perceptivity;
- their experience of balance, stillness, speed.

How might we honor the risks children take?
- physical;
- emotional;
- relational;
- intellectual.

How could we connect this moment to the developmental themes or schema of childhood?
- transporting materials; exploring trajectory;
- connecting and disconnecting;
- pretending and transforming;
- building and constructing; enclosing and enveloping;
- inventing and playing games;
- engaging in meaningful work.

These questions are broad-reaching; they don't all have resonance in every planning cycle. Some are more relevant than others to a particular course of study. You'll recognize which questions are most useful, as you move through the planning process.

Notice that there's nothing in these questions about "What would be the most fun, or cute, or immediately pleasing thing to do? How can I generate a quick product for children to take home for the refrigerator? What will let me tick off the most boxes on the assessment?"

• • • • • Our commitments are to thinking, to inquiry, to generative investigation, and to complexity. We're involved in a constant cycle of planning, not a one-time blow-out, as we continue to join our attention to the children's attention through our ongoing practice of observation and reflection.

As we consider action we might take and offerings we might make, our focus is on representational languages, materials, and the environment. We avoid planning to "talk about" an idea with children, but, instead, offer invitations for engagement with experiences like drawing, building, painting, sculpting, dancing, and pretending. Young children's ideas—like ours—are often vaguely formed, not fully articulated. Sometimes, children's work is anchored in intuition or instinct; they aren't so much thinking about what they're doing as simply doing it. A child can give an idea form by drawing, painting, sculpting, or building it. In doing so, she begins to clarify her ideas; she considers details and wrestles with inconsistencies. When her idea is visible, other children and adults can engage with it, thinking with her about its nuances and complexities, its gaps and incongruities. (You can read more about the potent role of representational languages in inquiry in my book, *The Language of Art*.[5])

Back to the kitty game. We've decided to explore the hypothesis that the children's kitty game is about being good and misbehaving; let's think about the nuances of that aspect of the game … The kitties' misbehavior is fabulously outrageous, bold and big and delighting to the children; they crack themselves up with their naughtiness. There are no severe consequences for their bad behavior: their mommy chastises them, but then she feeds them a nice meal and reads them a story and tucks them back into bed. She's demonstrating either great trust in her kitties' capacity to do better at being good or great naiveté about their propensity for mischief. The mommy and the kitties play two distinct roles in this game: the mommy holds out the possibility for good behavior and the kitties explore all sorts of possibilities for misbehavior—making a mess, making a ruckus, throwing things around, running away.

Given these shadings of the hypothesis about being good and misbehaving, what might we offer the children?

What could we offer that would deepen relationships? Tell the children a story about a time when you made mischief as a child, using photos from your childhood.

What could we offer that would invite children's self-awareness? Create a story about a time when you were mischievous and it was funny.

How could we help children see their own and each other's ideas? How can we make their thinking visible? Make a book of misbehaving and a book of being good.

What could we offer that would invite collaboration and contribution? What could we offer that would deepen children's relationships? How do children encourage each other to make mischief? How do children help each other to be good?

What could we offer that would invite children to take a different perspective? Draw a list of the things that moms think are misbehaviors. Do children agree that those things are misbehavior, or do they have different ideas?

How might we call forward children's emotional and spiritual ways of knowing and relating? How could we invite children's physical engagement? How might we honor the risks children take? Can you show with your body what it feels like to be good? What it feels like to misbehave? Is it scary to misbehave? Do you have to be brave? Can you show that with your body?

How could we connect this moment to the developmental themes of childhood, like pretending and transforming? Take turns being the mommy trying to teach good behavior to her kittens.

Sometimes, we might offer something that departs from the immediate focus of the original play, but that gets at the big idea that we think the children are exploring: our invitation may not have anything to do with kitty families, but everything to do with good and bad behavior. And sometimes, after considering a range of options for action, we might decide that we need to understand more about the children's play before we do anything, and so we commit to continue watching—which isn't the same as "doing nothing." We watch with a consciously articulated question in mind to focus our observation.

Expand, contract, expand, contract: following this planning rhythm, we generate a list of possible actions we could take, and then we choose one. How to choose?

We look for the offering that:
- is most lively and engaging, and invites expression beyond simple conversation or "talking-about";
- has potential to expand outwards in a range of directions, increasing complexity and generating new questions;
- expresses our values, and engages with the values of the children's families;
- has potential for strengthening the particular dispositions that we hope to foster in these particular children;
- spotlights children's strengths or the arenas in which we would like them to stretch and be challenged;
- brings children into collaborative relationships with each other in energizing ways;
- involves learning domains that we'd like the children to engage such as literacy, math, scientific processes, and ecological and social justice understandings.

As we plan, we'll likely get excited about possibilities for further exploration—questions about rule-making and rule-breaking, perhaps; consideration of why people misbehave and why they comply with standards for good behavior; questions about whether misbehavior sometimes serves a worthy purpose ... We can generate all sorts of ideas about where we might go—but we do that just to stay flexible and alert, knowing that there will be good surprises and unexpected directions that we can't imagine yet. We restrain ourselves from falling back on the old habit of planning a long way down the road, and we try not to get deeply invested in our enthusiastic ideas. We remind ourselves of our commitment to join our attention to the children's attention rather than asking them to join their attention to what we think they ought to pursue.

• • • • • • • • We choose one offering to make, in service of increasing the complexity of the children's and our own thinking. And then we thoughtfully plan for how we'll make that offering, with the lightest touch.

Planning the Nuts and Bolts

Once we've settled on a next step, we plan for it with precision:
- What will we do, specifically, to enact our offering?
- What materials will we need?
- When will we make this offering to children?
- Which children do we particularly want to engage with this invitation?
- How will we capture the experience for our next round of study and meaning-making and planning (audio- or video-tape, written notes, photos)?
- How will we communicate with families about our thinking, and about what's unfolding for the children in this round of exploration and invite their collaboration on the next round?

Part of our planning is for our on-going practice of research. What are we curious about, as we anticipate how the children might take up our offering?

What will we particularly watch for, as we observe children interacting with our invitation? What do we want to learn more about?

Because that's what comes next: another spin through the cycle of pedagogical documentation. We make a planned offering—and then we watch and listen, and make notes and collect traces of children's play, and study them to make meaning, to refine our initial hypothesis or to take up a different trajectory if our first offering didn't seem to land for the children. The Thinking Lens is a cycle. Our intentionally planned action spins us back to observation, and to the first step of the Thinking Lens, and on into study and further planning.

When we move through this cycle again and again, it spins us forward into long-term, in-depth investigations. More about this in Chapter 13.

A related note: In the explaining, the Thinking Lens cycle takes pages and pages. In its practice, it can take moments. Remember Mandie, with Austin on the table? Once internalized, the Thinking Lens can become instinctive practice. But it takes a while to internalize it, to replace old habits with new habits of mind and heart. As pedagogical leaders, we cultivate new habits in ourselves and in educators by moving methodically and deliberately through the Thinking Lens cycle, in one-on-one discussions with educators, during teaching team meetings and all-staff meetings—and when we're side-by-side with educators in the classroom. In the immediacy of classroom play, we can stand with an educator to observe children's play, and use the Thinking Lens to wonder aloud about its possible meanings and how we might respond right there and then, even as we encourage them to bring their thoughts about this play to their colleagues and to families for further development, in a quieter, slower-paced moment.

When we join our attention to children's attention, and become, with them, researchers and thinkers, we honor our right and the right of children to authentic, participatory, unscripted, and innovative expression. This mutual participation in generative creativity is an essential aspect of human dignity. Carla Rinaldi locates this in the context of human rights:

Children appreciate the fact that we are side-by-side with them in their search for answers: the child-researcher and the teacher-researcher … Only in this way will children return with full rights among the builders of human culture. Only in this way will they sense that their wonder and their discoveries are truly appreciated because they are useful. Only in this way can children hope to reacquire their human dignity, and no longer be considered 'objects of care.'[6]

When we plan from a stance of curiosity, when our offerings to children are intended as generative invitations into inquiry, when we act as teacher researchers, our classrooms become lively and enlivening places. Exploring real questions together, we and the children act as innovators and inventors, expansive in our thinking and in our expression.

Margie Carter

Our Plans are Queries

The notion that we should be planning from questions rather than creating lessons aimed at particular outcomes may be theoretically or personally appealing to you, but what about all that pressure to demonstrate outcomes through assessment results? What's the right thing to do when you believe in one thing and are required to do something else? Here's where you invite equanimity to join you in your base camp of disequilibrium. Without it, it's easy to lose your footing in the face of the avalanche of deadlines for gathering data for assessment tools.

Equanimity. Your thesaurus will show you that synonyms include composure, calmness, levelheadedness, and self-control. But I was first introduced to the term as part of my yoga practice. Equanimity was explained as one of the four limitless qualities we can have when we are mindful. More than just calmness, in the Buddhist way of thinking, equanimity comes from the word *tatramajjhattata*, which means "to stand in the middle," referring to a balance that comes from inner stability—remaining centered when we are constantly being pulled in one direction or another. For educators wanting to do "the right thing," Buddhist teacher Pema Chodron has wise words: "We are training in equanimity, in thinking bigger than right and wrong."[7] This is guidance I try to offer when I am working with programs that want to take the planning approach described here. You may have to complete those assessments, but you don't need to let that drive your practice. You can create plans that are queries and invent ways to document the observations (evidence) they are based on. At some point, you'll stand in the middle and drop in the codes for the assessment tool. Data for this purpose doesn't drive your pedagogy, it's just a passenger along for the ride. Wherever you stand, remember what to strive for: "keeping us connected to the children's thinking—and keeping children connected to their thinking."

Ann offers several thoughts to guide your planning efforts and efforts to articulate your approach from a proactive stance:

> We have an active role, but not a directive role: an exploratory role, the role of experimentation and inquiry. We form hypotheses and we test them. We add to our knowledge even as we support children adding to their knowledge. We participate in the project of learning, alongside

the children. We seek to increase the complexity of our thinking about children's thinking, as we join our attention to the children's attention, and move from a stance of tentativeness and curiosity.

[Planning is a] co-created project of investigation, questioning, and understanding, in which children pursue ideas of meaning and substance with educators' companionship and mentorship, and educators strive to understand and strengthen children's thinking about their pursuits.

Plan offerings that speak to questions children are holding, ideas they are exploring.

Plan with precision.

A pedagogical leader works closely with educators to be proactive, precise, and prepared to describe the thinking behind decisions they are making. Rather than a teacher saying, "I thought it would be fun if … " or "I thought the children would like to talk about … " she says, "When we saw that the children were … we wondered … and we decided to explore the question … because … " Thinking this way, let alone being able to describe one's thinking, takes practice. As a pedagogical coach, I often use still photos from the life of the classroom to generate ways to talk about our wonderings. I ask educators to "read the photos aloud."

Initially I might offer sentence starters such as:
- When I noticed … I felt … and I wondered …
- The questions I'm most intrigued with about this pursuit are …
- Because I don't know much about … I would like to get a perspective from …
- Because I value … I want to try … so that I can discover more about …

Sentence starters can serve as a scaffold for educators who are learning to first reflect before responding. I find the Thinking Lens a useful tool to help me formulate these sentence starters. The conversations that these sentence starters spark bring to life the notion of bringing intentionality and values to our practice.

Active, not Directive Roles

When I think of teachers taking an active, but not directive role in the planning process, I think about the foundation we lay when we plan the physical and social/emotional environment. Right from the start, the teaching team considers the classroom culture you want to create by applying your values as you plan routines, language, celebrations, and rituals. This same approach applies to planning the physical environment, both at the macro and micro level. For instance, if you value children developing strong relationships and negotiating conflicts, you might choose to put benches rather than chairs at tables. Benches require more than one person to move them, and children can work together to move them around the room. At the micro level, teachers take the lead in offering materials: you may offer props to encourage ongoing exploration of ideas that the children are pursuing, or to provoke a new course of investigation, or to bring an educator's interest or curiosity into the classroom. This last point is sometimes confusing to people who have the idea that materials offered should always be in response to something that is an observed interest of children. Certainly, you want to be responsive to children, but educators have an important role to play in provoking children's thinking, sometimes by offering materials, a question, or a challenge.

Learning is not Teacher-Directed nor is it Child-Directed

When I think of Ann's reminder that the learning we strive for is a co-created project of investigation, the work of a New Zealand educator, Bridgette Towle, comes to mind. I have visited her program many times, and each time, I've witnessed the extraordinary collaboration that the educators engage in with each other and with the children. Bridgette once knocked my socks off with the statement that she could no longer say she believes in child-centered curriculum. What on earth could she mean? I wondered, because Bridgette centers all her work on meeting up with children's minds. Bridgette explained her thinking like this: "It would be wrong to say my room is child-centered because that leaves me out of the equation."

For a taste of the pedagogical work of Bridgette and her colleagues at Kids' Domain, see her book *Cup*, part of the collection, *Reimagining Our Work*, edited by

Ann and me.[8] With stunning images and storytelling, *Cup* describes the interplay between children, educators, and materials as protagonists, which propels an unexpected, long-term investigation, and brings to life Ann's description of co-constructed learning:

> Learning is not teacher-directed—following the model in which educators plan learning activities with the goal that children will achieve measurable outcomes. Nor is it child-directed—following the model in which educators organize the environment and then step back, not structuring children's play or offering direction for their pursuits. Instead, it's a co-created project of investigation, questioning, and understanding, in which children pursue ideas of meaning and substance with educators' companionship and mentorship, and educators strive to understand and strengthen children's thinking about their pursuits.

* *

How can we keep our planning focused on keeping us connected to the children's thinking—and keeping children connected to their thinking?

* *

What would it take to make it so?

* *

As you reflect on these questions, consider your own dispositions, skills, and knowledge, along with the culture and structures that support working this way.

* *

We are now ready to start on our way down the Great Unknown.

We have an unknown distance yet to run, an unknown river yet to explore. What falls there are, we know not; what rocks beset the channel, we know not; what walls rise over the river, we know not.

Ah, well! We may conjecture many things.

*—**John Wesley Powell**[14]*

The Thinking Lens:
Making Thinking Visible

We talk about documentation a lot in early education, often in ways that are reductionist and clinical and generic. *Documentation* has come to mean evaluative descriptions of children's learning and their developmental progress, or minimally imaginative, caption-like accountings of a child's game or of some aspect of her character, general and generic: "Liza, you had a fun time in the sand box today. You really like to play in the sand!"

What we *could* be doing when we create documentation, though, is telling stories that matter: the tender kindness of a child's compassionate gesture towards a crying friend; the muscle of perseverance that a child calls on when he stacks blocks even though they keep toppling; the bold courage that a child musters as she jumps off the climber. These are the stories that we can capture in our documentation, calling the insides of an experience forward, making them visible, honoring them with story.

The author Cheryl Strayed says that there are two questions to consider when writing: What happened in this story? What is this story about?[1] In the typical approach to documentation, we get caught up in the first question—what happened? We recount what a child did or said, and if we tend at all to the second question—what is this story about?—we often reduce the meaning of a story to what a child learned.

• • • • • • But the question, *what is this story about?* is a bigger, deeper question than how a child demonstrated learning. It asks us to dive deep, to find the human meaning in a moment of life. *What is this story about?* What does it tell us about being human?

We've been sitting around campfires telling stories for as long as we've been human. It's not "what happens" in a story that keeps us next to the campfire, leaning forward to hear a story. It's our desire to make meaning that keeps us there: our awareness that stories help us understand what it means to be alive. We gather around campfires to tell stories that offer insights and wisdom. What would change in our documentation practice if we imagined ourselves gathered around a campfire telling stories that matter?

Stories, we think, begin with a storyteller's first words: "Once upon a time … " But that's not right, that's not when stories begin. Stories begin in experience, and in witness of experience. To make a story, we live: we participate in the unfolding life around us, and we pay attention to what we experience. We observe, we wonder, we are astonished and humbled, we're perplexed, we're surprised, we're curious—and then we find language to give voice to our experience and to the thinking and feeling that it sparks. Not with lists of learning outcomes, not with benchmarks and standards, but with story born in careful attention and full-hearted feeling and thoughtful reflection. Stories, like teaching, begin with witness.

Writing as Witness

What does it mean to witness the world? To witness the daily unfolding lives of children?

The word *witness* comes from the Old English word meaning *knowledge* and *understanding*—knowledge and understanding derived from observation and experience, knowledge and understanding that we gain when we are present and attentive, open, curious, tentative about making conclusions— when we bear witness.

Witness is also a noun: a person who gives testimony. Which is what a story is: *testimony* to the world, to each lived moment. Creating a story is a way of testifying about what we observe and experience, and about what stirs in us—feelings, ideas, questions, revelations—because of what we witness.

Here's how Anne Lamott describes the practice of witness and writing, in her book, *Bird by Bird: Some Instructions on Writing and Life*:

> In order to be a writer, you have to learn to be reverent. If not, why are you writing?
>
> Let's think of reverence as awe, as presence in and openness to the world … Think of those times when you've read prose or poetry that is presented in such a way that you have a feeling of being *startled* by beauty or insight, by a glimpse into someone's soul. All of a sudden everything seems to fit together or at least to have some meaning for a moment. This is our goal as writers, I think: to help others have this sense of wonder, of seeing things anew, things that can catch us off guard, that break in on our small, bordered worlds. When this happens, everything feels more spacious.[2]

This can be our intention in our documentation practice: to pay attention, to bear witness, and to tell the stories of what we see and experience in ways that invite others to have the sense of wonder that we have, to see things anew, to stand with us in our reverberant regard for children and childhood.

This notion of witness is embedded in the description of teacher research that we've been referencing, by Daniel Meier and Barbara Henderson:

> Teacher research is systematic, critical inquiry made public. As an approach, teacher research provides a habit of mind and a set of tools that help educators to stop reacting, and begin to see that by just looking, and then telling others what they see, they begin to deepen and clarify their role as early childhood educators.[3]

Habits of mind: reverence and awe, marvel and wonder, presence in and openness to the world.

Looking and then telling others what we see: bearing witness to the inquiry and insights of children, and then crafting stories that invite new ways of seeing, more spacious understandings of teaching and learning.

A pedagogical leader can offer the Thinking Lens to help us tell others what we see—and what moves us and leaves us curious, and what questions rise up in us, and what we think might be happening from the children's perspectives, and what other understandings we want to consult, and what we might do next, and what we hope to learn from families as we take our next steps with children. In a pedagogical approach to documentation, we tell stories to make thinking visible—our own thinking as well as the children's thinking. And we make thinking visible in order to think more, all of us, children, teachers, families, thinking more together.

Documentation stories are the "public" part of "systematic inquiry made public." Notice that Meier and Henderson's description of teacher research doesn't say "a child's learning made public." It says "systematic inquiry" made public—our questioning, experimenting, musing, analyzing. We make public our thinking about children's thinking.

• • • • • • Documentation is not reporting on what children know, or can do, or have learned; documentation is making visible how we educators think about a moment of a child's life that we've witnessed, and the insights and questions that it holds for us. We do this in service of expanding our awareness and our capacity for responsiveness.

Traditionally, documentation has been oriented towards creating a record, however minimal or superficial, of how much or how well children have achieved predetermined outcomes—how many boxes we can tick on a checklist. But when conceptualized as an element of pedagogical practice, documentation serves as a provocation for thinking and study, an insight into both educators and children, an expression of relationship.[4] It is "a process for making pedagogical work visible and subject to interpretation, dialogue, confrontation (argumentation) and understanding," says Peter Moss—systematic inquiry made public.[5] It's not about a piece of paper or pretty display, it's not a report at the end of a project, but the active process of reflection and study. Documentation is not a finished story, but a reflection on a moment in time, made while time continues to flow forward, and the story continues to be lived. In making our inquiry public, in offering it into the community for interpretation, dialogue, confrontation, and argumentation, we hope to get our thinking stirred up, we hope to see new possibilities for understanding and action, we hope to become more responsive and aware.

Why We Write

We write documentation stories for children. The stories we tell offer an entry point for children to revisit their experiences, to re-engage their inquiry or to invite other children into an extension of their earlier work. Louisa Schwartz and Janet Robertson write that: "When revisiting the documentation together with children, we focus on what kind of problem is under construction, what questions have been produced so far, what kind of tools and materials have been tried out and most importantly, to find where the potentials for continuing the construction of the problem are located."[6] Using our documentation stories as launch points, children are invited to study the cognitive knots and tangles of contradiction embedded in their theories, and set course for continued exploration and research.

We write documentation stories for ourselves and our colleagues, to give language to—and, so, to sharpen our thinking about—the experiences we share with children. When I have to write about the meaning of a moment I observe, I'm challenged to think more deeply than I otherwise would, with more precision and less vagueness or generality. Our writing is an act of thinking.

We write documentation stories for families. Our stories are windows through which they see into their children's experiences during their time apart, and through which they come to know us, the people to whom they've entrusted their children's well-being. And, importantly, our documentation asks families to think with us about the meaning of children's play, and to help us shape our offerings to children.

We write documentation stories for our community. Our stories change how people understand and value children and childhood; they can catch people off guard, as Anne Lamott says, and break in on small, bordered ways of thinking about childhood and the purpose of early education and the roles of adults in children's learning.

Our documentation stories are tools for reflection, dialogue, and understanding. They're not simply pieces of paper that we post on the walls of our classrooms or add to children's portfolios. Our stories are about relationships and the exchange of ideas. Documentation stories are thinking out loud on paper, and they speak to the active, engaged process of observation and study, collaboration and planning, that we share with children, co-teachers, and families.

Documentation, Not Assessment

Documentation is different than traditional approaches to assessment. Documentation captures stories that we can share, revisit, reflect on, and add to, an on-going part of the teaching and learning process. Assessment uses observations to evaluate children's learning and our teaching, often in relation to pre-established learning outcomes and at the end of an experience, and with consequences (referral to special services, moving up a grade level; school funding; teacher pay).

Documentation is lively and engaging—witness, revelation, surprise: stories told by a teacher who is self-reflective and self-revealing. It is in service of relationship: we come to know how each of us thinks, feels, wonders. Documentation emphasizes particularity and uniqueness. Assessment is narrowly focused and prescribed, with measurements completed by an evaluator with some detachment, comparing a child to normative standards.

Documentation stories are always in motion, never complete. Assessment happens at particular times during an academic year, in discreet parcels, and, once completed, can be tied up with a bow and put on a shelf alongside other measures and markers. Documentation makes thinking visible and informs further inquiry. Assessment makes measurable learning visible and informs further instruction.

Volumes have been written about documentation and assessment. I won't try to capture, here, the many nuances of the discussion about documentation in our field—or even to recap the highlights and headlines. My intention is to locate my thinking and values within the overarching conceptual frameworks, and to call forward what I believe has been neglected in the conversation: the art of telling stories that matter.

The gentle and insightful Fred Rogers said that, "What really matters is whether the alphabet is used for the declaration of war or for the description of a sunset."[7] This wonderfully captures the difference between the emphasis of assessment and of documentation: How many letters can this child identify? What does this child notice and care about, think about and pursue?

What Makes for Good Stories?

Traditionally, documentation has been destination-driven. Educators put pen to paper with an end already in mind: illustrate a child's competency with counting to ten, or with identifying five colors, or with recognizing her printed name. In the pedagogical practice embedded in the Thinking Lens, however, documentation stories serve our intention to wonder and to ponder. We begin a story with a moment that catches our attention, and we write about that moment as a way to think our way into a rigorous encounter with the questions and insights and self-awareness and new perspectives held in that moment. Rather than covering a child's learning, we uncover new ways of thinking, we discover insights and understandings that we may not have recognized until we began to write.

In our documentation stories, we don't force the revelation. Anne Lamott says that writing is like watching a Polaroid image develop: "You can't know exactly what the picture is going to look like until it has finished developing. First you just point at what has your attention and take the picture ... Stay with that long enough for it to show you what it is about."[8] This is a liberating way to approach our documentation practice. We can start with what has our attention—Jamie's quiet exploration at the water table, Austin standing on the table, the three-year-olds mounding toys into a castle in the sand box, the children enacting and re-enacting the drama of kitten mischief. We begin by capturing the moment that has our attention with deliberate language, and we pay attention to what begins to reveal itself as we write.

What this means in practice: Begin writing the immediate, physical, sensual reality of the moment that has your attention; linger in the details and avoid the conceptual and interpretive. Instead of writing that "Liza had a great time playing in the sandbox today," write what you saw Liza do …

———

Liza sat square in the center of the sandbox, by herself and apparently contentedly so. She nestled her bottom into the sand as she settled herself in. There were a couple different shovels and scoops within reach; Liza chose a trowel, shallow and pointed at the tip, and dug into the sand, bending low over the hole she'd begun, her tongue poking out of the corner of her lips in her trademark token of concentration and effort.

———

How did she dig? When we challenge ourselves to use specific language, interesting language, we often startle ourselves into unexpected insight.

Ways to describe how a child might dig:
- excavating;
- exhuming;
- foraging;
- scraping;
- etching;
- fossicking;
- burrowing;
- tunneling;
- ploughing.

We aim to match this specific language with other details of Liza's time in the sandbox that caught our attention. The inwardness of Liza's gaze. The way she hummed under her breath. Her apparent disregard for the sand trickling down her arms and spilling onto her lap with each shovelful of sand she moved. Write these details: their specificity is illuminating.

There's a classic injunction in writing to "show, don't tell." We do that when we use these sorts of specific, vivid images and precise language, rather than the broad brush strokes ("digging," "playing," "a great time") that generalize and neutralize a moment. The emphasis with this isn't to get the words right, but to attune ourselves, through our language, to the nuance of details, which is what sparks insights and puzzlement. Burrowing is a different act than excavating: each conjures a particular intent and energy. Using precise language not only communicates the fullness of this moment to the reader, but it tells us something we may not have articulated by simply watching Liza in the sandbox.

Another strategy for writing our way to revelation—and to a good story—is to tighten the lens, bringing one moment, one gesture into focus. Anne Lamott suggests writing into a "one-inch picture frame."[9] Poet and essayist Kim Stafford suggests writing a postcard: "The whole work of writing is to hone the habit of selection. We find the small, rich beginning that speaks, and we let it grow according to an imaginative logic of its own."[10] Both of these writers are pointing to the value of starting close-in, writing on an intimate scale, and near to the moment that has our attention. Rather than writing about Liza putting on her coat and walking out to the play yard and heading towards the sandbox, we start with her already seated, bent over the hole, trowel in hand—the moment that caught our attention, the moment that we want to consider.

We can capture a whole ocean coastline by describing one rocky patch of beach and the movement of waves onto that beach, we can capture a whole forest by describing the way the sun dapples the underbrush and the scent of dust and pine. When we write small, we can capture the big more fully. Intimacy—of time, of seeing—communicates more than the generalities that we fall back on when we write big ("Liza had a great time playing in the sandbox"). "It is only by selection, by elimination, by emphasis, that we get at the real meaning of things," declared the painter Georgia O'Keeffe.[11] And, so, we write about Liza burrowing, and, as we write from "the small, rich beginning," we listen for the resonance of meaning, the connections and surprises that offer themselves as the story unfolds.

Stories Tell Us Who We Are

As the narrators in our documentation stories, we write our way into revelation. New ways of understanding a child's pursuits are revealed as we mull over the details and the language for those details and the meaning that sparks from the details. And we are revealed: our ways of seeing, our questions and puzzlements, our insights and intentions.

• • • • • • The stories we tell expose us. Documentation is not simply relaying the observable facts of a moment in a child's day; it is making our observing, our feeling, our wondering, our thinking, our valuing visible.

We're present in our documentation from the get-go: we choose what story to tell, what moment we're willing to honor with the effort of writing about it. And we choose how to tell that story. Our documentation stories are as much about ourselves as they are about children: they speak volumes about what we find meaningful, worthy of our attention, our witness, our reverence. The people who read our stories know us better after reading what we've written. It's a good thing to acknowledge: we are as present in our stories as are the children.

This is not what most of us were taught about documentation. I was taught to erase myself from my documentation, to "keep my ideas and feelings" out of it and write only about the children. This erasure was intended to keep documentation "objective," an accurate measure of a child's learning. But a pedagogical approach to documentation acknowledges that we participate in the moments that we write about. The intention of a pedagogical approach is to use documentation as part of our teacher research, and, so, we, the researchers, are present front and center in what we write.

Why Liza? Why the sandbox and not the block area? What caught my attention, and what does that tell me (and you, the reader) about what I'm interested in, what I value, what touches my heart? What does my story-telling reveal about what I notice and what I don't notice? About the trajectory of my thinking and meaning-making? A reader will have a sense of Liza from my story, sure, but perhaps even more than that, he'll have a sense of the process of teacher research as I'm living it in relation to this moment in Liza's and my shared life.

By way of encouragement for us to claim, without squirming, this compelling stance of a first-person narrator, this meditation on writing by naturalist and essayist Terry Tempest Williams:

> I write to discover. I write to uncover. I write to begin a dialogue. I write to honor beauty. I write to remember. I write as a form of translation. I write because it allows me to confront that which I do not know. I write to record what I love. I write to listen. I write as a witness to what I have seen. I write by grace and by grit. I write knowing words always fall short. I write past the embarrassment of exposure. I write because it is a risk, like love, to form the words, to say the words, to be touched, to reveal how vulnerable we are. I write as though I am whispering in the ear of the one I love.[12]

What would change in your documentation practice if you approached your writing in this spirit?

The Thinking Lens as a Protocol for Writing

The Thinking Lens can serve as a writing protocol to guide our documentation practice. We can turn to the questions in the Thinking Lens and write through them to new insights. The Thinking Lens doesn't become a template for a report about a process that's already happened, but a protocol for clear and articulate thinking. Writing with the Thinking Lens carries us to nuance and questions and contradictions and puzzlements; the very act of writing our thinking—when done honestly—leads us to new terrain.

Know yourself, directs the first step of the Thinking Lens. This can be the entry into telling a story that matters. We begin our documentation with a story of something that caught our attention, something that gave us pause, something that made us sit up and pay attention—that "small, rich beginning." What happened in this story? As we write the intimate details that capture this moment's immediacy and specificity, we notice what sparks for us.

Know yourself; open your heart to this moment. Why am I telling this story? Why, of all the things I witnessed today, do I choose this story? What about it caught my heart, sparked with my values, challenged me, made me laugh, made me teary? What is this story about?

We write in the first person—another divergence from the strictures of documentation as traditionally taught. We write from our hearts and our bodies, from our curiosity and our concerns, from our sense of humor and our sensibilities; we write from memory and from anticipation. We write in the first person to acknowledge our participation in this moment as the observer and as the story teller, and to take our place as the narrator of this story …

———

As I watched Liza excavate, watched her gaze turn inward, watched the sand run down her arms and fill her lap, I felt my body's recognition of the visceral pleasure of digging in sand. I've been Liza in the sandbox! One of my earliest memories is from the sandpit in my childhood backyard: I remember the grit of the sand, and its warmth, and the sense that this was the whole world, this was everything—the rest of the backyard, the house, the neighbor's dog, the traffic on the street, none of it existed. There was only the sand, and the sun on my skin, and the hole that I dug and dug deeper and deeper. Awakened by memory, I watched Liza more fully, and with curiosity.

———

We are the narrators of our documentation stories, and we are teacher researchers using story "to discover, to uncover, to begin a dialogue, to confront that which I do not know, to listen." And, so, we write our way into the child's perspective: What is the story from the child's point of view? We don't have to have this neatly figured out before we begin writing; our writing will lead us to understanding.

Take the children's points of view. Offer our reading of the children's intent ...

————

Is Liza's experience like mine? What does her skin feel, what does her body know right now, right here, in this sandbox? What does she see of the rest of the play yard, of the raucous game of tag unfolding on the grass? How does she see her hole?

————

Examine the environment. As we write, we look around inside the scene that we're describing. What do we notice, now, about the environment, about the way time is unfolding? When we pay attention to these sorts of details, we find questions and connections that support our intention to understand a child's experience ...

————

I'm curious about Liza's choice of a trowel: it's sharp-tipped and shallow, a contrast to the big scoops and the buckets also near at hand. A trowel doesn't hold much sand, but it makes precise cuts—though the sand quickly streams into those cuts and blurs them. A scoop would have been more effective at moving sand in quantity enough to have an immediate impact on a hole's depth. Why did Liza choose the trowel?

————

Consider other perspectives. As we write, we locate this moment in relation to what we know of child development and early learning research, cultural identity, and cultural knowledge. This is challenging: our efforts to give language to our understandings of theory show us places where our knowledge is incomplete, places where we have cognitive tangles. And we find contradictions and puzzlements as we write about other perspectives.

Families' perspectives are among the perspectives we consider. This doesn't mean asking, "Have you seen your child do this at home?" It means asking real questions: What catches your attention in this story? What insights does this story give you about your child? About me? What question does this story leave you with? ...

———

I learned about the value of sand play when I was studying early childhood education. It's good for physical development, I was taught: muscles put to work to thrust a shovel, to lift and move sand, enhance a child's gross motor capacity. And I was taught that being in the sand is a good arena for "sensory play," which was presented in a pretty fusty way, more clinical than sensual, but an important aspect of children's learning. And there's the classic childhood story that everyone has of "trying to dig to China," told as illustration of another valued aspect of sand play: it is purposeful play, and holds opportunities for children to develop persistence and determination, to learn about setting a goal and moving towards it.

What does any of this have to do with Liza? The bit of all of this that has the most resonance for what I saw in her play is the angle about "sensory play," but her encounter with the sand seemed more immediate and compelling than those stale words imply. Her play certainly engaged her in a sensorial way, which, we've learned from brain science, is valuable for neurological development. But beyond the tactile sensory quality of the play was sensuality, it seems to me, and that's sure what I remember of my childhood sand play—that fully embodied experience of touch: the caress of the sand, the tickle of it, the grit of it, the warm and cold of it, the dry and moist of it. Liza was alive to the sand.

She sure seemed oblivious to the buzz of the rest of the world around her—the children playing tag on the lawn, the occasional child moving into and out of the sandbox. That makes me think of the notion of "flow": the experience of immersion, of giving oneself over to an experience. That's what it looked like Liza was experiencing: intense focus on her excavation in the sand. She didn't seem to be driven by an intention to dig "all the way to China." Her gaze was both soft and far-away, though the sweet tuck of her tongue at the side of her mouth conveyed solid concentration.

What is the value of experiencing flow? What is the value of sensual encounter—of "sensory play"? I have a body sense that "this stuff matters," but, as I try to find words to explain why, I find myself stumbling. Will you think with me about this? Why does Liza's experience in the sandbox matter?

———

Reflect and take action. This is the "So what?" part of our writing. What does it matter that we just spent this time thinking about this play? How are we changed? What will we do now, because of having spent this time thinking and writing? How will we move in the world differently? How will our teaching change? How does this time spent in consideration of this child's play help us be as human as we can be? …

———

What, if anything, can I offer Liza to honor her experience of flow, of sensual engagement?

As I got ready to write this documentation story, I did an internet search asking "Why do children dig in the sand?" It was not particularly helpful. Seven of the first nine websites that popped up warned about the "hidden dangers of playing in the sand." The website about early childhood growth and learning described ways that teachers can use children's sand play to strengthen their learning about spatial relations, math, and measurement, and to teach the concepts of lines and circles which are important for literacy learning.

I don't feel worried about Liza's safety, nor am I willing to seize her play and tether it to instructional purposes. What I value most in her play is the inwardness of it, the embodied nature of her experience, her un-self-consciousness. I don't know that she needs anything from me, other than my respectful witness of her experience. This story, perhaps, and the deep regard that I hope it captures, may be enough. Mostly, I want to wrap my arms protectively around this sort of spacious, uncompromised time for Liza and for the other children—for all of us, really. That's probably the best action I can take, as a teacher: look for ways that I can create space and time for sensual flow.

I'm curious what you make of all this, as you read—of Liza's time in the sandbox, of my thinking about it, of what I might do, going forward. I welcome a note or a chat, to learn from and with you about this play and its reverberations.

———

The Thinking Lens calls us to reflect, wonder, explore a range of perspectives. It asks that we stay tentative and humble, authentic and present, intentional and self-aware. When we use the Thinking Lens as a writing protocol, it invites a narrative arc that begins in the immediacy of a moment observed and carries us to the human heart of the moment. The Thinking Lens helps us tell stories that matter.

Stories Worth Telling

Good writing is immediate and personal. It tells a compelling story that has readers leaning forward wanting more. It transforms us. When we read a story that catches our hearts and minds, we feel connected to the characters, like we know them, like we've become friends; we want to know more about them and about what happens to them. We care about them. This is what our documentation stories can do: connect us to each other and to our shared life, to our shared humanness and the ways in which we express that in community together.

This approach to documentation foregrounds an educator's perspective and values her or his questions, observations, and conclusions, however tentative. There is no objective narrative to strive towards. If we each stood in the play yard watching Liza in the sand pit, and then went off on our own to write a documentation story, we'd have as many different stories as there are observers. We each watch Liza through the lens of our childhood memories, of our engagement with the world, our relationships, our values, our longings, and it's those lenses that helps us see what the story is about. We are human beings seeking to understand life, and living, and human being-ness. In our documentation stories, we can write our way to big ideas, to real questions and considerations, in a way that expands the humanness of all of us. We braid ourselves and the children into a moment of life, and ask: Why does this moment matter?

Those are stories worth telling. And those are the stories that children want us to tell about them, the stories that parents want us to tell—not jargon-filled assessments of discrete arenas of learning and development. We write our way to the human heart of the moment as we see and live it. When we offer those stories to each other, and consider them together, we begin to know what it is to be alive in this world. And the threads that bind us together in community grow stronger, and luminous.

Herb Kohl writes: "Not only children have stories: parents and communities have stories, and teachers, too, have tales to tell. In a learning community where everyone cares about everyone else's story, respect and affection can flourish."[13] Documentation stories are in service of relationship marked by respect and affection, and by the generosity of stories shared.

Documentation is in Service of Relationship

Good writing about stories that matter is not always cheery and bright. Especially when our subject is the daily life of young children, there will sometimes be fights and blood and snot and tears. You may have been taught that documentation ought not to include anything that's not glowingly positive; I certainly was. We're coached to write about the successes, about children's moments of discovery and accomplishment, their breakthroughs in learning and in friendship. But breakthroughs come after effort, after some measure of toil and struggle and not getting it and screwing up and getting confused, and that's what makes a breakthrough such joy, such release.

The stories of our efforts to figure things out are defining stories about our character, our humanness. To avoid telling those stories is to disrespect the fullness of accomplishment, the satisfaction of growth. Our orientation, always, is one of regard for children's capacities, and an unwavering commitment to an image of children as resourceful and resilient, intelligent in both mind and heart, worthy of our devotion and tenderness. From that orientation, the stories we share, whether of accomplishment or challenge, honor the ways in which children are becoming as human as they can be.

We may worry that parents will freak out if we write about an argument between children or about a child's failed efforts to master a game. But it's no big revelation to parents that their children have fights and fail at things. I was challenged early in my teaching by a mom who said, "You're so positive all the time. I know that my daughter's got a stubborn streak and that she bumps heads with other kids because of it. I want to hear the whole picture; you don't have to leave out the stuff that's not pretty." In our documentation, we can tell real stories about real children, and, with those stories, honor children's humanness, their bold spirits, their striving. These real stories have the arc of authenticity, and in telling them, we communicate to families that we hold their children's lives with tenderness and regard and generosity of understanding.

Sometimes, the real stories we're called to tell are the stories of our own wrestling to understand something, our own uncertainties or confusion. We may be reluctant to reveal ourselves as anything less than fully assured. But the pedagogical practice we're striving towards asks us to be researchers and collaborators—and researchers certainly don't have everything figured out. Researchers ask questions that compel them, questions with reverberations of possibility. They commit to thinking about those questions, knowing that they'll get mired in confusion, perplexed and puzzled and uncertain—and that they'll have breakthroughs of understanding, when a cognitive knot is untangled and insight shines bright and meaning is revealed and birds sing and the sun shines. The Thinking Lens doesn't direct us to have everything figured out before we collaborate with families; it asks us to offer our best thinking and our most resonant questions to families, to consider together with them. Our documentation stories are invitations into dialogue with families. Written with self-awareness and humility, they are doorways into relationship.

This is especially true in our documentation stories about social justice issues. When we write about the ways in which cultural identity, privilege, inclusion and exclusion, justice and injustice show up in our classrooms, our writing will not be easy and bright; there will be plenty of self-revelation and complexity braided into our documentation stories. Though they're the least comfortable moments to write about, we surely do need to write about the children's conversations about "pretty" and "ugly" skin colors, about the game that's "only for boys," about what makes a real family. These sorts of conversations and play touch on children's social and moral development, and the ethical tenor of our classrooms, and the ways in which we will all—children, educators, and families—come together to wrestle with the issues at the heart of community. Documentation stories about social justice issues contribute mightily to the quality and strength of relationships in our classrooms.

When we write about social justice issues, we use the Thinking Lens as a writing protocol, as with other documentation stories, with a particular emphasis on seeking families' perspectives and values, and planning together with them what we'll offer children.

An example, by Kendra PeloJoaquin, written when she was an educator at Hilltop Children's Center …

———

On the playground after school today, several of the children and I had a conversation that startled me. Here it is in our words:

Carl: You know, most of the kids who go to John Hay School are richer than us—richer than the kids who go to Coe School.

Kendra: But there are families from Hay who don't own their own homes.

Carl: Yes, but Drew and Molly (who go to Hay) get all the toys that they want.

I'd been startled by Carl's initial comparison between the children at the two schools, and found myself disputing his statement before I thought about what I was saying. In hindsight, I wish that I had gone more slowly and asked more questions. Class and economic status are a trigger for me, and in this case, I reacted to the trigger, instead of managing my reaction. My suggestion of class markers (owning a home) had nothing to do with Carl's measurement (buying more toys), so he disregarded it almost immediately. The conversation continued:

Kendra: Some people might buy more toys than other people, whether they're rich or not.

Carl: No, you only buy more toys if you have more money.

Oliver: Yeah, that's true. Lukas buys all of his toys and he's rich. His parents give him all the money to buy them.

Carl: He has hundreds of dollars in his piggy bank!

At this point our conversation shifted to something more innocuous, and eventually we made our way back to Hilltop for snack.

The conversation has stayed with me, though, and has left me unsettled. I want to redouble my efforts to pause to think about children's words before I react in situations like this, and work with my co-teachers to make my own assumptions and emotions more visible as I work with children around these intense and personal issues of wealth and ownership. When I was a child, my family didn't have extra money at all; we were poor and we knew it. That experience has left me quick to react in conversations about wealth and its meaning in people's lives.

I want to understand this conversation from Carl's and Oliver's perspectives. How do they feel about themselves, in the equation they laid out? What possibilities do they see for friendship across social class differences? How do they think about the access that's available to people with plenty of money and not available to people without much money?

Please think with me about this conversation. What does it spark for you as parents? The children named their perception of families' differing economic resources: they've stepped into territory that we adults usually avoid, because it's really uncomfortable.

What values do you hold for children's learning about social class differences? How do you wish I'd responded to this conversation? How would you hope I respond in the future?

Talking about wealth inequalities makes me squirm. But I want to do right by the children as they try to figure out the meaning of money and ownership, and so I invite your thoughts, and I'll continue to share mine.

————

Writing is the practice of witness and revelation. Our documentation stories about social justice issues are no exception; they, too, bear witness to a community's life together, and to the values, intentions, and concerns that, when braided together, make the character of that community.

When the great American writer, poet, and playwright Maya Angelou died, there were many remembrances of her artistry and activism. Here's what Bill Clinton said about her at her memorial service:

Her great gift was that she was always paying attention. In her writing what she was doing was calling our attention to the things she had been paying attention to. And she did it with a clarity and power that washed over people. She just kept calling our attention to things, like a firefly that comes at unpredictable times and makes you see something you otherwise would have missed.[14]

This can be how we approach our documentation practice: to make visible what would otherwise go unnoticed; to call into story the things that have our attention; to invite new ways of seeing and thinking about children, and their lives. To be fireflies, telling stories that matter, stories that illuminate.

Telling the Stories that Matter

Margie Carter

Education scholar and visionary Peter Moss says that when we examine "contrasting stories confronting each other, offering listeners conflicting alternatives," we begin to critique our practice in necessary and fundamental ways.[15] He challenges us to scrutinize the dominant story that has shaped early childhood today: the story that investing in early childhood will lead toward our national success in a fiercely competitive global economy. Moss says this story tells us:

> Invest early and invest smartly and we will all live happily ever after in a world of more of the same—only more so. Reassured by this story of early childhood education as a solution to some of our most immediate problems and anxieties, it is tempting to sign up to it rather than ask difficult questions about what sort of world we want to embark on the hard, messy and political task of clearing the deepening slough of inequality and injustice that breeds so many of the social problems that early childhood education is supposed to solve.[16]

I want to put this quote from Moss in front of every policy maker and funder who speaks with pride about investing in early childhood. I want us to say *No* to the dominant story that says our role is to get children ready to compete in the marketplace. We say *No* to teacher-proof curriculum packages with assessment tools that will "fix" the children (and teachers) that we have failed to respect, to invest our hearts and minds in. *¡Basta!* We know that this worldview leads us down a destructive path, and we have had enough. We have enough evidence that another world is possible, and *this* is the world we want our work to create. We say *YES* to a narrative of joy and beauty, of wonder and tears and music. We will tell stories that matter, stories that ask questions, stories that call forward our dearest values and biggest vision.

The creators of Te Whāriki, the curriculum used in early childhood programs in New Zealand, offer an example of creating new stories about learning.

Margaret Carr writes:

> When we began, I think the practitioners and I wanted to seize the notion of assessment, shake it around a bit, turn it upside down, and find something that was part of enjoying the company of young children. The practitioners liked the idea of starting with stories. So this journey towards a different way of doing things began.[17]

A journey towards a different way of doing things, yes! Buddhist teacher Thich Nhat Hanh reminds us that we have alternative stories to tell, to help us shape our lives:

> The good news
> they do not print.
> The good news
> we do print.
> We have a special edition every moment,
> and we need you to read it.
>
> They only print what is wrong.
> Look at each of our special editions.
> We want you to benefit from them
> and help protect them.
>
> The latest good news
> is that you can do it.[18]

Throughout this book, Ann brings us good news, suggesting we can tell a different story to guide our thinking about the purpose of education. She offers numerous gems for how we can take up a different narrative to craft our daily practice. This chapter, in particular, reminds us that our endeavor of pedagogical documentation involves finding and telling the stories that matter, the good news of becoming as human as we can be. How else will we survive? I don't know about you, but just accepting how things are isn't a story I want to live by.

When educators tell stories that matter, this animated news becomes a living testimony that serves as a mirror in which children see their beautiful capacities, and which offers reassurance and pride to families. These vivid accounts are the *real* outcomes that we've been waiting for. Ann not only challenges us to get below the banal but shows us ways to pay homage to courage, doggedness, and invincibility. I found so many notions to spend time with in this chapter:

- Honor the children and our relationships with them through stories.

- Give testimony to what we have witnessed, learned from, and been changed by in our examination of children's engagement with materials, people, and ideas.

- Use the Thinking Lens as a research tool, making systematic inquiry public, rather than falling back on traditional approaches to documentation that are destination driven.

- Approach your story-telling as a gathering around a campfire to find the stories with potential to "call forward what has been neglected," to reshape understandings.

- View your writing as "calling the insides of an experience forward."

- Write your way to the human heart, into revelation of what it is to be alive in this world.

- Allow the very act of writing your thinking—done honestly—to lead you to new terrain.

. . . .

Linger over this chapter, revisiting sections that make you want to light a candle, pour a glass of wine, or settle in with a fragrant cup of tea. Perhaps put on some quiet music.

. . . .

Choose several of the ideas in the preceding list that provoke you to remember, reclaim, and rewrite the story of yourself as the educator you want to be.

. . . .

Invest in 30 minutes of expressing this story in reflective writing.

. . . .

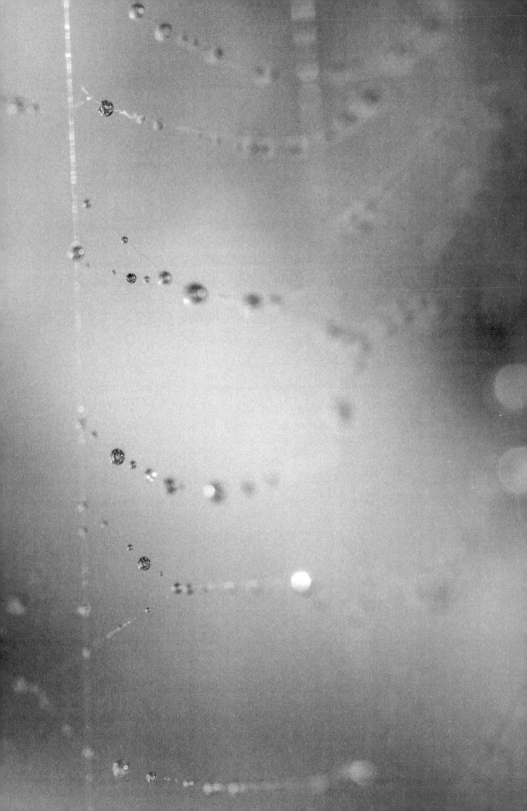

The fact is that there are more stories in the world than there are fish in the sea or birds in the air ... You could be sad at how many stories go untold, but you could also be delighted at how many stories we catch and share in delight and wonder and astonishment and illumination and sometimes even epiphany. The fact is that the more stories we share about living beings, the more attentive we are to living beings.

—*Brian Doyle*[15]

13

Slapstick Literacy and the Music *of* Friendship: The Thinking Lens in Action

Here's a story, not about anything fancy or jaw-droppingly extraordinary, but, rather, about the riches available—for us and for children—in the typical, ordinary experiences that we share every day. Drawn from my time as the pedagogical leader at Hilltop Children's Center it offers a peek into the pedagogical practice embodied in the Thinking Lens. In the story, I've bookmarked aspects of the Thinking Lens, as well as principles for pedagogical leadership.

As you read, remember: the practice of inquiry sustains the spirit of inquiry. You don't have to wait until you've got everything figured out to do this work. The pedagogical practice captured in the Thinking Lens helps develop the skills of teacher researchers. We learn inquiry by doing inquiry: it's on-the-job training …

Ellen was one of three teachers for a group of eighteen three-, four-, and five-year-olds. One morning, during the course of the usual open-ended play in the classroom, three-year-old Hank caught Ellen's attention. Lying on his stomach in the middle of the block area, propped up on his elbows, Hank was drawing a train track on a clipboard. It was his process of drawing that pulled Ellen close: he wasn't drawing representationally, but physically, capturing a train in motion. His pen circled around and around on the outside edge of the paper, as Hank chugged and whistled and rumbled around the tracks, breathing life and movement onto the paper. His drawing didn't look like much more than scribbles, but his act of drawing told an eloquent and articulate story of a train in motion.

Hank moved through four or five sheets of paper as he wrote his train story. He'd finish one fast-paced circuit, pull that drawing off the clipboard and toss it to the side, then launch into another fast-motion drawing. Ellen watched from a discreet distance, curious. When Hank finished and began to gather the sheets of paper into a rumpled bundle, Ellen approached Hank and commented that she'd been watching, interested, as he drew about a train. She asked if she could borrow one of the pages to make a copy of it to remember what he'd drawn. "Sure," he said, nonchalant and generous. "You can have them all." And he thrust his bundle into her hands and, calling out to a buddy across the room, ran over to launch a game with him.

At Hilltop, we held an expectation that each educator would bring an observation to the weekly meeting of her or his teaching team. We wanted the practice of teacher research to be the focus of those team meetings, rather than housekeeping and logistics, and, so, we asked each educator to come to the meeting with notes about something that had caught her or his attention during the week. We used the team meeting to study and plan from those observation notes, taking up each educator's observation for a portion of the hour. My role, as the pedagogical leader, was to facilitate our study, anchoring our conversation in the Thinking Lens. [**Principle:** *Anchor organizational systems in vision and values.*]

Ellen brought Hank's stack of drawings and the notes she'd made about his process to her teaching team's meeting. When it was her turn to share her observation, she spread the drawings on the table and described how Hank had made them, running the pen on the paper like a train along its tracks. "Hank doesn't spend much time writing or drawing," Ellen said. "That's why this caught my attention. He's a guy on the go, always in movement. I was surprised to see him lying on the floor drawing for such a long stretch of time."

Following the protocol of the Thinking Lens, we began by reflecting on what moved us about it, what caught at our hearts, in a personal and immediate way. [**Thinking Lens: Know yourself.** *What is your immediate response to the children's play and conversation? What feelings stir in you? What touches your heart as you watch and listen? What in your background is influencing your response?*]

Ellen said, "I was moved by the way Hank just fell into another world. I know that feeling, when I'm doing art, or knitting, or working in the garden."

"I loved trains as a kid," Rich offered. "I played with them for hours. It was like meditation."

Suze remembered, "My grandpa was obsessed with trains. He had an elaborate train that he put up around his Christmas tree every year, and he was always dragging us kids along to a train show. I loved my grandpa and so I loved trains."

We started our study with this personal sharing as a way to bring our full human selves to the discussion, and to be sure we were showing up all the way, not just as "educators." From that stance, we turned our attention to Hank, and our responses to his drawing, calling out the values and commitments that we held. [**Thinking Lens: Know yourself.** *What values are influencing your response? What adult perspectives, i.e. standards, health and safety, time, goals are on your mind? What leaves you curious, eager to engage?*]

Rich jumped in. "I love Hank's silly, physical games. He's like a puppy! This train drawing has some of that energy that I love in Hank—that movement and noise."

Ellen added, "Yeah, I think that's part of what drew me to this moment: it was pure Hank, but on paper."

Suze: "I'm interested in the literacy aspect of this work. It seems like Hank might be ready to write stories."

Rich: "I care about that learning, sure, but I feel protective of Hank's cheerful, goofy spirit. I don't want us to make more of this than it is—a kid drawing about a train because he loves the movement and noise of a train."

This seemed a good bridge into the second step of the Thinking Lens. "Let's think about this from Hank's perspective," I suggested. "Rich, you just offered one way to understand what was going on for Hank: this drawing was a way for him to translate his physical play onto paper, acting out a train. How else could we think about this drawing, from Hank's perspective? What might Hank be exploring?" [**Thinking Lens: Take the children's points of view.** *What are the children trying to figure out?* **Collaborate with others to expand perspectives.** *How do your colleagues understand the meaning of the children's play? What child development or early learning theories might you consider?*]

Suze said, "I think it's cool that he's drawing a story about something that he'd usually be doing with his whole body, running around like a train, or making a train track with the blocks and using a toy train on it."

"I think this is a foray into writing for Hank," Ellen mused. "He knows that marks on paper tell stories. And that's what he's doing—telling a story about a train."

Rich was unsure. "It's like Hank was acting out a story about trains, on paper. But he didn't try to write letters or make his drawing into the format of a book; I don't think he's super-interested in formal writing."

Suze suggested, "What I think Hank's doing is the first stage of literacy learning—not the formal writing, like you say."

Rich: "I agree with you. But literacy starts with representation, and that's what Hank was doing."

Ellen added, "Yeah, that's all that writing is, really: we make the lines into letters, but it's the same thing Hank was doing—using lines to tell a story."

"I'm intrigued by how self-contained this act of expression was for Hank," I offered. "He's usually goofing around with other kids and doesn't do much play by himself. But writing is something that people usually do by themselves, to tell a story to people who aren't there. It seems to me that it's significant that Hank was by himself when he was drawing—his solitude communicates something about his understanding of the power of writing."

Ellen countered, "But he didn't seem much invested in the actual drawings that he'd made. It's not like he wanted to read them to me, or to anyone else. He didn't even want to hold onto them himself, but gave me the whole pile of papers without any caveats about returning them or putting them in his cubby when I was done with them."

"Good point," I said. "I may be over-reaching, trying to make significance where there isn't any. But it also could be that, while Hank wasn't consciously trying to carry his story into a bigger context, he was demonstrating an aspect of writing that we value—that it is about connection."

Rich: "I think that, for Hank, it's more about him connecting with his physical play in a different way, not about connecting with other people."

This sparked a quick consideration of the environment, the third step of the Thinking Lens. [**Thinking Lens: Examine the environment.** *How are the organization and the use of the physical space and materials impacting this situation? How are schedules and routines influencing this experience?*]

Ellen: "He was drawing in the block area, where he's played games about trains plenty of times. He's built tracks with blocks and run trains along the tracks, and he's lined up chairs like seats on a train and been the train conductor. The block area is where his train play has happened. I think it's neat that he used that space to draw about trains."

Rich: "It's interesting that he grabbed a clipboard and a pen instead of blocks. I'd have expected blocks."

Suze: "That's what makes me excited about this—it's a foray into a new way of representing trains for Hank."

I wanted to call in other perspectives beyond early education, and so I asked, "What do we know about how choreographers notate dance? I'm trying to think of other circumstances where people write about physical movement." [**Thinking Lens: Collaborate with others to expand perspectives.** *What other arenas of knowledge and insight might you consult?*]

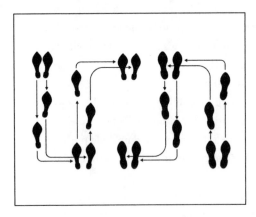

Ellen added, "That question makes me wonder not just how to write a dance, but how to read a dance."

We did a quick internet search for "choreography notation" and laughed at what we found.

Ellen: "That sure looks like a train running around a track to me!"

More laughter, then a moment of quiet, and then Rich ventured an idea. "This may be a sidetrack, but I keep thinking of Hank's friendship with Celia, which has really surprised me. She's such a serious and thoughtful kid, and spends a lot of time drawing and writing songs and dances. But when

Celia hangs out with Hank, she becomes a goofball. She and Hank are all about slapstick comedy and belly laughter."

Rich's introduction of Celia into the conversation was the catalyst for intriguing connections and possibilities. [**Thinking Lens: Reflect and take action.** *What action might you take to help the children see their own and each other's ideas? What might you do to deepen children's relationships with each other?*]

Ellen jumped in with a possibility. "What if we invited Celia and Hank to mix up their goofy playfulness with the serious work of writing—something that Celia's really good at?"

I wanted us to stay clear and aware of the values inside our planning, and so I said, "Let's think for a minute about why we'd head in that direction. What would our intentions be?" [**Thinking Lens: Reflect and take action.** *What values and intentions do you want to influence your response?*]

Ellen: "I think that doing some writing together would stretch Hank's and Celia's friendship in a new direction, give them new possibilities for how to be together."

Rich: "I can see how that would honor Celia's strengths—but I feel cautious about doing too much engineering of their friendship. Maybe Celia really needs their friendship to be just about goofing around, because she is so serious most of the time: maybe it's a way for her to chill out and relax."

I suggested we think about how we might invite Hank and Celia to come together. [**Thinking Lens: Reflect and take action.** *How will you invite collaboration?*]

"I wonder if they could write together in a goofy way," Rich said. "That'd be the best of who they each are."

Suze was excited. "Writing matters most when we have something to share with someone we care about—I think that's what you were getting at, Ann, when you talked about writing being a way to make connections."

Ellen said, thoughtfully, "I really like this direction. I want to be careful, like you say, Rich—I don't want to manipulate Hank and Celia's friendship. But I think they'd enjoy doing something 'special' together, something that acknowledges their friendship."

Ann: "Let's brainstorm some possible next steps."

Suze had an idea. "Maybe we could use Hank's train drawings—he could read his drawing to Celia and they could play out that story."

Ellen was unsure. "They don't usually play games like Hank's train-on-the-tracks drawing. They do more spontaneous play, with slapstick and rolling around on the floor. I think it'd be sort of forced to ask them to act out Hank's drawing."

"We could go the other direction," Rich suggested. "The next time we see them playing together, we could invite them to draw the story of their game. That'd be more spontaneous."

"That might be too spontaneous!" said Suze. "It'd require one of us to be nearby and able to jump in with them, and it'd need plenty of time beyond their play."

"Yeah, I agree," Rich conceded. "And it would interrupt or redirect their game, and I really want to protect that goofy, impromptu, unscripted play."

I had a thought. "What about inviting them into the studio and suggesting that they write or draw a surprise for each other? That would get around the problem of interrupting their play, and it would honor the quality of spontaneity and unpredictability that we value in their play. They'd be operating from that same spirit, only on paper."

That's what we decided to do: for our next step, Ellen would invite Celia and Hank into the studio together to write a surprise for each other.

We figured out the set-up of the space and materials. Ellen would arrange two tables to create private space for the children to make their surprises. Each table would have a stack of paper and a choice of drawing and writing pens. I'd join Ellen and the children in the studio, to support Ellen's learning about ways to talk with children to help them see their thinking, and to help make notes and take photos. We finished our planning by choosing a day in the coming week when both Hank and Celia would be at Hilltop and when the studio was available. [**Thinking Lens: Reflect and Take Action.** *What will we do, specifically? What materials will we need? When will we make this offering? How will we capture the experience for our next round of study and planning?*]

Into the Studio with Hank and Celia

Here's what unfolded when Ellen, Celia, Hank, and I met in the studio.

We sat on the floor in a little circle, and Ellen began to create some context for the intriguing invitation she'd made to Celia and Hank to join her in the studio. She held up Hank's drawing: "Hank, I brought this work that you did last week—"

Hank: "Train tracks! The train went around and around, then it crashed. But workers fixed it. Chugga chugga choo choo!"

Ellen took out another sketch that Hank had made; before she could say anything about it, Hank pointed to the paper and laughed: "Hey, Celia, that's the song, 'Stomach, gooey, and eyeballs'!"

The two children dissolved into belly laughter and a rousing chorus of a wacky improvisation: "Stomach, gooey, and eyeballs!" They sang the song over and over, laughing and laughing: "Stomach, gooey, and eyeballs!" Their delight in the song and in each other was wonderfully evident as they sang together.

Eventually, their laughter quieted enough for Ellen to make a suggestion: "I thought you two good friends might want to write surprises for each other—maybe songs like 'Stomach, gooey, and eyeballs,' maybe stories like Hank's train story. I made a table for each of you, where you can make your surprise."

And that was all the invitation that Hank and Celia needed. They each scampered to a table and made a production of sitting so their drawing couldn't be seen. Then the room got quiet and the children got to work.

At his table, Hank drew in rhythm with the song he sang under his breath: "Stomach, gooey, and eyeballs! Stomach, gooey, and eyeballs!" He coordinated the movement of his marker on paper with his singing, and it looked not much different from his spiraling tangle of lines that he'd drawn as his train tracks.

Meanwhile, Celia had begun drawing an intricate design for Hank. When Ellen checked in with her soon after she began drawing, Celia sent her away, saying that she wanted to draw in quiet with no one watching.

Hank finished his drawing first, and was eager to share his surprise with Celia. He jumped up and began moving towards Celia's table, which irritated Celia. She snapped at Hank, "Go away! I'm not ready!" Ellen moved to coach Hank about waiting and patience; I used that moment to re-contextualize Ellen's role from managing Hank's impatience to deepening the work at hand. I suggested to Ellen and Hank that Hank could write a note to Celia to let her know that he was done and ready to show her the surprise that he'd made.

Ellen jumped in with Hank to support his note-writing, which refocused him on the landscape of literacy, sidestepping a clash with Celia or with Ellen. Hank's simple note was a wriggling line that he read to Ellen: "It says, 'Celia, I'm done.'" He walked quietly to Celia's table, and slid the note onto it, then respectfully retreated to his table to wait for his friend.

While Ellen waited with Hank, I offered my help to Celia. "I'd be glad to read Hank's note," I said. I pointed to Hank's writing as I read it: "Celia, I'm done."

Celia shook her head. "That's not how to write my name," she said, studying Hank's line.

I explained, "Hank made marks on paper that matched the idea he wanted you to know. That's how writing works. Would you like to write a note back to him?"

Celia: "I don't know how to write letters."

Ann: "You could make marks on paper to match your idea, and I'd be glad to read your note to Hank."

Celia hesitated a moment, then wrote, in a wavy, sprawling line similar to Hank's, "I'm almost ready."

My intention in this exchange was two-fold. I wanted to help Hank and Celia see themselves as writers. And I wanted to model for Ellen the practice of calling attention to the children's learning, making explicit for the children what they were doing: writing to communicate ideas that matter.

Celia eventually finished her drawing, and she and Hank met in the center of the room to reveal their surprises to each other.

Hank held his drawing up for Celia to see, grinning hugely, singing, "Stomach, gooey, and eyeballs!"

Celia laughed and laughed. "Read it again!"

I was delighted by this exchange, whispering to Ellen, "She said *read* it again, not *sing* it again! How fabulous is that?"

Hank read his song several more times to Celia, who sang along with his reading. But he was eager to receive the surprise that Celia had made for him, and after a few more rounds of "Stomach, gooey, and eyeballs," he set down his drawing and asked Celia, "What did you make for me?"

Celia quietly, almost shyly, offered Hank her drawing, describing the details to him: "It's a butterfly and a egg in a nest made of twigs."

Hank exclaimed, "I know this song! It goes, 'Butterfly, egg, and twig and nest.'" Hank sang these words with the same melody as his goofy song, ending with a rousing, "Won't you be my darling?"

Celia and Hank sang this song several times to each other in an exuberant and heartfelt exchange of humor and friendship.

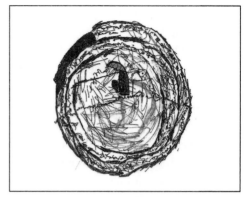

To support both the children's learning and Ellen's, I described the children's dynamic exchange of writing and reading: "You drew a picture, Celia, and Hank read the song in it!"

That launched the children into more singing, and, in no time, they were jumping around in a wacky slapstick operatic dance, with a mash-up of "Butterfly, egg, and twig and nest" and "Stomach, gooey, and eyeballs" and "Won't you be my darling?" Ellen and I cleared space for the children to goof and sing, pushing the tables out of the way to make room for Hank and Celia's playful and intimate reconnection with each other after their focused individual work. As the children danced their goofy dance, Ellen and I seized the opportunity for a quick in-the-moment planning conversation. We still had time available in the studio before lunch, and we considered whether and how to use it.

We thought back to our conversation at the team meeting, and the values and intentions that we'd called forward. "I'm tickled by the way that the children are 'reading' each other's writing—and using that as the catalyst for their puppy-dog goofing." I said. "Remember Rich's idea about having the children draw their silly play? This might be an opportunity to do that. That'd be a way to carry the writing that they've already done forward." [**Thinking Lens: Reflect and take action.** *What could we offer that would invite children to take a different perspective? How could we invite children's physical engagement?*]

Ellen suggested, "What about inviting them to create some writing together? Maybe they could write a song together, since they're already singing each other's songs." [**Thinking Lens: Reflect and take action.** *What could we* *offer that would invite collaboration and contribution? What could we offer that would deepen children's relationships?*]

"Fabulous!" I exclaimed. "Let's offer them some really big paper to match their big-sized goofiness."

And so, after this on-the-spot exchange, that's what we did. Ellen watched for an opening in the children's play, and jumped in with an invitation: "I wonder if you'd like to write a song together?"

The children were intrigued, and helped Ellen get a very long piece of butcher paper off the roll and lay it out on the floor. Celia and Hank lay on their bellies, markers near to hand. Hank began to hum.

Celia: "Hank, you keep singing so I can draw."

Hank added the familiar refrain into the melody he'd been humming: "Stomach, gooey, and eyeballs!" As he sang, Celia began to draw. He joined her, and, side by side, they drew and sang and drew. They didn't create a drawing together; their experience of collaboration seemed more about drawing next to each other, each riffing on the familiar song in her or his own expressive voice.

Lunchtime arrived, and we left the studio, and there it was—a morning's engagement with friendship and literacy, and with the joyful merriment of children's full-bodied play.

Another Round of Meaning-Making and Planning

A few days after our morning in the studio with Hank and Celia, Ellen and I met during her planning time to study our notes and the two children's drawings. We wanted to deepen our understanding of literacy, of friendship, and of goofy, slapstick play, and to prepare to write a documentation story about our experience with Hank and Celia. We used the Thinking Lens during this one-on-one conversation, just as we used it during our teaching team meetings, moving through the protocol step-by-step.

As our conversation unfolded, we called each other's attention to the two children's quite distinct ways of creating and offering their gifts for each other. While Hank was quick to create a written representation of their shared song, affirming their relationship in this new medium, Celia was private and internal with her work. We were glad to see the children goof around during their studio time, glad for their rollicking wrestle and screwball bellowing of silly songs—glad to see them able to move between the seriousness of writing for each other and the wackiness of their physical play. It reassured us that there was room for our invitation in the scope of Hank's and Celia's friendship.

We planned several next steps to extend and deepen Celia's and Hank's experience, and to carry their experience into the whole group of children. Ellen would watch for opportunities during daily life in the classroom to invite Hank and Celia, as well as the other children in the group, to record their experiences on paper—sketching their block structures, for example, or writing down the story of a drama game. And, with the two children's permission, Ellen would bring Celia's and Hank's written songs to the whole group's daily classroom meeting, reading the songs and teaching them to the whole group, to honor the children's literacy work and their friendship in a playful and public way.

After the meeting, Ellen and I worked together to craft a piece of written documentation to share the story of this experience—the children's experience, and the experience of teacher research. We wrote the documentation story together, as part of my on-going support for Ellen's learning.

We shared the documentation story with Hank and Celia's families, and asked them to share their thinking about what had unfolded [**Thinking Lens: Collaborate with others to expand perspectives.** *What insights do the children's families have? How does this play reflect or challenge their beliefs, values, or practices?*]:

We welcome your thoughts about this adventure that Hank and Celia shared. What's your take on our invitation into a more focused exchange between the two friends? How do you weigh the balance between that sort of intentionally crafted experience and their spontaneous play? In our conversations as a teaching team, we discovered a tension in our thinking: How do we honor children's right to shape their play and the content of their friendships, alongside our commitment as teachers to stretch children into new arenas of experience and thinking? How do you hold that tension, as a parent? How would you like us to hold it, as teachers? As always, you can email or call, or jot a note here, with your thinking.

Why Tell this Story?

This simple story illustrates the depth of inquiry that's possible when we anchor our teaching with the Thinking Lens. The richly complex experience that Ellen, Rich, Suze, Hank, Celia, and I shared began with the most ordinary of acts: a child making train sounds while he drew a scribbly sort of picture. When we stepped into that drawing, all of us together, we found ourselves in a nuanced and intricate landscape; our journey there helped us to know ourselves, and each other, more fully. And we came away with a deepened understanding of the value and challenge of speaking into and writing down what we care about.

This experience held deep intellectual and authentic engagement for us educators—more than we'd find in administering a pre-formulated writing activity from a scripted literacy curriculum. This experience held deep and authentic intellectual engagement for the children—more than exists in reciting the alphabet or copying letters. The children's whole selves were involved in their learning: hearts, minds, humor, bodies.

• • • • • • • • All the learning in this story happened in the context of relationships: educators with children, educators with each other as fellow researchers, children with each other, educators with families. It was an embodiment of inquiry at its most lively and enlivening, spinning us all forward into new questions and new possibilities.

But all this for two children?
Yes and no.
With three educators on the teaching team, each bringing an observation for us to study together at the weekly team meetings, we did deep dives for five or six children each week. These deep dives impacted our teaching and the life of the classroom in a range of ways. They compelled us to join our attention to

children's attention in intimate and specific detail, and this, in turn, helped us craft offerings to the children aimed at supporting their pursuits, their imbedded intent. Our curriculum was resonant with meaning and substance, with the energizing zing of relevance.

Our deep dives sharpened our understandings of things like literacy learning and friendship and the value of goofy play; we were better able to support that learning and play for all the children, after exploring it in the context of a few children's experiences. And our deep dives helped us become more self-aware of the values, convictions, and experiences that shaped our teaching. That self-awareness made us better educators.

We kept track of which children we'd spent time talking about at each team meeting, and of who we'd not taken deep dives with recently. This accounting alerted us to children we were overlooking; we'd commit to seeking out those children, to bring stories of their play to our team meetings for study and responsive planning.

The plans we generated during team meetings were one strand braided into the life of the classroom. There were other strands as well, which together, formed our curriculum. Educators offered materials rich with possibility throughout the classroom; they invited children into the art studio space for explorations with art media; they planned for play outdoors, and for neighborhood walks. Families brought materials, stories, and experiences to the classroom. There were community celebrations, and regular fire drills, and unfailingly fascinating garbage trucks in the alley. Classroom life was a blend of the deliberate and the spontaneous, the planned and the unexpected; it grew from the delicious intermingling of attention on an intimate scale and attention to the collective, bold and big.

This is complex weaving, this work of being an educator. Complex, and challenging, and energizing, and sustaining—with occasional forays into slapstick comedy.

Margie Carter

Attention and Generosity

This story found me both smiling with delight and harboring some unnamed discomfort. It took me some time to sort that out. What's going on here? Ah ha! Another opportunity to put the Thinking Lens to work to untangle my responses and learn from them. Perhaps other readers will want to join me, to explore this protocol in action as part of our reflections on this story.

Know yourself: What is your immediate response to the children's play and conversation? What feelings stir in you? What touches your heart as you watch and listen? What in your background is influencing your response? What values are influencing your response? What adult perspectives, i.e. standards, health and safety, time, goals are on your mind? What leaves you curious, eager to engage?

I know I strongly value children's self-initiated unscripted play. Sometimes I appreciate and join in their impromptu goofy antics, but, honestly, I often find this clowning around a bit tedious, if not annoying. There is only so much potty talk I can have fun with, and I never could hang in there to get even close to 99 bottles of beer on the wall. (Nineteen is about my limit.) Perhaps this low threshold is influenced by the scarcity of goofiness tolerated by adults in my own childhood?

I am, however, totally fascinated by the description of Hank's initial rapture as he expressed the train's movement with his body and with marker and paper. I'm especially curious about that having read Ursula Kolbe's *It's Not a Bird Yet: The Drama of Drawing.*[1] And Angela Hanscom's *Balanced and Barefoot* has made me more curious about how active bodies develop brains.[2] So, what connections are happening in that little guy's brain, I wonder?

I also recognize feeling protective of our readers who work in settings with conditions that make this story seem impossible to relate to. Who has time to indulge in delighting in the explorations of one or two children? How could precious, hard-to-secure team meeting time focus on something as trivial as slapstick comedy? Seriously, there's a budget that could allow a pedagogical leader to devote time to working with only one teacher and two children? Will our readers be able to get past "yes … buts" and see possibilities for themselves?

When feeling overwhelmed by a sense of the impossible, I often turn to poetry and music, so I dipped into my files for something to re-ground me in my fundamental values and aspirations. And there, tucked away as if waiting for me, was Simone Weil saying, "Attention is the rarest and purest form of generosity."[3] Yes, yes, isn't that what every child, every group of children deserves—our attention and generosity? At its core, this slapstick tale is an inspiring story about a pedagogical leader supporting educators to work with careful attention, intention, and generosity. This isn't relevant only for well-resourced programs serving privileged kids. Children, families, and teachers shackled with the disparities and complex challenges of poverty and racism all the more deserve careful attention to their minds at work, their resourcefulness, clever humor, and talent. Their early childhood programs should overflow with experiences of generosity and new possibilities.

Of course, wherever they work, teachers face challenges, and we should be empathetic to the demands on them, the hardships and frustrations, but we can call them to a place of generosity with our time and attention. Ann shows us that while pedagogical leaders seek to meet up with the hearts of educators, this is different than going down a rabbit hole when discouragement shows up. Pedagogical leaders must be attentive to avoid letting conversations with educators devolve into venting sessions. This is an opportunity to recommit to the program's core values about what children deserve from us, despite the challenges of bringing that to fruition.

In this story, we see Ann invite teachers to consider their own childhood experiences which might offer insights into what they see Hank doing. They seem keen to do this, which is terrific, but their enthusiastic sharing could lead them down a side road too far from a focus on Hank and this observation under consideration. Mindful of time and the intention to focus on the practice of teacher research, Ann uses these teacher stories to weave a path into meeting up with children's minds and we see the engagement that the Thinking Lens protocol offers for studying an observation in search of meaning.

We started our study with this personal sharing as a way to bring our full human selves to the discussion, and to be sure we were showing up all the way, not just as educators. From that stance, we turned our attention to Hank, and our responses to his drawing.

Pedagogical leaders learn to be nimble and attentive in these settings, keeping the protocol near at hand to guide conversations. Like learning to dance within an ensemble, play in a band, or row in a crew shell, it takes practice to master your own skills even as you work to find a rhythm that moves the group forward. Sometimes finding the right metaphor opens up a way to uncover something we already understand about what's needed. You might think of a pedagogical leader drawing on a protocol for these conversations like weaving a tapestry. While bringing focus and discipline, the Thinking Lens serves more as a weaving shuttle than a set of lock-step questions to answer.

Ann is a pedagogical *listener*, sensing where a move to other aspects of the protocol might be useful; she picks up threads, pays attention to possible discoveries of patterns. She is an occasional participant and stays alert for where her role as a facilitator or critical friend might be useful. Transparency with these skills and intentions helps educators see new possibilities, for the children and themselves.

Take the children's points of view: What are the children trying to figure out? What child development or early learning theories might you consider?

I'm thoroughly intrigued by Hank and find that what he and Celia undertake to further their friendship quite fetching and deserving of respect with protection from other agendas. When we really give our attention, we see that Hank and Celia are figuring out how to use their bodies as tools of expression, along with using materials, lines, singing, and humor to collaboratively craft and tell a story. We more often recognize this as what artists, dancers, and designers do, but we'll find it every day when we're paying attention to children. They are constructing understandings and creatively expressing them, just as we see in the work of photographers, landscapers, chefs. In the here and now, they show us how to recalibrate our own thinking because their perspectives are less constrained and more fluid than ours. Toward the future, they are building brain muscles and the skills of forensic detectives, scientists, philosophers, artisans, gamers, and even late-night comedians. (We'll possibly find Hank and Celia writing for or starring in Saturday Night Live or The Daily Show when they come of age!)

Being goofy is a gift of childhood and if we enjoyed it more, perhaps we wouldn't take ourselves so seriously. But serious endeavors, tenderness, and exuberant big body play are also hallmarks of childhood. I love how these teachers see and value that, how well they know and delight in Hank, how they recognize that this budding friendship brings out a new side of Celia and could do the same for Hank.

> Rich jumped in. 'I love Hank's silly, physical games. He's like a puppy! This train drawing has some of that energy that I love in Hank—that movement and noise.'

> Ellen added, 'Yeah, I think that's part of what drew me to this moment: it was pure Hank, but on paper.'

> … then Rich ventured an idea. 'This may be a sidetrack, but I keep thinking of Hank's friendship with Celia, which has really surprised me. She's such a serious and thoughtful kid, and spends a lot of time drawing and writing songs and dances. But when Celia hangs out with Hank, she becomes a goofball. She and Hank are all about slapstick comedy and belly laughter.'

In our search for and screening of new teachers, what would help us spot that disposition to notice details and delight in who children are? We're focused on resumes, degrees, and criminal background checks, often to the neglect of uncovering whether a potential staff member treasures the time of life called childhood, understands the importance of relationships, and sees their work as thinking rather than teaching. It's a crying shame that so many adults (parents, educators, politicians, and policy makers) are focused on taming and protecting and accelerating children's journey into adulthood.

The educators of Reggio remind us that children are *today's* citizens, not just tomorrow's. Our humanity is in jeopardy when we fail to slow down, savor, and celebrate life with them. At the risk of sounding cliché, I confess that somedays my confidence about the survival of our species is only sustained when I shut out the media news and tune my ears to children at play. The exuberance and full-on living in the tone of children's voices down the street reassures me and helps me regroup. Yes, there are outrageous things we must be actively countering (think: the preschool to prison pipeline for African American children, families seeking asylum being torn apart from each other at the border, or the societal mindset of racing to the top). In this frantic world of pain, fear, and terrible trouble, a song of "Stomach, gooey, and eyeballs!" can bring us some levity, as well as the courage and stamina to carry on.

Collaborate with others to expand perspectives. How do your colleagues understand the meaning of the children's play? What other arenas of knowledge and insight might you consult?

I've mentioned Ursula Kolbe's book, *It's Not a Bird Yet*, as a resource to help us deepen our understandings of Hank's physicality and drama in his drawing, as well as the work of occupational therapists like Angela Hanscom who apply neuroscience to understanding physicality; but let's give a shout out to the discovery of choreography notation! Who knew? (Was the person who invented it named Hank?) How brilliant of these educators to even consider such a web search. What a testimony to the power of thinking with others and considering perspectives that are not regularly present in your band width.

And notice the role Ann played throughout this story. In the search for meaning in the children's play, a pedagogical leader can collaborate with educators in small group settings, with the full classroom group, inside, outside, or on a community excursion. Together, they make guesses, challenge, and expand each other's thinking. They choose a possibility to test out. In her side-by-side work with Ellen, Hank, and Celia in the studio, Ann shared in the "precision planning" for the set-up of the space and materials, and clarified the intention of the invitation. She collaborated in listening and observing, in taking notes and photos. She offered insights and examples to support Ellen's learning about ways to talk with children to help them see their thinking. We see her dance in, do-si-do, and move back out.

> My intention in this exchange was two-fold. I wanted to help Hank and
> Celia see themselves as writers. And I wanted to model for Ellen the practice
> of calling attention to the children's learning, making explicit for the children
> what they were doing: writing to communicate ideas that matter.

From holding the big picture, grounded in values and intention, to assisting with the careful details of planning when the children and studio space would be available, Ann expanded understandings, skills, and self-confidence in the teachers. A pedagogical leader is an able collaborator: able to guide without taking over, able to challenge without intimidation, to keep the intention in focus, and to take on some tasks that serve as scaffolds for further learning and sustained enjoyment in working with children. Attention and generosity.

> **Examine the environment.** How are the organization and the use
> of the physical space and materials impacting this situation? How are
> schedules and routines influencing this experience?

Environments are physical, but also social and emotional spaces. While many elements are highly visible, environments also contain invisible structures that underpin an identity, an intention, opportunities, and possibilities. What I want to make transparent for our thinking about this story are the aspects of the environment created for educators to flourish as thinkers and collaborators. An organizational culture was painstakingly developed at this center, with structures created for the educators both to appreciate this moment with Hank and to respond with the generosity of time and attention.

In this organizational environment, there is time planned into the budget and staffing patterns for teaching teams to meet with a pedagogical leader. The expectation set for this time, as well as for regular time with the children, is to engage in the practice of teacher research. Structures (again with the resources of time, schedules, and physical space) are in place to orient and support new teachers into this practice. This didn't happen overnight, but was steadily plotted and scrapped together over a number of years, fueled beyond barriers and limitations, by a fierce determination to bring another vision into reality. Inch by inch, gaining ground, innovating, gaining skills, and know-how. There were blind spots and setbacks to be sure, but the longing and determination of the educators was relentless.

Because time and money are *always* in short supply, Hilltop learned that team meetings had to be thoughtfully supported with pedagogical leadership and protocols to support educators to study, listen, consider, and plan together; without these supports, it was too easy for the meetings to devolve into housekeeping and grousing. By the time of this slapstick literacy story, the educators had matured in their thinking and practice; they were at ease weaving through this pedagogical process several times during a short one-hour weekly meeting. In addition to these weekly team meetings, Ann's role as pedagogical leader was to orient incoming staff, offering them side-by-side coaching. Over the years, the budget crept toward the capacity to make the pedagogical leader position full time, adding responsibilities for monthly professional learning gatherings for the full staff, with the center closing at 3:00 the first Friday of the month. It took time and extended collaboration to help families understand the value of this time despite its inconvenience for them. Generosity on their part because attention was given to building that collaboration. You can see further evidence of this collaboration in the expectation that Hank and Celia's family will respond to Ellen and Ann's written documentation about their slapstick children.

> **Reflect and take action.** What values and intentions do you want to influence your response to what you've seen, learned, and make guesses about? What might you do to deepen relationships and how will you invite collaboration?

If you haven't done so already, go back through this story with the Thinking Lens protocol. Take some time to formulate your own reflections and action plans from what provokes you. Perhaps these questions will spur you on:

- Where are you in your longing for or experience with working in this way as a teacher, supervisor, coach, or consultant?

- The role of organizational culture and pedagogical leadership is often missing in the U.S. Quality Rating and Improvement Systems (QRIS), but there is growing evidence that it is a skeleton key to unlock many aspects of quality. States are now funding rating scales and coaches to improve scores, but what about funding pedagogical leaders and an adaptation of the Aotearoa New Zealand government's funding of teacher research to create "centers of innovation"? Where could you imagine opening the doors to that potential?

- The organizational structure of publicly funded and corporate programs always includes "educational coordinators" responsible for multiple sites. What if some of these roles were reinvented as pedagogical leaders, not in name, but in actual practice? How might community-based programs come together in a shared services model to provide organizational development support, pedagogical leadership, and back-office business services to clusters of programs?

• •

As you reflect, develop an action plan. It won't cost a dime to go to work with a different mindset tomorrow. What goals might you set for yourself?

• •

This time next year, what do you hope is true for you as a pedagogical leader?

• •

. . . .

Where will you find support for yourself, as you move forward with this work?

. . . .

What strength or gift do you bring to moving this work forward?

. . . .

The aim of life is to live, and to live means to be aware, joyously, drunkenly, serenely, divinely aware.

—Henry Miller[16]

14

Voices from the Front Lines: A Call to Reimagine Our Work

In a branch of the Chinese system of medicine and philosophy, the place in our bodies just behind our navel is thought of as the door of life. The related martial arts practice of Qigong often begins by swinging one's arms to knock on that door to free up life energy. From there, practitioners mobilize their spines, and move any restrictions between their heads and hearts, especially in times of decision making. There is wise metaphor here, as we turn ourselves to the work of reimagining early childhood education: we must move forward with strong spines, clear minds, and open hearts.

We struggled at times, as we worked on this book, with the tension between the stifling press of compliance that is the reality for too many educators and our commitment to creating another reality. We didn't want to write from a place of willful ignorance, skirting past the hard challenges in educators' daily lives, waving as we hurried by, and calling a too-cheerful invitation to "just change how you're doing things, and you'll feel better." At the same time, we didn't want to give over to the current systems, yielding to "the way things are" by putting a superficial shine on accountability and outcomes. Our intention with this book is to move towards transformation rather than resignation—to write a new story about children and childhood, about early childhood education and about educators.

In the gap between our biggest aspirations and most challenging current realities, we have some serious choices to make: we can blame, attack, or withdraw; we can go numb and normalize what is unacceptable; or we can mobilize the courage and confidence to imagine another world. We can knock on the door of life, straighten our spines, clear our minds, open our hearts, and reach beyond the limitations of who we are now to stake a claim for new possibilities.

We're looking for co-conspirators in the move to transform early childhood education. In common usage, conspirator is understood as a person who joins a secret plot to do something illegal. The word, though, grows from potent roots: its Latin origins connote "breathing together," acting together toward a shared purpose. In this spirit, we issue a call for conspirators—for people across the early childhood landscape who are ready to join together, breath and muscle and imagination, to reclaim our work.

In this chapter, we hear from people who are conspiring to keep playful inquiry, imagination, intellectual agility, curious and critical thinking, and eager collaboration at the center of early childhood education. We take heart from these educators who continue to be innovative and who act from deep integrity, holding true to their values about childhood, about the purpose of education, about who educators can be in the lives of young children. We invited these folks to offer responses to our book, in order to call forward a range of roles and contexts, perspectives and stories. We asked them to share their thinking about the role of pedagogical leadership, the use of protocols, the challenge of disequilibrium—and the power of knocking on the door of life, choosing to act from a place of hope and vision. With gratitude, with deep regard, we offer the voices of these educators, breathing together in a conspiracy for transformation.

Pitching a Tent in the Land of Disequilibrium

By Shaquam Urquhart Edwards

As a community college faculty member, I consider myself a pedagogical leader. I've been in the field of early childhood education for 34 years. I believe in what Margie and Ann refer to as "keeping the dynamics of visions, values and practice in continual motion." It is all so clear when my mind doesn't have to reconcile with the realities of what I see in the field, or the stories that I hear from my college students. I value children and families together, similar to the way that Ann refers to as seeing families in three dimensions, with a lens that illuminates their humanity. Those beautiful words make me sing and twirl. But then the music stops and I am dizzy from the dance. I am seriously off balance, in a state of disequilibrium as I seek to make sense of what is my vision, what promise this book is offering, and what is actually happening in preschools across America.

A Story to Tell

I believe in telling the stories of my community. Here's one, not at all uncommon, from a recent visit to a preschool class of two-year-olds. I was not in the room in the role of an educator. I was there simply as a family friend, and the teachers were not aware of the work that I do. Of course, I am always wearing my invisible hat of pedagogical leader and I observe with that perspective. It was early morning, and the teachers were welcoming families, exchanging warm greetings and asking how the children's nights had been. Hugs and kisses and a few too many parents sneaking out without good-byes caught my attention. Some children were looking around the room, appearing to be searching for the adult that had brought them to school. As early care and education professionals, we know about attachment and trust. How are these young educators still encouraging families to sneak out? I wonder if they have taken ECE classes.

Have they learned about attachment theory, and the importance of creating good-bye rituals that children can come to expect and count on, to help them feel empowered and trusting of the adults in their world?

The pedagogical leader in me yearned to pull these young teachers to the side and engage in on-the-spot coaching, offering them emotional support, environment consulting, and potential scripts to use with families. This could all be so different! I envisioned last-minute cozy cuddles in the book corner (which was actually dismal, bare, and lacking seating), and tiny hands gently pushing grown-ups out the door, while teachers validated feelings of sadness for children and families who were experiencing separation anxiety. These young teachers needed fundamental knowledge and support!

After breakfast was served and cleared, the children were told to go to circle: an area on a rug where there were no materials and no adult waiting to engage them. Those dozen two-year-olds were running circles around the room as the two teachers tried to corral, cajole, and bribe the children to sit. I was under the impression that this was a regular routine. It seemed familiar to the children, and the teachers appeared to expect the children to behave as they did. I secretly wished for these educators to have pedagogical leaders, classes, or ongoing training to help them learn the developmental needs of two-year-olds. I wanted the teachers to experience the joy of being with young children at group time, and not just the frustration. My inquiring mind wanted to know if these energetic young woman had any coaching or mentoring on how to have age-appropriate, engaging, circle times. If so, chances are that they would know that the first step is to be ready for the children, seated, and with inviting materials to draw the children in, rather than attempting to lasso them as they circle around.

One teacher had a computer tablet in her hand. She was taking photos. When most of the children landed, a teacher sat near the children, and also in reach of the CD player. When at last all the children landed on the rug, a teacher put on fast music; the toddlers responded by jumping and dancing—until they were made to sit again. The teacher gave children rhythm sticks and put on a song with rapid instructions that involved naming colors, though no actual colors were offered to help the children make a connection. The song ended, the sticks were collected, the bodies wiggled. Next came the weather check: one little one ran to the window to make her report, the others concurred. Suddenly the teacher with the tablet said to her co-teacher, "I didn't get that on the tablet, could you do it again?" I blinked a few times and took a deep breath.

It was crystal clear to me that for these two teachers, the photo documentation that occurred throughout the day had very little to do with the children. The teachers sent photos with little captions such as, "I'm learning my colors!" along to the families. The children were the subjects of the photos, but they really were innocent bystanders of drive-by documentation and assessment. Neither the children nor teachers were engaged learners in a culture of inquiry. There was no joint attention happening in that classroom. The teachers were not "walking with" the children as Ann discusses in Chapter Two. They were not even speed walking. There was no "with" going on. There was only co-existing with the intent to manage, control, and send smiling photos to show parents how much learning was going on.

What am I to Do?

Though they were not, these teachers could be my students. These young women who look happy and proud to be with children are the faces of many early care and education teachers. How do I engage these teachers who have been taught that their job is to clean and corral, rather than to engage, promote inquiry, practice authentic assessment, and wonder with children? When the focus is on superficial images of learning and not actual learning, how do I reach them? How do I reconcile the idea of exploring a year-long concept with teachers who work for schools that are satisfied with the one-and-done tablet assessment training and a curriculum centered around dominant culture holidays, and color or letter of the week themes? Families see a clean, sterile environment and get photos of smiling children and believe that their children are getting a quality early childhood experience. But I know better, and it keeps me in a state of disequilibrium. Ann writes that "disequilibrium is a lively place to make camp." That may be true, but it is certainly not a comfortable place to pitch a tent.

So what do I do? I keep reading books like this one for inspiration, possibility, and fuel for my own intellectual vitality. I soak in stories like the one Ann shares of Hank and Celia, and the way that their teachers supported friendship and goofy writing surprises with such loving intention and anticipation of what might unfold between the children. I wrestle with stories that give me opposing thoughts, like the one about Jamie in Chapter 10, where Ann mentions that labeling his work as merely "sensory play" is dismissive and disrespectful. I understand that perspective, and yet, for some of my students, getting them to see this as sensory play rather than merely "cute" is a big step in their understanding of child development. I read and re-read sections that help me hold on tight to the notions of embracing complexity and uncertainty because that gives me strength to keep building little bridges between ideal pedagogy and the realities of the schools that students work in. I pause at the poetry and verse between chapters because it affirms the importance of creativity in my work and highlights the artistic aspect of teaching.

This book pulls me into my community. It reminds me of the good work that is happening in preschools around the country. I am reminded that there are early care and education professionals who are eager to learn, who want to push past the old models of busying children with cute and meaningless projects and who embrace real learning in ways that honor young children. I need to be part of this community that continues to learn and is willing to sit in the brave spaces even when it is not comfortable. Being in a state of disequilibrium is not easy. I much prefer balance, but what I know for sure is that being off balance pushes me to seek knowledge. In order to right myself again, I need information, new perspectives, insights, and self-awareness, all of which leads to forward motion and positive change. I am energized and inspired by teaching and learning.

One of my favorite things about working at a community college is the diversity of students. I've had students as young as 16, and as seasoned as 80 years old. Some have very little formal education and others have advanced degrees. They come from all parts of the world and every socioeconomic level. And we are all there learning together, immersed in the spirit of inquiry that Ann and Margie discuss. Invigorating learning is catchy. I keep catching it and tossing it to my students. Many of them are up for the joyful challenge of learning about young children, and that ignites my passion as a pedagogical leader. I just have to embrace the feelings of uncertainty that go along with teaching and learning, and pitch a comfortable tent since I will be camping in the land of disequilibrium for a long season.

QUESTIONS BEFORE DARK

Day ends, and before sleep
when the sky dies down, consider
your altered state: has this day
changed you? Are the corners
sharper or rounded off? Did you
live with death? Make decisions
that quieted? Find one clear word
that fit? At the sun's midpoint
did you notice a pitch of absence,
bewilderment that invites the possible? What did you learn
from things you dropped and picked up
and dropped again? Did you set a straw
parallel to the river, let the flow
carry you downstream?

—**Jeanne Lohmann**[1]

Trying on the Idea of Being a Pedagogical Leader

By Nadiyah Taylor

As I read through this wonderful book, I move between two sets of sometimes contradictory experiences. First, I feel reflective, inspired, and renewed. I'm reminded that some of my best times as a community college instructor are when I am engaged in dialogue with others; imagining a bright future for children and their families and considering our role in supporting teachers to help make that vision real. I am appalled that someone attempted to prevent Ann from pursuing a calling to teach children, thinking such a choice was beneath her. Yet, Ann's story strengthens my passion for supporting my students to feel pride in their work and to stop referring to themselves as "just a preschool teacher." I am inspired to think about my values as a teacher-educator and consider if my day-to-day work is in line with these values. I wonder, have I explored "the purpose of education" with my students, not as a study of history, but as an exploration of deep values, hopes, and dreams? I think so, but if not, what's holding me back? I also find myself looking forward to building on Margie's suggestions given throughout the book to engage in new ways to "spark the spirit of inquiry" in myself, my colleagues, and my students.

Reading Ann's description that inquiry is "a consideration of questions that move us and questions that matter," I consider questions that matter most to me as an educator. Am I:

- supporting my students as thinkers and explorers, who think deeply about the importance of their work in the lives of children and families?
- empowering my students to see themselves as competent learners and researchers when so many of them have not been acknowledged as thinkers in their previous educational experiences?
- supporting teachers to explore and even embrace the complicated and complex issues of identity, their own, and those of the children they will one day teach?

- encouraging my students to stay in the early childhood field, despite low pay and low respect, while also helping them to develop their skills as advocates?
- helping to change the culture of education so that teachers really see families as partners?
- helping to change the current direction of early education that seems so focused on turning our young children into robots who can read by age five, but who have the joy of reading taken away by the time they finish 3rd grade?
- clearly identifying the values that our community college program holds and ensuring our courses reflect these values?

I am excited to explore these questions, while trying on the idea of being a pedagogical leader in my program. What would be tangibly different if I moved into a space where my focus in the classroom changed to thinking with my students, rather than teaching them? What would it mean on a departmental level for me to support other educators to move in this direction? Am I comfortable stepping into a new space, a new role?

Am I Perpetuating the Cycle of Drill and Fill?

Alongside my eagerness to engage these questions, another, perhaps contradictory, set of feelings wash over me, feelings of hesitation and some resistance. How can I possibly do what is being suggested within the structure that I am working in? I am struck by the many parallels between challenges faced by early childhood educators and those of the community college faculty who teach them. "A culture of inquiry is rooted in the immediacy of what is unfolding, rather than oriented towards the achievement of learning goals, or the eventuality of assessments, or the replication of routines." This statement jumps out to me because in the community college world there is a hyper-focus on assessing "student learning outcomes" and moving students through their education as quickly as possible. Colleges are responsible to legislators who determine priorities and connected funding, some of which match my values as a teacher, but many of which are oppositional to them. As instructors take on larger class sizes and more administrative tasks, we have less time ourselves for reflection and exploration. I want to be creative and visionary, but am often swamped with meetings, grading and completing reports, many of which drain me and push me to focus on someone else's agenda rather than my own or my program's values. How do I engage students in a practice of reflection and inquiry when I often cannot engage in these practices myself?

When I reflect on my daily life as an instructor, with upwards of 225 students a semester, am I unintentionally falling into behavior patterns that are at odds with what I believe my work should be? I read Ann's description of the:

> ... reality that has come to dominate our field, in which curriculum is created to be 'teacher-proof' because teachers are seen as the weak link between learning goals and measurable achievement on assessments. A reality in which professional development is focused on health and safety mandates, compliance issues, and accountability to state rating systems. A reality in which children's days are overrun with activities that orient them towards learning outcomes on which they'll be evaluated in the name of 'quality.'

At first reading, I feel confident that I do not reinforce this message in my classes. I don't see teachers as the weak link at all and spend a lot of time bolstering their confidence to see themselves as leaders and actors in their own lives. But on second reading, I wonder if there's some hard truths here for me to consider. During some quarters I've given up written reflections because they take too long to grade. There are times when I resist requiring that students visit me during office hours because I cannot envision how to actually meet 200+ students. I have some big questions to ask myself. Am I perpetuating the cycle of "drill and fill" with my adult students as they learn theories and teaching strategies from me? Am I becoming bitter at having to advocate constantly for the needs of our students and program, for the importance of a lab experience for our students? Do I misplace blame? Does my passion for wanting to change the world turn into frustration with students who "just don't get it?"

These are sobering thoughts and it is seductive to throw my hands up and let the system take over, to say, "It's not my fault: I have to prepare students for the world they will be teaching in." "It's not my fault if I cannot show high levels of productivity and get students through the sequence of courses, because otherwise our program won't survive, and that will serve no one." "I just have too much work. What more do you expect me to do?" But as these feelings of exhausted despair tug at me, my better-self reminds me that I do want to change the world, and that requires hope, dreaming, hard work, and advocacy. Margie's story of working with Luz is especially enlightening as a path forward. I am able to see how one director, working within mandates similar to those that press on my work, navigated her way to both meet those mandates and to provide pedagogical leadership.

Being Transparent to Change my own Thinking

At the start of the last quarter, I opened my course Child, Family & Community with an activity borrowed from a colleague. For our first days of the session, I asked students to bring five items to class that represented events or memories in childhood that helped them to be the person they are today. Students took turns sharing their shoebox of items, and their stories were fascinating, moving, sad, funny, and inspiring. On the third day of sharing, I realized we'd taken 45 of the 75 minutes of the class session with this activity and I began to feel nervous. "Are the students bored?" "Am I taking too much time with this activity?" "Is this relevant?" "It's the end of the second week of class and we haven't gotten into 'content' yet!"

In that moment, I chose to be transparent with my students, *in order to change my own thinking.* I acknowledged that this activity was taking a lot of time (we have a large class) and also identified the importance of telling our stories, of being seen. I shared my belief that we bring our whole selves to teaching. The shared experiences of our childhoods remind us that none of us get through life unscathed, or without happiness or anger. The children in our care are beginning their life journeys and need to share their stories and experiences with us. It takes time to listen, but we learn so much from one another, and we become better listeners. This

IS the content. This IS what I want to teach, and what I want students to carry away with them. I'm teaching for dispositions as much as for content knowledge.

This experience exemplifies fundamental questions that I have as a teacher educator:

- How do I face up to the realities of education today and still hold my values as an educator? What *are* my values?
- What do I want to share with students?
- What are my hopes and dreams for children, families, and educators; for our society?
- What is my role in setting a foundation with students, many of whom are uncertain about whether they want to teach or who are already looking beyond what they expect to be a fun, but ultimately fleeting job as they move on to more "important," respected, and ultimately higher paying work?

I don't want to leave my students feeling unprepared for the classrooms they will enter, even if those classrooms do not align with my vision for early childhood education. The reality is that many teachers don't have the option to hold out until they can work in the best programs. Their choices are constrained by financial realities, and their need for job security. And, sadly, there are not that many programs that practice the sort of *inquiry-driven, responsive, joyfully collaborative* teaching and learning that I want for children—and for their teachers. So, teachers stay where they are and suffer in silence, sometimes fearing that they will lose their jobs if they speak up. Or they move from job to job, trying to find a philosophical fit, increasingly dismayed by their experiences, but not ready or confident to act as change-makers in the programs where they work. Or perhaps, the most concerning outcome for me is that teachers begin to disbelieve in the importance of educating children in this manner and stop resisting altogether.

Not "Can I do this?" but "How can I do this?"

All of this makes me think of Lisa Delpit's challenge that teachers help students become bicultural, to understand the "codes of power."[2] For me as a college instructor, this means identifying that there are systems and realities in early childhood education that students need to know. Some of these include: having a working understanding of the current assessment systems and learning foundations; being aware that funding is often tied to measures such as the DRPD, CLASS™, and ECERS; that funders and policy makers and agency administrators too often define quality for us, in ways that we may disagree with. Alongside helping students learn these early childhood education "codes of power," I must also support students to hold strong to their values and beliefs and passion for making a just and fair educational system. I need to both enable them to navigate the current system, *and* give them the skills and permission to critique/problematize/resist those same systems. For example, I can help students see that assessments can be used to inform our teaching, when used in appropriate and culturally competent ways—*and* there are also many other ways to evaluate and understand our work as teachers.

How do we move from where we are to where we want to be? We want teachers to focus on who children are now, not only on the expectations for getting them "ready for school." Teachers need time to think and plan. They need to be financially secure. Teachers need to have a vision for themselves as professionals and advocates for change.[3]

Paulo Freire writes that "Knowledge emerges only through invention and re-invention, through the restless, impatient, continuing, hopeful inquiry human beings pursue in the world, with the world, and with each other."[4] I turn to Freire's concept of praxis or reflective action as I consider how I might carry forward the thinking that Ann and Margie's book has sparked. I've been reminded that I, like teachers, need time to reflect, and to dream. Time to reflect, and to act.

As I hold these questions and commitments to action, I expect that I'll continue to move between inspiration and hesitation, renewal and resistance. This "restless, impatient, continuing, hopeful inquiry" will provide a framework for my current and future work, professionally and personally, helping me to remember that without hope there can be no change. I know that very few truly meaningful things in life happen without hard work, self-awareness, and action.

My Reflection	*Actions I Can Take*
What does a culture of inquiry look like in a college setting?	Talk with others; seek out new ideas; spend time creating a vision statement for my college teaching.
Do I have the skills to put inquiry at the center of my courses?	Identify what skills I need—and what I'm missing. Find a mentor or critical friend to help me.
Do I believe/behave as if inquiry is just for a subculture of privileged teachers and children, but not pertinent for most early childhood programs?	Examine my hidden biases. Find a way to examine and discuss a possible class/race component to inquiry-based programs.
How can I work with empathy about the work/life conditions of my students, while at the same time motivate them to rise above limitations, and mobilize their passion and power?	Make space for students to share their stories. Build in stories of teacher activists, researchers, and leaders into the curriculum.
Do I let textbooks determine the content of my classes in limiting ways?	Continue to include relevant, thought-provoking, current materials that will support students as thinkers and researchers. Be transparent with students about my own biases and point out information that is incomplete, or too focused on "drill and fill."

Another world is not only possible, she is on her way. Maybe many of us won't be here to greet her, but on a quiet day, if I listen very carefully, I can hear her breathing.

—Arundhati Roy[5]

To Inspire Thinking

By Christina Aubel

I no longer make a New Year's Resolution. Instead, at the end of a year, I begin listening in on conversations, rummaging through articles and books, slowing my pace to meet the mountains and saltwater near my home, searching for an idea to hold onto throughout the year. Sometime between the end of the old year and the beginning of the New Year, I write my idea into a small notebook that I place on my desk for safekeeping. In a few weeks, the small notebook disappears under the weight of papers I save with a pat and a promise to sort later. My carefully written idea sits at the bottom of the pile floating up occasionally into my consciousness at unexpected moments during the year, and then retreating, tucking into the grooves of my uncertainty. My idea takes time to unfurl and lay open for public viewing. I've come to know that over time, my gentle, yet radical idea will surface, letting out capacities within me long silenced by doubt and fear (Who am I to have an idea to champion?).

"Inspire and be inspired" was the idea I wrote in my notebook last year. My intention was to inspire my students and to be inspired by them. I didn't stop to consider how to inspire; I only knew I felt a sense of urgency to inspire teachers to become thinkers, innovators, explorers, and seekers of ideas. The early learning field is being overridden by those who believe every aspect of our curriculum and instruction should be folded inside the rigid contours of a box and labeled "easy to use—no thinking required." Listening to teachers who work in childcare programs talk about the pressure they feel to fit lesson plans inside tight small spaces reminds me of my first years as a teacher when I wrote weekly lesson plans in tiny letters to fit into tiny squares on the required planning chart. I'm certain my thinking was also tiny—perhaps even teeny-tiny since I used the same unchanged lessons year after year for several years.

That changed when I continued my education and met an ECE college instructor who took my thinking seriously. She observed me in my classroom, listened to my ideas about changing the "housekeeping area" into a "dentist office," challenged me to wait for a child's response, corrected my papers on the theories of Vygotsky and Piaget: in all these ways and more, she showed up for me because I was her student. She sat next to me in a preschool-sized chair and coached me to wait, listen, and think. I stopped writing tiny and began thinking big. Well, at least not so small.

Inspiring Teaching and Learning

Now I am the instructor listening to my students' concerns—which leave me concerned for them. Too many teachers are spending what little planning time they have filling out lesson plans with activities linked to standards and memorizing curriculum rather than learning about children and families. They are weary from the requirement of completing daily, weekly, and monthly safety, health, and nutrition checklists. They are weary—and I feel weary after visiting their classrooms.

> *Do I still hope I can inspire them?* Yes.
> *Do I know how?* I'm working on this part.
> *Do I know when I am inspired?* You bet.
> *Do I still believe in them?* Yes.

With this clarity, I challenged myself to design online assignments for my Creative Expressions class with the intention to inspire my students to see beyond boxed-in and one-time activities. My goal was to help them remember the childhood exhilaration of venturing into the wilds of creativity, and inspire them to offer the children in their care an abundance of experiences and materials to intentionally further their creative thinking.

In an online discussion, I asked my students to recall a time from their childhood when they felt creative—and when they didn't, when they'd felt their creative spirit squashed or dismissed or ignored. How do these early experiences show up now, I asked, in how you see yourself?

Nearly every student in the class had a vivid recollection of feeling confident about a creation when they were young and equally clear feelings of being hurt by a disapproving comment or an absence of comment about that very creation. Although they had found joy in their early lives in drawing, writing, painting, or performing, they rarely created anything anymore.

And so, I challenged them with another assignment to connect with their creative selves. I asked them to create something inspired by their childhood memories—make a video, write a paper, paint, take a photograph, sculpt. As I viewed and read their work, I was witness to their vulnerability, frustration, and joy. I was inspired as I read twenty-seven poems submitted by one student, took in a majestic blue tree painted by another, marveled at a delicate rose woven from cedar bark to commemorate the death of one student's co-teacher, and got acquainted with a charming and spunky yellow chick designed by another student. I laughed and wept and felt their trust in me. I wondered if trust is at the heart of inspiring and being inspired. What I believe is that creative inspiration is the muscle needed to lift us out of a boxy way of thinking, and help us remember how to think, innovate, explore, and seek ideas alongside the children we care for each day.

Losing Our Way in the Thicket

Alongside many other educators, I have spent the last several years saying to whoever would listen, "We are working to lift the quality of early learning, because we must see ourselves as professionals—and we hope that people in education, politics, business, and society in general will see us in the same way." But somewhere along the way, the focus of the movement towards quality narrowed to collecting data and developing assessments in an effort to prove our importance and professionalism.

Our research and methodology as we pursue quality early education for all children must, of course, be as stellar as that in other arenas of education, to demonstrate that early childhood education is worthy of receiving public and private funding. Data and assessments are valid evidence of our work to support early learning. But data and assessments are not everything, and they are not enough. As a field, we have lost our way in a thicket of graphs and charts. Next to every line, number, and box is a story about a child, a teacher, and a family, and without those stories there is nothing to graph or chart.

Teachers need time to tell the stories that will illustrate the significance of children and childhood. Time should not be a gift teachers are granted by happenstance whenever a meeting ends early to open a crack of extra time to write a lesson plan or two. Taking the time to consider an intentional plan or to write a thoughtful documentation story is not only a teacher's right—it is the right of a child to experience a well-intended plan and be the highlight of a beautifully crafted documentation story. It is a significant problem that early learning educators are devalued because they choose to spend their days with the youngest children. And our youngest citizens are devalued simply because they are the youngest and smallest. Their cuteness is currency in our economic markets, but the worth of their minds and potential is considered too insignificant to count. How often must we debate the fact that teachers need more time to accomplish meaningful work and that children and childhood should be valued in our society?

Our teachers will walk away from early childhood education unless we find a way to come together to raise their spirits and fill their hearts. This book is our pathway. It is pure inspiration. Within it is a protocol, a "Thinking Lens," that opens wide our potential to inspire thinking like a window on a bright morning inviting a blaze of light to chase away our hesitancy. The Thinking Lens illustrates the potency of knowing ourselves as educators by asking us to self-reflect, take other perspectives, and think collaboratively. In years past, I thought knowing myself was a solitary walk, but along the way I realized it is in the lively interactions with others where I learn the most about myself and all of us together. The educational beliefs on which I stand and my desire to inspire thinking in teachers come from this energetic confluence of ideas.

Let's construct courses that embolden our students to rise up and stand strong as leaders for the rights of children, families, and teachers. I am not a physical risk taker, but I am an emotional risk taker. I will not jump through the air with you, but I will take a leap of faith with you so that, together, our capacity to inspire our students and be inspired by them will become legendary.

NEST FILLED

Use your whirling wings to find the right tree.
Use your pert eye to choose the level limb.
Use your nimble feet to cherish the hospitable fork.

Use your fearless beak to gather twigs, leaves,
grass and thistledown to weave your basket-house
open to the wuthering sky.

Use your body to be the tent over tender pebbles,
lopsided moons. Then wait—warm, alert, still
through wind and rain, hawk-shadow, owl night.

Use your life to make life spending all you have
on what comes after. And if you are human, a true
citizen, fully awake, then learn from the sparrow

how to build a house, a village, a nation. Use instinct
to find the right place. Use thought to know the right
time. Use wisdom to design the right action.

In the era of stormy weather, build your
sturdy nest, and fill it with the future.

—Kim Stafford[6]

Which Wolf Will You Feed?

By Karyn Callaghan

Ann and Margie paint a different picture of what it means to be a leader in this time when standardization, assessment, and compliance are creating a vortex, a strong "undertow" that has diminished the joy, the intellectual challenge, and the surprises that nourish us all.[7] They offer an antidote. Ann's portrait, enhanced through the dialogue with Margie that weaves through the book, is of a thoughtful, sensitive pedagogical companion who walks alongside educators and children. As I read the book, I felt strong empathy with the desire to interrupt what Moss refers to as the "gravitational pull" of the dominant discourse.[8]

Faith Hale, a cherished colleague and Indigenous educator, shared with me a traditional teaching about the two wolves inside us; one is our negativity, our cynicism, our anger and disappointment, and the other is our optimism, our hope, our determination. The question is: one wolf must die, and one wolf must live, which one wins? The answer is: the wolf we feed. The one that we seem to be feeding in our current context has grown to demand the bulk of our attention, time, and energy. It is the one that views children as needing to be managed, fixed, readied. And we should not be surprised that educators get pulled down into this undertow, because they are being viewed in much the same way. I have seen the light go out in educators' eyes under the burden of enforced compliance with teacher-proof standardized curriculum, state-mandated learning outcomes, "quality" checklists.

Feeding the Wolf of Positivity

There is a place for standardization when such issues as health and safety procedures are involved. (Even then, we must oppose the strong inclination to cast everything as a safety hazard!) However, if we are talking about education, we can push back against the current context by feeding the wolf of positivity. This may require us to stand not in the middle, but firmly on one side, beside children, insisting that there are other perspectives—we can choose to hold a view of children, educators, and families as capable of complex, creative thinking. We can show the richness of a pedagogy that foregrounds relationship.

Ann does this throughout the book with excerpts of documentation that she offers for reflection. We are invited into relationship with what she has documented. Ann has recorded what caught her eye and ear, perhaps because it delighted, or puzzled, or surprised, or challenged her. She is feeding that wolf, holding its negative counterpart at bay. This is documentation that gives and gives. We can return to it repeatedly, and each time, because we and our context have changed, we may see something differently. The desire is not to standardize, to fit children into tick-boxes, but to seek complexity, to encounter the particular children as they make meaning and order of their experiences through relationship. What is revealed is not only the intelligence of the children, but also of the educator. Not only supporting, but participating in this work alongside children and other educators, is the life-affirming role of a pedagogical leader.

A Question about Protocols

The pedagogy that is foundational to this book is also invaluable for inviting others to see an alternative perspective to the one that has been both onerous and a betrayal of the rights of children and educators to have agency in their own learning. It is vibrant and compelling, pulsating with its own rhythms. It shows life in classrooms, not just symbols in the form of scores and ratings. This documentation gives those in decision-making roles in our communities wonderful stories to share, inviting others into the mix, contributing to a context where we can have dialogue about the purpose of education in our society.

It is in this spirit of the particularity—the uniqueness of each child and educator, and the ongoing dance within an ever-changing context—that I resist protocols. Perhaps it is just my rebellious spirit that causes me to see them as an effort at fencing an open landscape. Perhaps it is my experience with compliance that compels me to have reservations about their impact. I say this knowing that many like and depend on protocols. They are a tool, and in a skilled hand they may produce a desired outcome. I worry that they become something rote—applied to every dialogue, gone through because … that's the protocol.

For example, in my experience in our culture, it is challenging for adults to keep children at the centre of our focus. They are not invited to the table. If the beginning of a protocol invites reflection of yourself, it can be very difficult to bring the dialogue back to consider the perspective of children. I think Ann and Margie have done the tough lifting involved in coming to know themselves well, and so perhaps beginning here provides for them a solid foundation from which to launch into deeper reflection. For many, this level of introspection has not happened; our culture seems to conspire against it. Therapists spend years with adults, trying to help them unravel their motivations and identity. I believe that if we place ourselves resolutely beside children, listening, documenting, creating documentation that is shared with the children, colleagues, families and perhaps even the community, inviting other readings, by the end we will come to deeper understanding of ourselves, our assumptions, our blind spots, our fragility, our sense of justice. Deeper knowledge of self is revealed *through the process* of creating pedagogical documentation—i.e., it comes at the end, not at the beginning.

Seeking Complexity and Embracing Uncertainty

I have a video recording of Loris Malaguzzi addressing the first Canadian group on a study week in Reggio Emilia in late spring of 1993. He invited them to look at a grouping of photographs of children's feet, seemingly enacting scenarios, making friends with the foot next to them, arguing, moving apart, reuniting. He asked the participants how they might describe what they had seen, and after speculating about possible responses, he provoked them to consider the photos through different theories: science, design, space, dance, geography, mathematics, music, relationship. He challenged the educators not to limit their reading of documentation to what they already know—to be always reaching, broadening their search, curious about the world. As an alternative to what we would call planning, he urged us to be prepared for the hundred possibilities in order to be ready for the hundred-and-first, which may come from a child—the improvisation of which Ann writes. The process of meaning-making and preparation would be different each time, depending on the children and adults who are involved, and on the context. There is an expectation that each participant will bring a perspective and come away changed by the deep listening that is involved.

This nimbleness and creativity both challenges and appeals to me. We can choose to take responsibility for our learning and the learning of those around us, children and adults, and responsibility to embrace uncertainty, to be open to surprise, to be responsive. This should be accompanied by an expectation that others will also enact that responsibility toward us, inviting courageous conversations, helping us to recognize our own assumptions and subjectivities and consider other possibilities.

This is how I view the Thinking Lens that Ann and Margie have offered— multiple possibilities for opening dialogue rather than a sequential protocol. Perhaps just one of the stars in the constellation they have pointed us to will be sufficient at a given meeting, or for personal reflection, one that resonates at that time, with those people, thinking with and about particular children. Or two that connect. Or others not on the list that arc in as a surprise. Just as we can begin to trace the Big Dipper from any star, and can also veer away from it, we can use prompts to help us attend to what and why (and why not), as we find ways to think with others about questions that unsettle us. "Rather, there are from time to time magic moments where something entirely new and different seems to be coming about."[9] We can animate Kozol's entreaty that Ann quoted, and "join with children as the co-collaborators in a plot to build a little place of ecstasy and poetry and gentle joy"[10]; then we will have co-constructed an alternative that will feed the wolf of joy and optimism, a vibrant context for learning and living that honors our search for meaning.

There is more to life, and ought to be much more to childhood, than readiness for economic function. Childhood ought to have at least a few entitlements that aren't entangled with utilitarian considerations. One of them should be the right to a degree of unencumbered satisfaction in the sheer delight and goodness of existence itself. Another ought to be the confidence of knowing that one's presence on this earth is taken as an unconditioned blessing that is not contaminated by the economic uses that a nation does or does not have for you.

—Jonathan Kozol[11]

Finding Hallways and Building Bridges

By Kristie Norwood

As I sat down to read *From Teaching to Thinking: A Pedagogy for Reimagining Our Work*, I did so with excitement. I have read many of Margie's and Ann's books; these are two of my heroes. But when I got through the first chapter, I felt something I had never felt before when reading their work: hopeless. Why? What would cause me to shift from excitement to hopelessness?

Me, a person of strong faith, who draws inspiration from Reverend Victoria Stafford's writing about standing at the gates of hope. Me, who has considered writing a book about hope. Why did the opening of *From Teaching to Thinking* have me teetering on hopelessness? I turned to Stafford's poem to ground myself:

> *Our mission is to plant ourselves at the gates of Hope—*
> *not the prudent gates of Optimism, which are somewhat narrower;*
> *nor the stalwart, boring gates of Common Sense;*
> *nor the strident gates of Self-Righteousness, which creak on shrill and angry hinges*
> *(people cannot hear us there; they cannot pass through);*
> *nor the cheerful, flimsy garden gate of "Everything is gonna be all right."*
> *But a different, sometimes lonely place, the place of truth-telling,*
> *about your own soul first of all and its condition,*
> *the place of resistance and defiance,*
> *the piece of ground from which you see the world both as it is and as it could be, as it will be;*
> *the place from which you glimpse not only struggle, but joy in the struggle.*
> *And we stand there, beckoning and calling,*
> *telling people what we are seeing, asking people what they see.*[12]

I think it can be overwhelming at these gates of hope, "the piece of ground from which you see the world both as it is and as it could be." Standing at those gates, the place of truth-telling about your soul, I realized that, when I'd read Margie and Ann's work in the past, I was in an organization that fully aligned with the ideas and principles brought forth in the book. Now, I am in a position where those principles frequently lose any place of prominence due to standards and requirements. So now I find myself on the outside looking in.

Part of the protocol for thinking that Ann and Margie introduce emphasizes the importance of seeking other perspectives. I took that to heart, and I began to embrace my new "outsider" perspective. Now, I could give voice to the "naysayer," the one that says, "Oh, that's nice but we could never … " I continued to read *From Teaching to Thinking* from the perspective of someone working in a federally funded program, where compliance with standards equals funding. If you work in that context, you may, like me, find yourself overwhelmed with the possibility of something new and full of potential, while you have to continue to deal with the reality of today.

Overwhelmed by being in that space myself, I had a hallway moment—a phrase I use to describe the experience of being in-between what is and what could be. I remember hearing Ann and her colleague at Hilltop, Sarah, talk about sitting in the hallway between their classrooms talking about collaborating in new ways; the hallway was the place where they started dreaming and scheming about how to make a way outta what seemed like no way, so that they could begin teaching in a different way. As I read *From Teaching to Thinking*, I began looking for that hallway, that passageway between the full realization of the ideas and principles of this book and the reality of where many programs are. Hallway moments are needed in my context because it is a federally funded program and we don't get to exist apart from the mandatory work required to keep our funding. The requirements are extensive. I have to think about what is possible within the context of what is. I can't add something else.

Creating a Culture of Inquiry

So how do I create hallway moments in my organization? Here's an example. Three times a year we have to collect assessment data to describe our outcomes. Each teacher has to work with the Education Coordinator for their site to create an outcomes report. This report used to start with a sentence like, "As you can see, we are XX% below expectations." In the past, these reports focused heavily on the numbers. As the organization's Education Manager, I began having conversations with the coordinators and raising the idea of the power of "why" as a question. I walked them into a way to "look through" the numbers. "You can see the percentages, but start going deeper with the question of 'why.' What do you wonder about when you look at these numbers? What do you see as possible reasons for these numbers? What do you think the causes are?"

I decided to re-write the guidelines for how to do these reports, and I took out the charts that reported the numbers. I replaced these charts with questions like, "What did you notice when you read the data? What surprised you about the data? Why do you think the numbers turned out like that?" Reports are now based on questions, not numbers, to encourage the teachers to think. I also wanted to promote thinking for Education Coordinators, who review the reports with teachers, so I asked, "Tell me who your children are. Tell me who your teachers are. Don't just focus on the numbers. I have the numbers. What do you think you need in order to support your teachers?"

Making these changes helped to build relationships. I built relationships with my coordinators because we had conversations, instead of just reviewing reports. Our conversations gave them a platform to go back and have those same kinds of discussions with their teachers and parent coordinators, which strengthened those relationships.

Our Work as Pedagogical Leaders

Ann and Margie remind us we can use our jobs as Education Coordinators to fulfill the purpose of pedagogical guidance, which I think of in the context of creating hallway moments. We can talk about looking at our required documentation from a research perspective, studying it, not just turning it in. This is like CSI work, I tell my coordinators. You have all this information in a teachers' observations, and our pedagogical work is to dissect this documentation to learn as much as we can, and then see how it all fits together to give you a complete picture of the child and his or her learning. Someone in the organization has to provoke and promote this (in large organizations like ours, this is the job of the Education Coordinators, who work with teachers at a number of sites).

Education Coordinators have to learn how to lead the investigation; they have to provide the space for it and make the case for it with the center directors. They have to request time to be in the classroom and sit with the teaching team and talk with them about their practice. And I'm their partner in doing that.

It is so important to engage educators' hearts and minds. Working with them to make meaning of the work should be our goal. When I am training, leading, and coaching, I am present with teachers. I am with them in their triumphs and challenges. I am both cheerleader and provocateur. In my current role as an Education Manager, I support Education Coordinators to do this same thing with their teachers, by modeling for and mentoring the Education Coordinators on how to take on the role of a pedagogical leader.

When I meet with coordinators, I talk about compliance issues for 15-20 minutes, then the rest of the time I'm checking in on how they're doing their work as pedagogical leaders. I caution my coordinators not to be led by data. Remember, I tell them, your GPS informs you on where to go, but it is not driving your car! Start your work with teachers by focusing on children and families first and you'll find the data will be responsive to that. Instead of letting the data lead us, we can look for ways to ask questions and observe more.

In the Head Start context, we are working to balance out the influence of our required curriculum with giving teachers the freedom to be teachers. So, for example, when we offered teachers training specifically focused on lesson planning, I decided to challenge how we put this together. I said, "Let's go back to a time when lesson planning had nothing to do with technology and was done with a pen and piece of paper." I challenged teachers to start their planning by considering what they know about themselves, their children, child development, early childhood education, the families, community, and the world. These considerations should be guiding our planning, not the activities suggested by the computer program when observation data is electronically entered.

I want to give teachers a strong foundation, so despite what the system does, they can still do right by the children. I really want to get to the place where teachers are emotionally and intellectually engaged in learning with children. Then planning is no longer a burdensome task, a necessary evil. Planning for a journey is very different than planning for compliance. The enjoyment is there and you look forward to it. I coach my Education Coordinators to take these messages to their teachers. "Let's talk about circumstances and issues," I urge them.

I'm getting more explicit about how to be a pedagogical leader. I'm learning to call out the elements of my conversations with Education Coordinators so that they can apply those to their conversations with teachers. I tell my coordinators, "Do you see how I just walked you through that? That is something you can do with your teachers. You can use questions to guide your conversations." I see the outcomes for teachers and know this approach is working. I have noticed changes when teachers come to trainings. They show they are used to being asked to think. They are more engaged.

Clarity of Purpose

People have suggested that I consider going to teach at a college or private preschool setting to get out from under all the limitations of a publicly funded early education organization. But I chose to stay working with Head Start because I want to be a bridge. I know all the mandates and regulations, but I also know another world is possible, and I can help teachers get over the hurdles and cross into it.

The idea of knowing my larger purpose has helped me clarify the difference between my job and my work. It helps me not settle into a feeling of hopelessness. My job is about tasks that I complete. It's laid out in my job description. My work is about purpose. It informs me on how to do my job. My purpose helps me to work as a bridge between how things are and how they could be, especially in some of the toughest areas like inner cities.

The distinction between your job and your work applies not only to individuals, but the organization as a whole and the culture it develops. That's why Ann and Margie stress how important it is to define, write, and revisit your true purpose. Doing this helps to get you outside your current paradigm, to see different possibilities that help elevate your thinking. As an organization, do the work of defining your purpose. Think about your identity as an organization. What is your culture and how does it set the climate? Ask yourself: Who are you and what do you want to be known for? How much of your focus is truly on the children and families? Then, spend some protected time reviewing your purpose. This is how your work can inform your job.

In early childhood education, our shared purpose is to have a positive impact in the lives of children and families. We must hold ourselves accountable to the impact that we are making, but we need to broaden our lens. It's about more than measuring skills attained. What about citizenship, belonging, connection to the world, and a sense of joy? These are all factors that impact lifelong success. I think these questions are related to the refrain in Tom Hunter's song, about helping children be "as human as they can be" to prepare them for a future world we cannot see.

Seeing Ourselves as Change Agents

Many publicly funded programs serve families who are living in poverty and families of color. That means that those of us who work in those programs have a responsibility to use a social justice lens in our work, as Margie and Ann describe. We have to see that an important part of our work is to be change agents, not simply to accept the status quo. We can't stay silent when we see things that aren't right. We have to be informed, open, and not blind. Our work is to call out where the battles really lie. We have to call out how we see things like racism and white privilege embedded in our systems. For instance, we have to recognize how we have been viewing little black boys as "problems" who "we gotta get right." No one benefits from a deficit, dumbed-down approach.

In our organizations, we need to remember that poverty is a condition; it does not define a child or a family. Poverty definitely has an impact on the child and family, but so do rich experiences, provocative and engaging environments, and quality interactions. Poverty creates enough restrictions for people. Why would we contribute to those restrictions by eliminating time to learn from play? Why would you not feed children's brains with opportunities to explore and investigate? While the condition of poverty must be addressed, children deserve the benefit of quality, enriched experiences. All children deserve engaged learning experiences, and children affected by poverty, more so.

Unfortunately, most publicly funded programs have approached poverty from a deficit orientation. The mindset often is, "These kids are in poverty; they can't handle anything else that's challenging." This shapes a mentality, an identity for kids who begin to think, "Poverty is who I am, not where I am." Instead, we need to help them see that, "Wherever you are, you can go beyond that." We have to see the need for a paradigm shift. We need to see teachers as an integral piece to this puzzle for change. Instead of the mindset that focuses on correcting the child's behavior, the focus shifts to the teacher's perception of the child.

From Hallways to Bridges

So how do we start that paradigm shift in publicly funded programs? I believe that each teacher needs the hallway moments that I spoke of. Even short pedagogical conversations feed your spirit, comfort your soul, and, most important, fuel your fire. I also believe that our ECE field needs bridges. After the hallway moments happen, we need people willing to step forward and be bridges. We have to provide safe and stable passage that leads from where many programs are, stuck in mandates and requirements, to where they can be, creating a culture where process and inquiry are the principle and practice.

From Teaching to Thinking provides not just hallway moments but tools to construct the bridge from there to here. The stories in the book come from practical experience in real world circumstances. I see practical applications for creating cultures of inquiry and intellectual and emotional engagement of teachers; using the Thinking Lens to deepen understanding; and creating organizational systems that align with values. These all provide a foundation to make that needed bridge between what is and what must be.

There are many programs across this country that have standards to comply with and requirements to meet. Don't think this book ignores the realities for government funded programs. It offers many starting places for people in restricted contexts. As you read, I encourage you to remember that you don't have to try to change everything at once. Start with what you are already doing and begin to look at it differently. Begin to ask questions you've never asked before. You don't have to schedule another meeting to ask why. You are already going to many meetings where you can ask why, where you can ask people to consider other perspectives and possibilities. I see the power of one person who gets a bigger vision and starts to become a bridge. Others have done it. This is something you could do. Be a bridge to another world.

From Teaching to Thinking reminds us about the core of this work: teaching that is birthed in and enhanced by honor and respect for the ones that bear the name, Teacher. Teachers are invited to engage, think, learn, question, and grow. And those of us who work with and support teachers are challenged to see their strength and their boundless potentials. We are challenged to provide structures and cultivate communities that make the principles in this book become the norm. Join me at the gates of hope, and stand there with me, beckoning and calling, telling people what we are seeing, asking people what they see.

Keep walking, though there's no place to get to.
Don't try to see through the distances.
That's not for human beings.
Move within, but don't move the way fear makes you move.
Today, like every other day, we wake up empty and frightened
Don't open the door to the study and begin reading.
Take down a musical instrument.
Let the beauty we love be what we do.
There are hundreds of ways to kneel and kiss the ground.

—Rumi[13]

Teachers as Cultural Workers

By Eliana Elias

I was a preschool teacher for 12 years before I started my career as a coach and consultant. I worked in the laboratory school of a small college. In that setting, we had explicit conversations about how reflection should guide our practices with children, about the connection between social justice and education, and about the importance of the role of the teacher as an active learner. We benefited from the support of mentors and role models, and we had dedicated time for professional development. We had painful and transformative conversations about racism, homophobia, classism, and other types of bias, and explored the role we played in either standing against bias or contributing (directly or indirectly) to the inequities present in the system. We struggled to understand how to engage the children and their families in authentic conversations about how, with our diverse backgrounds, we could form a caring community of learners. We also experienced infectious joy as we baked with the children, did carpentry projects, and set up "campgrounds" in the playground. Together we marveled at how children's learning was visible in their play. This was before early childhood was "discovered," before companies flooded the market with expensive ECE products and trainings; before rating scales and assessment tools became tied to high stakes funding, before early childhood started being viewed as a "social investment," expected to solve most of the social problems afflicting our communities today.

I left that "little lab school bubble" 17 years ago to become a college instructor and to work as a consultant and coach in publicly funded programs. I have been serving programs that work with our most vulnerable children ever since. My experiences as a preschool teacher help me hold on to the notion that "another world is possible." And, I am fortunate to know many people who, like me, think of our profession not as an industry defined by numbers and assessments, but as a unique opportunity to honor the childhoods that our children deserve.

I've needed these anchors during these last 17 years as I have witnessed how the desire to increase the quality of care for all of our children has resulted in an excessive concern with assessment tools, and how this has resulted in unintended consequences, often drowning directors and teachers in paperwork, keeping them focused on compliance with requirements rather than their connections with children and families.

A Strange New Vocabulary

"Quality improvement" should fundamentally be intended to dismantle the inequities that plague our field, to support teachers and directors as thinkers and innovators, and to offer children early learning experiences that prepare them for a lifetime of citizenship. But it's hard to see those intentions in the strange new ECE vocabulary that our leaders and policy makers use to describe quality improvement. Rather than using words such as love, joy, authenticity, and connection, they use a language that is more appropriate for factory settings: measurable outcomes, data driven solutions, evidence based practices, and smart goals, to cite a few examples. We aren't instructed to look for the hearts of the communities we are supposed to support.

In quality improvement systems, I find that our most fragile children, programs, and teachers get reminded over and over of how their lives are not measuring up to the standards designed to measure success. As a coach, I am part of this engine, often asked to help programs improve their scores in order to continue to access resources. I have questioned my role in this system and have struggled to stay focused on my commitment to do my work always through a social justice lens. My beliefs about the purpose of education are strongly influenced by the thinking of Paulo Freire. I turn to him not only because of our shared history as Brazilians, but because his thinking so resonates with what I see as our challenges, mistakes, and bigger possibilities for finding our humanity in ECE.

The choice to work for social change is easily overshadowed by all of our obligations as coaches. But even in this context, we have a great deal of freedom to choose our focus and to continuously work to mitigate the injustices that we encounter. One of the ways I've been attempting this mitigation is with efforts to make our teachers' experiences visible. For instance, I created a project entitled *Teachers' Voices*, where I applied Freire's ideas to document and study the personal narrative of six immigrant early childhood educators, women who serve a diverse population of children and families in San Francisco. I asked the teachers to share stories from key moments in their lives; then, as these teachers studied their own stories, they recognized their resiliency, their ability to thrive despite powerful challenges.

I could see firsthand the value Ann and Margie ascribe to using a protocol. In the *Teachers' Voices* project, our use of a protocol helped us make powerful connections between educators' personal narratives and important concepts in ECE, an example of what Ann and Margie describe as inviting educators to bring their full selves to their work. Teacher Ariana, for example, told us the story of her immigrant father and his insistence on preserving his home language with his children: "When I was growing up I was made to speak Spanish; my dad forced us to speak Spanish at home and English was for school. I didn't see the value in knowing and speaking both languages. Now I do."

This short statement, when given the proper importance, and when probed further with reflective questions, provides the perfect context for educators to understand many of the central issues in our work with children of immigrant families today, issues such as: home language preservation and development; family identity and parental guidance; partnering with families; and supporting families in setting consistent practices in their home. Seeing my role as a pedagogical guide helps me invite rigorous investigation and provides teachers with a template for valuing each other's experiences to explore theoretical concepts. To me, this is central to their ability to succeed as educators in a diverse community.

Moving Towards a Pedagogy of Hope

My view of my work is reaffirmed by the ideas in *From Teaching to Thinking*. In it, I find pedagogical principles that encourage us to continue to reinvent a world where we get better at changing ourselves as we pursue our ability to change the world. I am convinced that the complexities of supporting and coaching teachers must not be reduced to a matter of scores and compliance. Even in the context where I work, where assessments have become so central to our professional goals, I can take these kinds of actions:

- Use my role as a coach to collect and reflect back to educators their individual histories to highlight the successes that are almost impossible to capture through numbers.

- Approach coaching with a high image of teachers, and use the same pedagogical principles I would like to see them apply when working with children.

- Continue to promote the view that humans are active learners, who learn best by interacting with others.

- Support programs and the people who live in them to focus on growing strong identities with intentional values.

- Encourage strong community connections that are reflective of the range of cultural expressions present in my very diverse context.

- Use *power with* teachers (rather than on teachers), and enter into explorations that share our curiosity towards their practices.

By anchoring my work in these commitments I create a context where teachers and coaches can routinely challenge each other as we explore the notion of educators as "Cultural Workers." This notion comes from Freire's book, *Teachers as Cultural Workers: Letters to Those Who Dare Teach*, in which he describes how teachers must be learners, be joyful and rigorous, serious and scientific.[14] He says, "It is impossible to teach without the courage to love, without the courage to try a thousand times before giving up ... In short, it is impossible to teach without a forged, invented, and well thought out capacity to love ... We must dare, in the full sense of the word, to speak of love without the fear of being called ridiculous, mawkish, or unscientific, if not anti-scientific."[15]

As I coach, I want to continue to follow Freire's advice: To dare to never dichotomize cognition and emotion. For me this means I can work within the systems of assessments and rating scales, measurable outcomes and data, *and* that I can do it with the full range of emotions needed to reflect back to teachers their unique strengths and passions, and my own humanity and aspirations. Obviously, this is not easy. The coach/teacher relationship mirrors the larger complexities that make it so difficult for humans to relate to one another. As we navigate the murkiness caused by powerful forces outside of our control, things like income disparities, low salaries, lack of time, racial discrimination, language barriers, we must resist the temptation to try to find simplified solutions that lie solely within the concepts of objectivity and reliability.

We can't "fix" these complex dynamics, and the accompanying discomfort and uncertainty we feel by proclaiming we are objective and thereby fair. We all know, deep down, that the world of human connection and human development is not guided by objectivity, clearly demarcated deadlines, and neatly arranged "smart goals." That is the world of commercial interests in the business world. Linear tools and strategies from this world might effectively help us achieve a certain level of improvement, but the real work lies on our own ability to come to terms with the infuriating and excruciatingly beautiful nature of what makes us so uniquely human: our ability to see things from our own cultural perspectives, our flawed, but sincere desire to understand the paths of others, and our ability to adapt and change to different conflicting cultural constructs.

Finding Critical Questions and a Useful Tool

Reading *From Teaching to Thinking* has been invigorating. Within the dynamic and poetic exchanges between Ann and Margie, I have renewed my commitment to fully engage the critical questions that are so central to my professional journey as an educator:

- How can I continue to see the role of Early Childhood Education as a building block for a more equitable and democratic world?
- How can I genuinely partner with teachers in their search to have strong professional and personal identities, and an ability to think critically about their role in building a better future?
- How might I use my power and knowledge on behalf of children and families who have been historically excluded?

Apart from inspiration and a prodding to think critically, Ann and Margie offer concrete tools, one of which I've been using in my work as a coach for a number of years, after first encountering it in their earlier writing. I often think of the Thinking Lens protocol as a road map capable of taking me on a journey from the depths of my emotions to the most rigorous of my academic training. The Thinking Lens helps me bridge the gap between reflection and action, and helps me model for other educators how we can use our whole thinking and feeling selves on behalf of the children and families, and also on our own behalf. This is essential in our role as Cultural Workers, co-creating responses to challenges that result in new discoveries and worthwhile changes. This is a gift. A gift that can help us discipline ourselves to go beyond the oversimplification of the assessment tools, and to dive into the complexities of our practices with the help of a collaborative mindset and a guiding tool. In my coaching practice, I now use the Thinking Lens often. I'll end with a story about that …

———

Several weeks ago I entered a classroom that sounded and felt very different than usual. I have been working with this team of teachers for at least three years. Despite the challenges (35% of the children in this program are homeless, 80% come from low-income families, 40% have special needs), this had been a relatively calm classroom, where the head teacher had established a language of respect and where joyful experiences, such as singing, dancing, and playing, had been incorporated into the classroom routines. On that particular day, however, the newest member of the teaching team was leading the activities, and two substitute teachers followed her lead. With the absence of the head teacher, the classroom descended into chaos, and the teachers' voices became strained and borderline abusive. "Guys … GUYS! Return to the rug NOW! I can't believe you are not listening! No snack for you, if you don't walk to the table respectfully! SIT DOWN!" As the teacher's voice became more and more stressed, I searched inside of me for what I needed to do.

*I turned to the Thinking Lens protocol, which I've internalized after several years of using it. I started with the questions about **Knowing Yourself**: I knew I was getting agitated. My agitation was starting to make me have negative feelings about the teacher—seeing her as grumpy, unkind, controlling. I wanted her to stop yelling directions and corrections. After this pulse and heart check, I moved to **Seeking the Children's Perspectives** and the answers were obvious: The children were suffering. I then moved to **Seeking Multiple Perspectives***

and Opportunities and Possibilities, *and considered my relationship with this teacher, what I already knew about the classroom, what I already knew about how the head teacher would have handled this situation; I recalled the theories that describe adult learning. I quickly clarified my short term goal: to relieve the children's discomfort and the teacher's irritation. And I clarified my long-term goal: to provide this teacher with opportunities to self-reflect and to make long lasting changes in her teaching practices.*

This disciplined way of thinking helped me get a handle on my emotions and make a plan for intervention. When the teacher made another alarming threat—"I am going to keep you here and not let you go play outside. We are going to sit on this rug till everyone is quiet"—I looked calmly at the teacher and said: "We can't do that. The children will go outside now." I moved towards supporting a quick transition, and then I figured out a way to have this teacher meet with me for one hour so we could reflect together. Rather than starting with the assessments, and how these negative interactions could have affected their site's qualification for funding streams, I again used the Thinking Lens as a framework to focus our conversation. I guided her by simply asking the questions: When you reflect on what happened, how do you feel? What was the children's point of view? How could we think about this in a new way and do something different next time?

After many tears, this teacher painted a compelling picture of how the stresses of being left with two inexperienced substitutes were magnified by her own personal stresses. She was able to share how she felt incompetent, inadequate. I was able to affirm her humanity and the unfair circumstances she found herself in, while sharing what is expected of us during such times to ensure the children's wellbeing. Together we collaborated on a plan for what she would do when she returned to the classroom and we openly talked about how she might go about repairing her relationship with the children. I stayed with her for the rest of the day to ensure that she had some time to play with the children. We made time to talk to the substitutes about our plan and how we would do transitions with children without resorting to the language that was being used that morning.

Ann and Margie offer the Thinking Lens as a pedagogical tool to study observations, but I have been able to use the Thinking Lens in many different situations in my work. As a result, the educators that work with me know that it is OK to share how they feel first, to mourn and to rejoice in the moments they share with children and their families. They know that I will often lead with a question about emotions and then we will also move methodically through the tool, exploring the children's points of view, practicing taking multiple perspectives, engaging with families, and finding opportunities and next steps for action. Teachers appreciate this disciplined way of shining a light into their practices, and of treating their ordinary moments (sometimes joyful, other times stressful) as worthy of attention and study. The Thinking Lens tool has helped me transform my coaching sessions into professional celebrations that elevate early childhood educators to their rightful place as Cultural Workers.

THE WAY IT IS

There's a thread you follow. It goes among
things that change. But it doesn't change.
People wonder about what you are pursuing.
You have to explain about the thread.
But it is hard for others to see.
While you hold it you can't get lost.
Tragedies happen; people get hurt
or die; and you suffer and get old.
Nothing you do can stop time's unfolding.
You don't ever let go of the thread.

—William Stafford[16]

Transforming Our Organisation

By Nicky Byres, Jennifer Chen, and Helen Lo

In our early years' organisation, the Society of Richmond Children's Centres (SRCC), we often reference the lyrics of a Tom Hunter song:

> *We've been waiting for you to come to this place,*
> *waiting for you to come to this place.*
> *Wherever you're from, we're glad that you've come.*
> *We've been waiting for you to come to this place.*[17]

We offer this welcome to new Educators, new families, and new opportunities because we believe that community is something that we create with intention, not leaving it to chance.

As we respond to this book at this particular time in our journey we respectfully paraphrase these words:

> *We've been waiting for this book to come to this place,*
> *Waiting for this thinking to come to this place.*
> *Wherever you're from, we're glad that you've come.*
> *We've been waiting for this to come to this place.*

The three of us administrative and pedagogical leaders of SRCC, a non-profit child care organisation, read *From Teaching to Thinking* together, and had common responses and some divergent thoughts. A perfect place to practice considering multiple perspectives! Nicky comes from the leadership perspective as the Executive Director of the organisation and Jennifer and Helen come to the book as Pedagogical Leaders. We braid these voices here to tell the story of how our child care service has evolved from a traditional themes-and-holidays program to one committed to the project of emergent, responsive, inquiry-based teaching and learning. Our hope is that our story helps you see that this work can be done by anyone prepared to do it. Our journey has been marked step-by-step, misstep-by-misstep, with victories and defeats, frustrations and delights.

We are always searching for the next right step to take towards fully living into our vision and values and doing THIS WORK of responsive, inquiry-based, co-constructing curriculum in our corner of the planet.

Our Journey

So how did our journey unfold? Over a decade ago, we had an Ah-Ha moment at a conference, as we listened to stories of children and teachers engaged together in long-term investigations about ideas that mattered. We caught a glimpse of a way of being and practicing that was strikingly different from our teacher-directed, thematic approach. This new approach gave children and families a voice alongside the Educators. We saw a more wholehearted way of living life together in a community of curious co-learners. From this lightening-strike beginning, we began to lean into a more democratic, co-constructed model for our work, grappling with the issues of power, territory, and inclusion that arose as we started to change our organisation. It was a revolutionary new way of seeing our work and we eagerly pursued it with our hearts beating loudly in our chests.

We've experienced several Ah-Ha moments since that first one; they've all been both daunting and exhilarating. Sometimes we dived into these new ideas without much planning or forethought. Sometimes we found ourselves quickly out of our depth; sometimes our huge enthusiasm for this new way of thinking and being kept us afloat. After awhile, we found ourselves looking for a more secure way of moving forward, tired of bobbing in the sea of new thinking without clear direction.

Our anchor came in clarifying our vision and values. We carefully crafted a clearly articulated vision with attendant core values that situated our work within a clear framework. Now, we had a point of reference to measure our work by: "Does this step/decision/direction align with our vision and values?" In many ways, all the work we did before we landed on a co-constructed community vision and a shared set of core values was ineffective and unsustainable (although sometimes quite fun, as when we transformed our physical spaces). After a year of carefully considering our vision and values, a process that involved the Board of Directors, Educators, and the leadership and admin team, we found ourselves on more solid ground that gave our work a secure and clearly articulated place from which to grow.

We embedded vision and values into everything we did. Our whole community in the SRCC can recite our vision statement in their sleep: "Changing the world by honouring childhood." Furthermore, we all know what that vision looks like every day in every classroom, in every ordinary moment. We have heeded Ann's questions that start this book: "What kind of people do we want to be? What kind of world do we want to live in?" We've taken the time to consider our answers to these foundational and pivotal questions. At times, we found it overwhelming to look at our work from such a wide perspective, but it sure helped us get to the core of who we want to be as an early childhood community and what we seek to offer to those we work with—children, families, and Educators most of all.

One significant change we've made is our approach to professional learning. We've taken to heart the practice of offering Educators experiences that we hope they will, in turn, offer to children. What better way to know how a four-year-old feels when she conquers a challenge and proudly declares "I did it!" than by having a similar experience? For some of our Educators, that's meant embracing new experiences like rock climbing, riding a bicycle, or sitting quietly and doing some art on a Professional Development day. We pay attention to nourishing our Educators' bodies, minds, and spirits, and see professional learning as a daily endeavour rather than a special event.

We have not been alone on this journey of figuring out how to do the work so well outlined in this book—this journey from teaching to thinking. We have sought colleagues, including the authors of this book, further along in the journey than ourselves, and they have graciously shone a light on the path for us. We have read a lot and talked to many, seeking to understand ways of fully living into this inquiry-based work. Our commitment is to strengthen our Educators' experience of their work and the experiences of children and families in our care as we work to deepen our commitment to joyful, curious childhood with meaningful discovery, authentic inquiry at its heart. We've recently begun to dig into representational work to strengthen learning and thinking, both for children and adults.

Several years ago, we began to work with the Thinking Lens as a tool to help us articulate and operationalise our vision and values. For too long, we used documentation as an end point rather than as a beginning for dialogue, and we struggled to help Educators find their role and voice. The Thinking Lens rightly starts with Educators' perspectives and thinking as the jumping-off place and takes the discussion through the steps that lead to a depth of clarity that illuminates the work the children and Educators do together.

We see the trajectory of our own journey in the pages of this book, and while we take delight in noting some of the things we have figured out, we take equal delight in seeing the things on which we have much work to do. In particular, we found the way that Ann and Margie call forward the social justice component of the work instructional for our work in an ethnically and linguistically diverse community that is grappling with honouring indigenous ways of knowing and being. We look forward to stretching into new thinking and practice on that front.

A Budget and Job Description for Pedagogical Leaders

Over the course of this journey, one of the key steps we took was to rework the budget so that we could fund first one, then two Pedagogical Leaders on our Leadership Team. We made that financial commitment because we believed that for our new approach to curriculum to grow with adequate support and mentoring, we needed a dedicated position to make it happen. It was a big commitment, but it was easily justified as it clearly aligned with our vision and values.

From Teaching to Thinking clearly outlines the important role of a Pedagogical Leader in holding the work of careful observation, thoughtful meaning-making, and responsive planning in its prime place of importance, not allowing the busy business of child care tasks and chores to derail it. When we read this book, we thought, "Yes! Here's the job description for our Pedagogical Leaders!" These leaders model for our organisation the parallel practice we believe in— offering to Educators the support and experiences we hope they will in turn offer the children. They keep us accountable to and rooted in our primary task of curriculum development by coaching Educators to think deeply, develop hypotheses about what they are seeing, and make new offerings to the children to deepen their thinking and experiences. They have served us so well in growing our curriculum practice; they visit each of our six program sites each week, to strengthen relationships with the Educators and children, and to participate first-hand in the work unfolding in the classroom. They model risk-taking and deep thinking in their side-by-side work with Educators, and facilitate collaborative reflection and study at each teaching team's weekly curriculum meetings where plans are made for next steps. We would not be where or who we are as a community of inquiry without them. And here they are with their perspectives on this book.

Jennifer writes:

When I started my career in the SRCC as an Educator of three-, four-, and five-year-olds, I taught the children based on what I felt they needed to learn. Classroom schedules were inflexible and curriculum themes were implemented from plans I made on my own. I was delighted to be in the company of children, but I was not coming from a place of curiosity or inquiry in my time with them. Rather than bringing in my values and experiences, I'd had it drilled into me when I was in College that I should remain objective when assessing a situation. I had not considered any other way of teaching ... a way that could be more fulfilling and rewarding.

Then our staff attended a conference that shone a light in a different direction. This different direction involved seeing children in new ways—seeing them as resourceful authors of their own learning. It was different from the way we worked at SRCC. I was drawn to it, inspired by it—but I created many barriers in my head that prevented me from moving forward. *There were too many daily tasks to do, we didn't have the right cameras, we didn't have access to laptops, it didn't work for our schedules* ... the list went on and on. My fear of change prevented me from seeing the possibilities. However, bit by bit, with the guidance and leadership of Nicky, our Executive Director, we slowly started making changes. We started with the aesthetics of the classroom, flexibility in the children's schedules, and writing documentation stories. I began to slowly change as I took down the barriers I had created.

Fast forward to a few years later, when I had the opportunity to go to Hilltop Children's Center in Seattle with some of my colleagues. In witnessing the work of Educators and children there, my eyes were completely opened. I felt the stirring within me of the desire to work with children in a way that let me really honour them for who they are. I witnessed how children are capable and deep thinkers, and I could see how the Educators walked alongside the children in their quest for the meaning of life. I knew that this was the work that I wanted to do. Shortly after visiting Hilltop, we decided at SRCC that we needed a Pedagogical Leader to lead this very meaningful work, and so we created a position on the administrative team. I was fortunate enough to be asked to step into these very big shoes.

Missteps in My Journey

But ... where should I start? When I read *From Teaching to Thinking*, I initially wished that I'd had something like it earlier in my journey as a pedagogical leader to guide me. However, I realize that this book needed to come at this moment because it is only now that I am ready for it. I know this book will be something I turn to over and over again—to revisit ideas and take in information as my practice as a pedagogical leader continues to grow.

Working with Educators, there have been many moments when they ask, "How do I take the deep dives when I don't know how to swim?" Ann writes:

Pedagogical leadership doesn't mean simply telling educators to 'do inquiry' and hoping for the best. Pedagogical leadership means that you begin with your own work, your own role, reshaping your days to support and sustain inquiry in educators, so that they, in turn, support and sustain inquiry in children. The work with children will stall out, and quite possibly fall apart, if the work with educators doesn't get attention; inquiry for children requires inquiry for adults.

These words really resonated with me because this is the area where I took a misstep in my journey. I came from a place of theory but I had not done the actual work with children and Educators. I used to *tell* Educators what to do rather than *showing* them what to do. While I knew that the Thinking Lens would be a good place to start in terms of mentoring Educators to take the deep dives into their thinking, I didn't use this thinking protocol while working in programs with Educators. It was only when I began to practice this protocol side by side with Educators as they worked with children that I began to see the changes I hoped for. As Ann writes, we can't expect children to do long-term investigations if we have not experienced them ourselves. It is crucial to parallel our practice: we will see progress in this work when we wholeheartedly pay generous attention to and learn alongside Educators, in the way that we hope Educators pay generous attention to and learn alongside children.

When I am in programs, the Thinking Lens has been useful for me in facilitating the thinking and the dialogue that helps us identify the imbedded intent of children's play. I think the word that Ann dreamt about perfectly sums up what the Thinking Lens has been doing for our work:

Hyperoppery: To look beyond the surface; to view exceedingly closely; to see over and through expectations and assumptions, into the depths of meaning available in each moment.

The Thinking Lens brings awareness to *how* we think. But in being aware of how we think, we also need some guiding lights which come in the form of vision and values. Having clear vision and values keeps us all accountable to the work that we do. We often reflect back to how our work aligns with our vision and values. Are we meeting up with what we say we do?

Being in dialogue with one another and with families also helps us stay within the framework of vision and values. It is a way to hear others' perspectives and really bring forward what our own biases are. Ann calls this:

looking beyond our familiar ways of seeing and thinking, looking past our habitual expectations and quick assumptions, into new vistas and intricate details glimpsed in perspectives other than our own. It can be unsettling, for sure, this expanding of our perspectives: it's startling to see that what seems an obvious conclusion to us is not at all the obvious conclusion for a co-teacher, startling to have our eyes opened to something that hadn't occurred to us at all until it was thrust into our consciousness by a child's parent. It's disquieting to have our assumptions flung back at us as only assumptions, not the one truth or the preferred truth or the desirable truth.

This idea leaves me with a lot to consider. In order for Educators and pedagogical leaders to do our work well, we have to feel deeply and deem ourselves worthy of taking part in this work. We have to be open to being vulnerable and not fear making mistakes. We have to be mindful of how we are listening to others and offering them the space that they need to feel heard.

I move forward with the notion that we all have the capability to find the imbedded intent in any moment that we share with children and in the daily happenings of our lives. I believe we all have a thinking protocol, much like the Thinking Lens, within us that helps us see below the surface of what we witness. It is when we become aware of our values and biases and seek others' perspectives that we can focus on the teaching and learning of social justice—when we can fully see the bigger picture. That is when we can live into being "as human as we can be."[18]

Helen writes:

As I read each chapter of this book, I felt immediately connected. It was as if this book was detailing my personal journey into pedagogical thinking and into the role of a Pedagogical Leader.

From thinking directly with children in the classroom to mentoring and thinking with my colleagues, the practice of deep thinking and reflecting changed entirely how I live on this earth. How did I first begin this practice? What drove me to do it?

I started this pedagogical journey at a vulnerable time in my life, a time where I experienced a lot of change, a lot of unplanned happenings in my life. I had to really search for the meaning of it all, look for the deeper, sustaining meaning. It became clear to me that connecting my personal life with my professional life allowed me to invest myself wholly. I wanted to be able to physically feel and grasp the purpose and meaning of life. That was all the push I needed. I wanted to see life for what it was. I wanted more! I wanted to feel more fully human.

When I began to dig deeper into my heart, I saw everything differently. I began growing an appetite for this practice, being able to share, reveal, and seek others' perspectives … It filled me. Every ordinary moment with the children to every ordinary conversation with my colleagues became a quest for more. There would be endless questions and endless possibilities … it was infinite … and it felt good!

It wasn't like I got this work right away; there were many blurry, confused days. I've always kept myself up to date with professional development: our non-profit Society invested in extensive training in emergent curriculum, and our constant meetings and discussions with one another always shined light and hope that I would one day get a full understanding of it all. It wasn't until one brief visit from Ann that the concept of "representational work" came into my life. I mean, I knew how to take photos and document things that were happening in front of my eyes, but was that all?

Something sparked inside: wait—what are the children trying to tell me without actually telling me? I began to see their work (their sketches, paintings, their constructions, their creations with loose materials etc.) as part of our investigation into big questions and intent, the BIG IDEA! Their representational work was how the children shared their theories with me. I just needed to give my generous attention to see it and hold it gently for us to look closer. The representational work from the children became another tool for me to see and reflect deeper, and became part of my practice with the children and with my colleagues. Representational practice doesn't come easy, and requires practicing how to use the many mediums (languages) offered. Both Educators and children need to gain confidence and knowledge on how to transfer our thoughts, feelings, ideas into something tangible. Harder than it sounds, trust me!

As a pedagogical leader, I began to weave the Thinking Lens and representational work together as a daily practice for my colleagues and myself. The investigations, the conversations, the Big Ideas have never been richer or more clear.

There is so much more to do and I see myself changing, learning, ever growing. This book has radiated through me and I feel more driven than ever before.

Welcome to the Journey

Yes! Yes! YES! This is the book we have been waiting for!

So here you have it ... If we could do this work at our organisation—diving deeply into vision and values, pedagogical leadership, representational thinking, everyday use of the Thinking Lens, finding time and space to document our work and invite families into the conversation—then, with this book on your desk, you can do it, too! And if you do invest in taking your next step, you will find yourself deeply fulfilled and sustained in the work. Your job is to make the effort to take the next step—however big or small. Forward motion is key! We are deeply grateful to Ann and Margie for all the ways they have inspired us over the years and for this book that will soon be dog-eared and full of sticky notes and never far from our reach. If we could be of service to any reader looking for fellow journeyers on this path, we would love to shine the light. (info@richmondchildcare.org)

FOR THE CHILDREN

The rising hills, the slopes,
of statistics
lie before us,
the steep climb
of everything, going up,
up, as we all
go down.

In the next century
or the one beyond that,
they say,
are valleys, pastures,
we can meet there in peace
if we make it.

To climb these coming crests
one word to you, to
you and your children:

stay together
learn the flowers
go light.

—Gary Snyder[17]

Conclusion
Telling a New Story:
The Work Begins

As this book ends, a new story begins: the story that you write forward from here. What will you carry from your reading into your teaching practice, your leadership, your life?

Our hope is that you are seduced by the spirit of inquiry. That you see inquiry as a way to live in community with children, educators, and families—delving, wondering, marveling, imagining, and inventing together. A way to be as human as you can be.

How will you start living into inquiry? What will you emphasize? Where will you commit your attention?

Pedagogical leadership doesn't mean simply telling educators to "do inquiry" and hoping for the best. Pedagogical leadership means that you begin with your own work, your own role, reshaping your days to support and sustain inquiry in educators, so that they, in turn, support and sustain inquiry in children; we sure saw this in each of the offerings from the contributors to Chapter 14. They recognize that the work with children will stall out, and quite possibly fall apart, if the work with educators doesn't get attention; inquiry for children requires inquiry for adults.

What organizational systems might you put into place to foster inquiry in educators? How will you cultivate the dispositions to pay attention and be curious and alert to ordinary moments that hold wonderful potential? How will you slow things down, so that educators become easy with taking time to reflect and mull and collaborate, rather than rushing to take action or to document learning? How will you create the space and set the expectation for reflection and meaning-making and deliberate, intentional planning?

As you hold these questions, remember Lilian Katz's instruction:

Some in-service educators are especially intent on getting something accomplished for the children, and seem to construe the situation as 'getting to the kids through the teachers.' If you want to help children, then do so directly. Try not to 'use' teachers. Instead, focus on helping the teachers as persons worthy of your concern and caring in their own right. Define your role as someone who helps and works with teachers for their own sakes.[1]

Pedagogical leaders work with teachers "for their own sakes," because teachers are worthy of attention and heart. This commitment is given eloquent voice by the contributing thinkers in Chapter 14. Each of them defines their role as "someone who helps and works with teachers for their own sakes"; indeed, this way of understanding their work anchors them as they move through challenge and discouragement and weariness.

As you strive to tune yourself to the educators with whom you work, committing yourself to working with them for their own sakes, you might use the Thinking Lens, re-configuring it according to the principle of congruity. Replace "children" with "educators," and see how the Thinking Lens could support you as you live into your role as a pedagogical leader, reimagining your work.

Know yourself. Open your heart to this moment.
- What is your immediate response to the educators' work? What feelings stir in you? What touches your heart as you watch and listen?
- What in your background and values is influencing your response to the educators' work?
- What administrative perspectives (i.e. budget, compliance issues, staffing schedules) are on your mind?
- What leaves you curious, eager to engage with educators' work?

Take the educators' points of view.
- How are the educators demonstrating their competencies, even when faced with discouraging barriers?
- What are the educators trying to figure out? What theories are they testing? What questions are they holding?

- What understandings are the educators drawing on? Are there patterns in their inquiry that reveal a trajectory of thought? Are there contradictions to explore further?
- How are the educators building on each other's ideas, perspectives, and contributions?

Examine the environment.
- How are the organization, use of the physical space and materials, and availability of (and skill with) technology impacting the educators' work?
- How are staffing patterns, schedules, and routines influencing the educators' work?

Collaborate with others to expand perspectives.
- How do your colleagues understand the role that educators' play in children's inquiry? How have your colleagues figured out how they can support educators to be researchers?
- What adult learning theories might you turn to, to help you support educators' growth and learning?
- What cultural perspectives should you be aware of as you engage with the educators?

Reflect and take action.
- What values, intentions, and desired outcomes do you want to influence your response?
- How might you help the educators see their own and each other's ideas? What might you do to invite the educators to take other perspectives?
- How might you support educators to give voice to their insights and questions in the documentation that they create?
- What might you do to deepen educators' relationships with each other and/or the community?
- How will you continue to seek out the educators' points of view?

Writing a New Story

A big part of work as a pedagogical leader is telling a new story about educators and their work, a story that illuminates the values that you are, together, striving to embody. It's a challenge, though, to create a new story while you live in the old story. We can learn from social movements, which strive to build new structures that embody the values of justice, equity, and peace, even as they work to dismantle current unjust and violent structures, until a tipping point is reached, and cultural change takes hold.[2] Transformation demands steady effort and a measured pace. It's sparked by vision and hunger, by fire in the belly; it's sustained by muscle and determination to create organizational structures that ground vision in practice.

That's sure been true of our experiences of transformation. When Ann joined the staff at Hilltop Children's Center in 1991, where Margie was the visiting staff coach, it was a fairly typical mid-sized full-day, non-profit child care center. The teachers were dedicated to their work and held good intentions, but didn't have a defined philosophical or pedagogical approach. In the mid-1990s, Ann and her co-teacher, Sarah Felstiner, began to learn from and with Margie about the teaching and learning that take place in the schools in Reggio Emilia, Italy. What we learned inspired us to begin reimagining our work, and we became determined to create an early childhood program that invited our intellectual and emotional engagement.

Fueled by conviction and desire, Hilltop educators worked with the administration and Board to build an organizational culture and structure to support new pedagogical practice. Changes unfolded in tiny steps, over many years, as we slowly wove continual professional learning and improved working conditions into the everyday life of Hilltop. We inched away from catch-as-catch-can staff meetings on the hallway floor during nap time, gradually adding weekly paid preparation and planning time. Then came monthly early closures for staff meetings that are organized around professional learning rather than logistics and regulations. Eventually, we added full-day closures four times a year for professional learning, and an annual staff retreat weekend held in a beautiful place to nourish our spirits, hearts, minds, and bodies.

At one point, teacher-leaders proposed trading some of their professional learning benefits to fund a pedagogical leader position. To strengthen the organizational support for our pedagogical practice, the Board worked with the administration to reorganize the administrative structure several times, during a decade of continuous evaluation. This effort grew from a commitment to align business practices with pedagogical practices, and to keep both business and pedagogy true to our vision.

This sort of transformation isn't only for communities privileged by class and race. Ann has worked as a consultant in the role of pedagogical leader with a consortium of publicly-funded early childhood programs that serve newly-arrived immigrant families and low-income families. The program administrator carved money out of the professional learning budget that would typically be spent on sending staff to conferences and workshops; with that money, he funded time for educators to meet together with Ann for study and planning. Margie has facilitated "cross-town" professional learning collaborations between centers serving families with very different cultural and financial resources. They built relationships across traditional cultural and economic divides, exploring the roots of their pedagogical practices and bringing new insights to each other. In cities across North America, centers have taken up a more formal shared services approach to administration, locating tasks like human resources, budget management, grant writing, and IT support in a central office to free up center directors to act as pedagogical leaders. We've seen communities in which directors have worked with their QRIS coaches to form communities of practice which meet monthly to study documentation and share their teacher research.

In each of these programs, educators and administrators came together to bring about the change they longed for. They asked the soul-deep questions, "To what will we be accountable? For what do we want to be known?" From those questions, they began to live into new stories for their work, and for their living.

Loris Malaguzzi, one of the founders of the schools in Reggio Emilia, offers a vision for the story that you can create: "We are part of an ongoing story of men and women, ideals intact, who realize that history can be changed, and that it is changed starting with the future of children."[3]

Starting here, now, how will you join this on-going, history-changing story? What ideals will you call forward, what effort will you contribute, what unwavering determination will you hold to, in service of the future of children? How will you begin the work of reimagining early childhood education?

Notes

Poetry/Prose Pages

1   Antoine de Saint-Exupéry (biography.com/people/antoine-de-saint-exupery-030816).

2   Dougald Hine & Paul Kingsnorth, *Uncivilisation: The Dark Mountain Manifesto* (The Dark Mountain Project, 2009).

3   John O'Donohue, "For Longing," in *To Bless the Space Between Us: A Book of Blessings* (New York: Doubleday, 2008).

4   Brad Aaron Modlin, "What You Missed that Day You Were Absent from Fourth Grade," in *Everyone at this Party has Two Names* (Cape Girardeau: Southeast Missouri State University Press, 2016).

5   Judy Brown, "Fire," in *A Leader's Guide to Reflective Practice* (Indianapolis: Trafford Publishing, 2008).

6   Katie Kissinger, "Wings of the Same Bird," in *Anti-Bias Education in the Early Childhood Classroom: Hand in Hand, Step by Step* (Abingdon: Taylor and Francis Group LLC Books, 2017).

7   Margaret Wheatley, *Finding Our Way: Leadership for an Uncertain Time* (Oakland: Berrett-Koehler Publishers, 2005), 58. (Prose text by Roger Rosenblatt redone as a poem by Wheatley).

8   Anne Lamott, *Bird by Bird: Some Instructions on Writing and Life* (New York: Anchor Books, 1994).

9   Jonathan Kozol, *Ordinary Resurrections: Children in the Years of Hope* (New York: Crown Publishers, 2000).

10 Maxine Hong Kingston, *The Fifth Book of Peace* (New York: Vintage Books, 2003).

11 Elie Wiesel, interview by Oprah Winfrey. *O, The Oprah Magazine*, November 2000.

12 Parker Palmer, *The Courage to Teach: Exploring the Inner Landscape of a Teacher's Life* (San Francisco: Jossey-Bass, 1998).

13 Jonathan Kozol, *Ordinary Resurrections: Children in the Years of Hope* (New York: Crown Publishers, 2000).

14 John Wesley Powell, "Down the Colorado: Diary of the First Trip through the Grand Canyon, 1869," in *The Early Grand Canyon: Early Impressions*, ed. Paul Schullery (Niwot: Colorado Associated University Press, 1981).

15 Brian Doyle, *Martin Marten* (New York: Picador, 2016).

16 Henry Miller, *The Wisdom of the Heart* (New York: New Directions, 1941).

17 Gary Snyder, "For the Children," in *Turtle Island* (New York: New Directions, 1974).

Preface: Writing a New Story

1   Loris Malaguzzi, "History, Ideas, and Basic Philosophy: An Interview with Lella Gandini," in *The Hundred Languages of Children: The Reggio Emilia Approach to Early Childhood Education*, eds. C. Edwards, L. Gandini, and G. Forman (Greenwich: Ablex, 1998).

2   Ibid.

3   Ibid.

4   Ibid.

5   Ibid.

6   Peter Moss, *Transformative Change and Real Utopias in Early Childhood Education: A Story of Democracy, Experimentation and Potentiality* (New York: Routledge, 2014).

7   Ibid.

8   Ibid.

9   Barry Lopez, "The Contemporary Writer and Social Responsibility," *The 2016 Maxine Cushing Gray Distinguished Writer Award Lecture* (Seattle: University of Washington, October 27, 2016).

Chapter 1: The Heart of Education

1   Tom Hunter, "As Human as They Can Be," in *As Human as They Can Be Tribute DVD* (Bellingham: The Song Growing Company, 2008).

2   Carrie Melsom, personal communication to author, 2013.

3   Ann Pelo, *The Language of Art: Inquiry-Based Studio Practices in Early Childhood Settings* (St. Paul: Redleaf Press, 2017).

4   *Webster's Third New International Dictionary, Unabridged* (Springfield: Merriam-Webster, 1993).

5   Elliot Eisner, "The Satisfactions of Teaching," *Educational Leadership: Improving Professional Practice* 63, no. 6 (2006): 44-46.

6   Ibid.

7   John Dewey, *Democracy and Education: An Introduction to the Philosophy of Education* (New York: Macmillan, 1916).

8   Sylvia Ashton-Warner, *Teacher* (New York: Simon and Schuster, 1963); Paulo Freire, *Pedagogy of the Oppressed* (New York: Continuum, 2000); Jonathan Kozol, *Death at an Early Age* (Boston: Houghton Mifflin, 1967), *On Being a Teacher* (New York: Continuum, 1981), *Letters to a Young Teacher* (New York: Crown Publishers, 2007); Maria Montessori, *The Absorbent Mind* (New York: Holt, Rinehart, & Winston, 1967); *The Discovery of the Child* (New York: Ballantine Books, 1967), *The Montessori Method* (Mineola: Dover Publications, 2002).

9   Paulo Freire, *Pedagogy of the Oppressed* (New York: Continuum, 2000).

10 Sylvia Ashton-Warner, *Teacher* (New York: Simon and Schuster, 1963).

11 Paulo Freire, *Pedagogy of the Oppressed* (New York: Continuum, 2000).

12 Parker Palmer, *The Courage to Teach: Exploring the Inner Landscape of a Teacher's Life* (San Francisco: Jossey-Bass, 1998).

Chapter 2: Creating a Culture of Inquiry

1   Carlina Rinaldi, "The Teacher as Researcher," *Innovations in Early Education: The International Reggio Exchange* 10, no. 2 (Spring 2003).

2   Carol Anne Wien, *Developmentally Appropriate Practice in "Real Life": Stories of Teacher Practical Knowledge* (New York: Teachers College Press, 1995).

3   Chris Gethard, interview by Terry Gross. *Fresh Air*, January 6, 2017.

4   Ibid.

5   Peter Moss, "We Cannot Continue as We Are: The Educator in an Education for Survival," *Contemporary Issues in Early Childhood* 11, no. 1 (2010).

6   Vea Vecchi, *Art and Creativity in Reggio Emilia: Exploring the Role and Potential of Ateliers in Early Childhood Education* (New York: Routledge, 2010) (citing Loris Malaguzzi).

7   Carlina Rinaldi, "The Teacher as Researcher," *Innovations in Early Education: The International Reggio Exchange* 10, no. 2 (Spring 2003).

8   The Australian Government Department of Education, Employment and Workplace, *Belonging, Being, and Becoming: The Early Years Learning Framework of Australia* (Barton, ACT: Commonwealth of Australia, 2009).

9   Ibid.

10 Larry Daloz, *Mentor: Guiding the Journey of Adult Leaders* (San Francisco: Jossey-Bass, 1999).

11 Antonio Machado, *Antologia Poetica de Antonio Machado*, ed. Andres Sorel (Madrid: XYZ, 1975).

12 Myles Horton and Paulo Freire, *We Make the Road by Walking: Conversations on Education and Social Change* (Philadelphia: Temple University Press, 1990).

13 William Ayers, *Teaching the Personal and the Political: Essays on Hope and Justice* (New York: Teachers College Press, 2004).

14 Margie Carter and Deb Curtis, *Training Teachers: A Harvest of Theory and Practice* (St. Paul: Redleaf Press, 1995).

Chapter 3: Rethinking Professional Learning

1   Parker Palmer, *The Courage to Teach: Exploring the Inner Landscape of a Teacher's Life* (San Francisco: Jossey-Bass, 1998).

2   Tove Jansson, *Moominland Midwinter*, trans. Thomas Warburton (New York: Farrar, Straus & Giroux, 1958).

3   Elizabeth Jones and John Nimmo, "Collaboration, Conflict, and Change: Thoughts on Education as Provocation," *Young Children* 54, no. 1 (1999): 5-10.

4   Lilian Katz and Sylvia Chard, *Engaging Children's Minds: The Project Approach* (Greenwich: Ablex, 1989).

5   Daniel Meier and Barbara Henderson, *Learning from Young Children in the Classroom: The Art and Science of Teacher Research* (New York: Teachers College Press, 2007).

6   Arthur L. Costa and Bena Kallick, "Through the Lens of a Critical Friend," *Educational Leadership* 51, no. 2 (1993): 50.

7   Larry Daloz, *Mentor: Guiding the Journey of Adult Leaders* (San Francisco: Jossey-Bass, 1999).

8   Tove Jansson, *Moominland Midwinter*, trans. Thomas Warburton (New York: Farrar, Straus & Giroux, 1958).

9   Ibid.

10 Parker Palmer, *The Courage to Teach Guide for Reflection and Renewal* (San Francisco: Jossey-Bass, 2007), 30.

11 Tove Jansson, *Moominland Midwinter*, trans. Thomas Warburton (New York: Farrar, Straus & Giroux, 1958).

12 Elizabeth Jones and Gretchen Reynolds, "Understanding Teachers' Use of Power," *The Play's the Thing: Teachers' Roles in Children's Play* (New York: Teachers College Press, 1992) (quoting Eve Trook).

13 Ijumaa Jordan, "The Real Power of Mentoring: An Interview with Ijumaa Jordan," interview by Margie Carter. *Exchange*, March/April 2013, 18-22.

14 Ibid.

15 Tenneson Woolf, personal communication to author, 2015.

16 Ibid.

17 Ibid.

18 Tiziana Filippini, "The Role of the Pedagogista," *The Hundred Languages of Children* (Greenwich: Ablex, 1998).

19 Brian Arao and Kristi Clemens, "From Safe Spaces to Brave Spaces: A New Way to Frame Dialogue Around Diversity and Social Justice," in *The Art of Effective Facilitation* (Sterling: Sylus Publishing, 2013), 135-150.

20 Elizabeth Jones and John Nimmo, "Collaboration, Conflict, and Change: Thoughts on Education as Provocation," *Young Children* 54, no. 1 (1999): 5-10.

21 Elliot Eisner, "The Satisfactions of Teaching," *Educational Leadership: Improving Professional Practice* 63, no. 6 (2006): 44-46.

22 Tiziana Filippini, "The Role of the Pedagogista," in *The Hundred Languages of Children* (Greenwich: Ablex, 1998).

23 Louise Boyd Cadwell, *Bringing Learning to Life: The Reggio Approach to Early Childhood Education* (New York: Teachers College Press, 2003).

24 Elizabeth Jones and John Nimmo, "Collaboration, Conflict, and Change: Thoughts on Education as Provocation," *Young Children* 54, no. 1 (1999): 5-10.

Chapter 4: A Principle for Reimagining Our Work: Anchor Organizational Systems in Vision and Values

1 Peter Block, *The Empowered Manager: Positive Political Skills at Work* (San Francisco: Jossey-Bass, 1991), 121.

2 Margie Carter and Deb Curtis, *The Visionary Director: A Handbook for Dreaming, Organizing and Improvising in Your Center*, 2d ed. (St. Paul: Redleaf Press, 2010).

3 Margie Carter, "Leadership Challenges in Publicly-Funded Preschools. An Interview with Luz Casio," *Exchange*, March/April 2016.

Chapter 5: A Principle for Reimagining Our Work: Understand Professional Learning as the Work of Culture-Making

1 Margaret J. Wheatley and Myron Kellner-Rogers, "Self-organization: The Irresistible Future of Organizing," *Strategy & Leadership* 24, no. 4 (1996).

2 Margie Carter, "Drive-through Training," *Exchange*, July/August 2010 (quoting Wendy Cividanes).

3 Slow Food USA (slowfoodusa.org).

4 Tenneson Woolf, "In Complexity All Stories are True?" *Tenneson Woolf Consulting*, January 22, 2015, *http://tennesonwoolf.com/in-complexity-all-stories-are-true/* (accessed January 22, 2015).

From Teaching to Thinking

5   Margie Carter, "Leadership Challenges in Publicly Funded Preschools," *Exchange*, March/April 2016 (quoting Luz Casio).

Chapter 6: A Principle for Reimagining Our Work: Engage with Educators as you Hope They Will Engage with Children

1   Lilian Katz, *Helping Others with Their Teaching* (Urbana: ERIC Clearinghouse on Elementary and Early Childhood Education, 1993).
2   Louise Boyd Cadwell, *Bringing Learning to Life: The Reggio Approach to Early Childhood Education* (New York: Teachers College Press, 2003).
3   Lilian Katz, *Second Collection of Papers for Educators* (Urbana: ERIC Clearinghouse on Early Childhood Education, 1975).
4   Margie Carter, "Conversations that Generate New Ideas," *Exchange*, July/August 2016.
5   Deb Curtis, Debbie Lebo, Wendy Cividanes, and Margie Carter, *Reflecting in Communities of Practice* (St. Paul: Redleaf Press, 2013).
6   Ann Hatherly, "Organizational Culture: Quality's Soul Mate," *Early Education* 23, (2000).

Chapter 7: A Principle for Reimagining Our Work: Come Together with Families as Collaborators, Colleagues, and Critical Friends

1   Louise Derman-Sparks and Julie Olsen Edwards, *Anti-Bias Education for Young Children and Ourselves* (Washington, DC: NAEYC, 2010).
2   Amelia Gambetti and Judith Allen Kaminsky, "The Fundamental Role of Participation in the Experience of the Reggio Emilia Municipal Infant-Toddler Centers and Preschools: An Interview with Paola Cagliari," *Innovations in Early Education* 8, no. 3 (Spring/Summer 2001) (quoting Paola Cagliari).
3   Ibid.
4   Jim Greenman, "Empowering Parents?" *Exchange*, March 2001.
5   Carlina Rinaldi, "The Relationship between Documentation and Assessment," *Innovations in Early Education* 11, no. 1 (Winter 2004).
6   Ibid.
7   Brené Brown, *Daring Greatly: How the Courage to Be Vulnerable Transforms the Way We Live, Love, Parent, and Lead* (New York: Avery/Random House, 2015).
8   Ibid.
9   Carlina Rinaldi, "The Relationship between Documentation and Assessment," *Innovations in Early Education* 11, no. 1 (Winter 2004).
10 Norma Gonzalez, Luis C. Moll, and Cathy Amanti, eds., *Funds of Knowledge: Theorizing Practices in Households, Communities, and Classrooms* (New York: Routledge, 2005).
11 Margie Carter, "Redefining Parent Engagement," *Exchange*, November/December 2015 (quoting Mary Jo Deck); PhotoVoice (photovoice.org).
12 Margie Carter, "Redefining Parent Engagement," *Exchange*, November/December 2015 (quoting Mary Jo Deck).

Chapter 8: Pedagogical Practice: The Thinking Lens as a Research Tool

1 Daniel Meier and Barbara Henderson, *Learning from Young Children in the Classroom: The Art and Science of Teacher Research* (New York: Teachers College Press, 2007).

2 Ibid.

3 Joseph P. McDonald, Nancy Mohr, Alan Dichter, and Elizabeth C. McDonald, *The Power of Protocols: An Educator's Guide to Better Practice* (New York: Teachers College Press, 2004), 4.

4 Margie Carter, Deb Curtis, and Ann Pelo, *The Thinking Lens© for Learning Together with Children.*

5 Comune di Reggio Emilia, Centro Documentazione Ricerca Educativa Nidi e Scuole dell'Infanzia, *To Make a Portrait of a Lion* (1987).

6 Carrie Melsom, personal communication to author, 2014.

7 Matthew Crawford, *The World Beyond Your Head: On Becoming an Individual in the Age of Distraction* (New York: Farrar Strauss and Giroux, 2015).

8 Ibid.

9 Mary Oliver, "Listening to the World: An Interview with Krista Tippett," *On Being*, October 15, 2015.

10 Ibid.

11 Albert Einstein, as quoted by Garrison Keillor. *The Writer's Almanac*, March 14, 2016.

12 Peter Moss, "Structures, Understandings and Discourses: Possibilities for Re-envisioning the Early Childhood Worker," *Contemporary Issues in Early Childhood* 7, no. 1 (2006).

13 Tom Hunter, "As Human as They Can Be," in *As Human as They Can Be Tribute DVD* (Bellingham: The Song Growing Company, 2008).

14 Peter Moss, "Structures, Understandings and Discourses: Possibilities for Re-envisioning the Early Childhood Worker," *Contemporary Issues in Early Childhood* 7, no. 1 (2006).

15 Joseph P. McDonald, Nancy Mohr, Alan Dichter, and Elizabeth C. McDonald, *The Power of Protocols: An Educator's Guide to Better Practice* (New York: Teachers College Press, 2004), 4.

16 Daniel Meier and Barbara Henderson, *Learning from Young Children in the Classroom: The Art and Science of Teacher Research* (New York: Teachers College Press, 2007).

17 National School Reform Initiative (SRI) Protocols (nsrfharmony.org).

Chapter 9: The Thinking Lens: Know Yourself

1 Australian Children's Education & Care Quality Authority, *Guide to the National Quality Standard* (Sydney, Australia: 2011).

2 Ibid.

3 Lisa Delpit, *Other People's Children: Cultural Conflict in the Classroom* (New York: W.W. Norton & Co., 1995).

4 William Ayers, *Teaching the Personal and the Political: Essays on Hope and Justice* (New York: Teachers College Press, 2004).

Chapter 10: The Thinking Lens: Making Meaning

1 Rick Bass, *The Wild Marsh: Four Seasons at Home in Montana* (New York: Houghton Mifflin Harcourt, 2009).

2 Carlina Rinaldi, "The Teacher as Researcher," *Innovations in Early Education: The International Reggio Exchange* 10, no. 2 (Spring 2003).

3 Pam Oken-Wright and Marty Gravett, "Big Ideas and the Essence of Intent," in *Teaching and Learning: Collaborative Exploration of the Reggio Emilia Approach*, eds. Fu, Stremmel, and Hill (Upper Saddle River: Pearson Education, Inc., 2002).

4 Ibid.

5 Ibid.

6 Carlina Rinaldi, "The Relationship between Documentation and Assessment," *Innovations in Early Education* 11, no. 1 (Winter 2004).

7 Australian Government Department of Education, Employment and Workplace, *Belonging, Being, Becoming: The Early Years Learning Framework for Australia* (Barton, ACT: Commonwealth of Australia, 2009).

8 Nikolien van Wijk, *Getting Started with Schemas: Revealing the Wonder-full World of Children's Play* (Christchurch, NZ: Playcentre Federation, 2008); Deb Curtis and Nadia Jaboneta, *Children's Lively Minds: Schema Theory Made Visible* (St. Paul: Redleaf Press, (in press)).

9 Margie Carter and Deb Curtis, *Training Teachers: A Harvest of Theory and Practice* (St. Paul: Redleaf Press, 1994).

10 Deb Curtis and Margie Carter, *Learning Together with Young Children: A Curriculum Framework for Reflective Teachers* (St. Paul: Redleaf Press, 2017) (quoting Kelly Mathews).

11 bell hooks, *Killing Rage: Ending Racism* (New York: Holt Paperbacks, 1996).

12 Australian Government Department of Education, Employment and Workplace, *Belonging, Being, Becoming: The Early Years Learning Framework for Australia* (Barton, ACT: Commonwealth of Australia, 2009).

13 Lisa Delpit, "The Silenced Dialogue: Power and Pedagogy in Educating Other People's Children," *Harvard Educational Review* 58, no. 3 (1988): 280-298.

14 Ibid.

15 Sweet Honey in the Rock, *All for Freedom* (Music for Little People: 1989).

16 Deb Curtis and Margie Carter, *Learning Together with Young Children: A Curriculum Framework for Reflective Teachers* (St. Paul: Redleaf Press, 2017).

Chapter 11: The Thinking Lens: Planning

1 Bob Strachota, *On Their Side: Helping Children Take Charge of Their Learning* (Turners Falls: Northeast Foundation for Children, 1996).

2 Carrie Melsom, personal communication to author, 2013.

3 Loris Malaguzzi, "History, Ideas, and Basic Philosophy: An Interview with Lella Gandini," in *The Hundred Languages of Children: The Reggio Emilia Approach to Early Childhood Education*, eds. C. Edwards, L. Gandini, and G. Forman (Greenwich: Ablex, 1998).

4   Flannery O'Connor, *The Habit of Being: Letters of Flannery O'Connor*, ed. Sally Fitzgerald (New York: Farrar, Straus and Giroux, 1988).

5   Ann Pelo, *The Language of Art: Inquiry-Based Studio Practices in Early Childhood Settings* (St. Paul: Redleaf Press, 2017).

6   Carlina Rinaldi, "The Teacher as Researcher," *Innovations in Early Education: The International Reggio Exchange* 10, no. 2 (Spring 2003).

7   Pema Chodron, *Comfortable with Uncertainty: 108 Teachings on Cultivating Fearlessness and Compassion* (Boston: Shambhala Publications, Inc., 2008).

8   Bridgette Towle and Angela Heape, *Cup: A Vibrant Vessel of Learning and Creativity* eds. Ann Pelo and Margie Carter (Lincoln: Exchange Press, (in press)).

Chapter 12: The Thinking Lens: Making Thinking Visible

1   Cheryl Strayed, *Tiny Beautiful Things: Advice on Love and Life from Dear Sugar* (New York: Vintage Books, 2012).

2   Anne Lamott, *Bird by Bird: Some Instructions on Writing and Life* (New York: Anchor Books, 1994).

3   Daniel Meier and Barbara Henderson, *Learning from Young Children in the Classroom: The Art and Science of Teacher Research* (New York: Teachers College Press, 2007).

4   Jason Avery, Karyn Callaghan, and Carol Anne Wien, *Documenting Children's Meaning: Engaging in Design and Creativity with Children and Families* (Worcester: Davis Publications, 2016).

5   Peter Moss, "Structures, Understandings and Discourses: Possibilities for Re-envisioning the Early Childhood Worker," *Contemporary Issues in Early Childhood* 7, no. 1 (2006).

6   Louisa Schwartz and Janet Robertson, "Materials Matter," in *Conversations Behind Early Childhood Pedagogical Documentation*, eds. Alma Fleet, Catherine Patterson, and Janet Robertson (Mt. Victoria, New South Wales: Pademelon Press, 2012).

7   Fred Rogers, quoted in ExchangeEveryDay, February 28, 2003.

8   Anne Lamott, *Bird by Bird: Some Instructions on Writing and Life* (New York: Anchor Books, 1994).

9   Ibid.

10 Kim Stafford, *The Muses Among Us: Eloquent Listening and Other Pleasures of the Writer's Craft* (Athens: The University of Athens Press, 2003).

11 Georgia O'Keeffe, 1922.

12 Terry Tempest Williams, "A Letter to Deb Clow," in *Red: Passion and Patience in the Desert* (New York: Pantheon Books, 2001).

13 Herb Kohl, *Should We Burn Babar? Essays on Children's Literature and the Power of Stories* (New York: The New Press, 2007).

14 Bill Clinton, "Remembering Maya Angelou," NBC News, June 7, 2014.

15 Peter Moss, "Structures, Understandings and Discourses: Possibilities for Re-envisioning the Early Childhood Worker," *Contemporary Issues in Early Childhood* 7, no. 1 (2006).

16 Ibid.

17 Margaret Carr, *Assessment in Early Childhood Settings: Learning Stories* (Thousand Oaks: Sage Publications, 2001).
18 Thich Nhat Hanh, "The Good News," in *Call Me By My True Names: The Collected Poems of Thich Nhat Hanh* (Berkeley: Parallax Press, 1999).

Chapter 13: Slapstick Literacy and the Music of Friendship: The Thinking Lens in Action
1 Ursula Kolbe, *It's Not a Bird Yet: The Drama of Drawing* (Sydney: Peppinot Press, 2005).
2 Angela Hanscom, *Balanced and Barefoot: How Unrestricted Outdoor Play Makes for Strong, Confident, and Competent Children* (Oakland: New Harbinger Publications, 2016).
3 Simone Weil, *Gravity and Grace* (London: Routledge, 2002).

Chapter 14: Voices from the Front Lines: A Call to Reimagine Our Work
1 Jeanne Lohmann, "Questions Before Dark," *The Light of Invisible Bodies* (McKinleyville: Fithian Press, 2003).
2 Lisa Delpit, "The Silenced Dialogue: Power and Pedagogy in Educating Other People's Children," *Harvard Educational Review* 58, no. 3 (1988), 280.
3 Marcy Whitebook, Elizabeth King, George Philipp, and Laura Sakai, *Teachers' Voices: Work Environment Conditions That Impact Teacher Practice and Program Quality* (Berkeley: Center for the Study of Child Care Employment Institute for Research on Labor and Employment, University of California, Berkeley, 2016).
4 Paulo Freire, *Pedagogy of the Oppressed* (New York: Continuum, 2000).
5 Arundhati Roy, *The Ordinary Person's Guide to Empire* (New Delhi: Penquin, 2005).
6 Kim Stafford, "Nest Filled," in *The Flavor of Unity: Post-Election Poems* (Little Infinities, 2018).
7 R. Khattar and K. Callaghan, "Beyond Professionalism: Interrogating the Idea and the Ideals," *Canadian Children* 40, no. 1 (2015), 5-19.
8 Peter Moss, "Micro-project and Macro-policy: Learning Through Relationships," in *The Hundred Languages of Children: The Reggio Emilia Experience in Transformation*, 3rd ed, eds. C. Edwards, L. Gandini, and G. Forman (Santa Barbara: Praeger, 2012), 101-113.
9 L. M. Olsson, *Movement and Experimentation in Young Children's Learning: Deleuze and Guattari in Early Childhood Education* (New York: Routledge, 2009).
10 Jonathan Kozol, *Ordinary Resurrections: Children in the Years of Hope* (New York: Crown Publishers, 2000).
11 Ibid.
12 Victoria Stafford, "The Small Work in the Great Work," in *The Impossible Will Take a Little While: Perseverance and Hope in Troubled Times*, ed. Paul Rogat Loeb (Philadelphia: Basic Books, 2014).
13 Rumi
14 Paulo Freire, *Teachers as Cultural Workers: Letters to Those Who Dare Teach* (Cambridge: Westview Press, 2005).
15 Ibid.

16 William Stafford, "The Way It Is," in *Ask Me: 100 Essential Poems* (Minneapolis: Graywolf Press, 2014).

17 Tom Hunter, "As Human as They Can Be," in *As Human as They Can Be Tribute DVD* (Bellingham: The Song Growing Company, 2008).

18 Ibid.

Conclusion: Telling A New Story—The Work Begins

1 Lilian Katz, *Helping Others with Their Teaching* (Urbana: ERIC Clearinghouse on Elementary and Early Childhood Education, 1993).

2 Malcolm Gladwell, *The Tipping Point: How Little Things Can Make a Big Difference* (Boston: Little, Brown, 2000).

3 Loris Malaguzzi, "History, Ideas, and Basic Philosophy: An Interview with Lella Gandini," in *The Hundred Languages of Children: The Reggio Emilia Approach to Early Childhood Education*, eds. C. Edwards, L. Gandini, and G. Forman (Greenwich: Ablex, 1998).

Bibliography

Arao, Brian and Kristi Clemens. "From Safe Spaces to Brave Spaces: A New Way to Frame Dialogue Around Diversity and Social Justice." In *The Art of Effective Facilitation*. Sterling: Sylus Publishing, 2013.

Ashton-Warner, Sylvia. *Teacher*. New York: Simon and Schuster, 1963.

Australian Children's Education & Care Quality Authority. *Guide to the National Quality Standard*. Sydney, Australia: 2011.

Australian Government Department of Education, Employment and Workplace. *Belonging, Being, and Becoming: The Early Years Learning Framework of Australia*. Barton, ACT: Commonwealth of Australia, 2009.

Avery, Jason, Karyn Callaghan, and Carol Anne Wien. *Documenting Children's Meaning: Engaging in Design and Creativity with Children and Families*. Worcester: Davis Publications, 2016.

Ayers, William. *Teaching the Personal and the Political: Essays on Hope and Justice*. New York: Teachers College Press, 2004.

Bass, Rick. *The Wild Marsh: Four Seasons at Home in Montana*. New York: Houghton Mifflin Harcourt, 2009.

Block, Peter. *The Empowered Manager: Positive Political Skills at Work*. San Francisco: Jossey-Bass, 1991.

Brown, Brené. *Daring Greatly: How the Courage to Be Vulnerable Transforms the Way We Live, Love, Parent, and Lead*. New York: Avery/Random House, 2015.

Brown, Judy. "Fire." In *A Leader's Guide to Reflective Practice*. Indianapolis: Trafford Publishing, 2008.

Cadwell, Louise Boyd. *Bringing Learning to Life: The Reggio Approach to Early Childhood Education*. New York: Teachers College Press, 2003.

Carr, Margaret. *Assessment in Early Childhood Settings: Learning Stories*. Thousand Oaks: Sage Publications, 2001.

Carter, Margie. "Conversations that Generate New Ideas." *Exchange*, July/August 2012.

_____. "Drive-through Training." *Exchange*, July/August 2010.

_____. "Leadership Challenges in Publicly-Funded Preschools. An Interview with Luz Casio." *Exchange*, March/April 2016.

_____. "Redefining Parent Engagement." *Exchange*, November/December 2015.

Carter, Margie, and Deb Curtis. *Learning Together with Young Children: A Curriculum Framework for Reflective Teachers*. St. Paul: Redleaf Press, 2017.

_____. *Training Teachers: A Harvest of Theory and Practice*. St. Paul: Redleaf Press, 1995.

_____. *The Visionary Director: A Handbook for Dreaming, Organizing and Improvising in Your Center*. 2d ed. St. Paul: Redleaf Press, 2010.

Chodron, Pema. *Comfortable with Uncertainty: 108 Teachings on Cultivating Fearlessness and Compassion*. Boston: Shambhala Publications, Inc., 2008.

Costa, Arthur L., and Bena Kallick. "Through the Lens of a Critical Friend." *Educational Leadership* 51, no. 2 (1993): 50.

Crawford, Matthew. *The World Beyond Your Head: On Becoming an Individual in the Age of Distraction*. New York: Farrar, Strauss and Giroux, 2015.

Curtis, Deb, and Nadia Jaboneta. *Children's Lively Minds: Schema Theory Made Visible*. St. Paul: Redleaf Press, (in press).

Curtis, Deb, Debbie Lebo, Wendy Cividanes, and Margie Carter. *Reflecting in Communities of Practice*. St. Paul: Redleaf Press, 2013.

Daloz, Larry. *Mentor: Guiding the Journey of Adult Leaders*. San Francisco: Jossey-Bass, 1999.

Delpit, Lisa. *Other People's Children: Cultural Conflict in the Classroom*. New York: W.W. Norton & Co., 1995.

———. "The Silenced Dialogue: Power and Pedagogy in Educating Other People's Children." *Harvard Educational Review* 58, no. 3 (1988): 280-298.

Derman-Sparks, Louise, and Julie Olsen Edwards. *Anti-Bias Education for Young Children and Ourselves*. Washington, DC: NAEYC, 2010.

Dewey, John. *Democracy and Education: An Introduction to the Philosophy of Education*. New York: Macmillan, 1916.

Doyle, Brian. *Martin Marten*. New York: Picador, 2016.

Eisner, Elliot. "The Satisfactions of Teaching." *Educational Leadership: Improving Professional Practice* 63, no. 6 (2006): 44-46.

Filippini, Tiziana. "The Role of the Pedagogista." *The Hundred Languages of Children*. Greenwich: Ablex, 1998.

Freire, Paulo. *Pedagogy of the Oppressed*. New York: Continuum, 2000.

———. *Teachers as Cultural Workers: Letters to Those Who Dare Teach*. Cambridge: Westview Press, 2005.

Gambetti, Amelia, and Judith Allen Kaminsky. "The Fundamental Role of Participation in the Experience of the Reggio Emilia Municipal Infant-Toddler Centers and Preschools: An Interview with Paola Cagliari." *Innovations in Early Education* 8, no. 3 (Spring/Summer 2001).

Gladwell, Malcom. *The Tipping Point: How Little Things Can Make a Big Difference*. Boston: Little, Brown, 2000.

Gonzalez, Norma, Luis C. Moll, and Cathy Amanti, eds. *Funds of Knowledge: Theorizing Practices in Households, Communities, and Classrooms*. New York: Routledge, 2005.

Greenman, Jim. "Empowering Parents?" *Exchange*, March 2001.

Hanscom, Angela. *Balanced and Barefoot: How Unrestricted Outdoor Play Makes for Strong, Confident, and Competent Children*. Oakland: New Harbinger Publications, 2016.

Hatherly, Ann. "Organizational Culture: Quality's Soul Mate." *Early Education* 23, (2000).

Hine, Dougald, and Paul Kingsnorth. *Uncivilisation: The Dark Mountain Manifesto*. The Dark Mountain Project, 2009.

hooks, bell. *Killing Rage: Ending Racism*. New York: Holt Paperbacks, 1996.

Horton, Myles, and Paulo Freire. *We Make the Road by Walking: Conversations on Education and Social Change*. Philadelphia: Temple Press, 1990.

Hunter, Tom. "As Human as They Can Be." In *As Human as They Can Be Tribute DVD*. Bellingham: The Song Growing Company, 2008.

Jansson, Tove. *Moominland Midwinter*, translated by Thomas Warburton. New York: Farrar, Straus & Giroux, 1958.

Jones, Elizabeth, and Gretchen Reynolds. "Understanding Teachers' Use of Power." *The Play's the Thing: Teachers' Roles in Children's Play.* New York: Teachers College Press, 1992.

Jones, Elizabeth, and John Nimmo. "Collaboration, Conflict, and Change: Thoughts on Education as Provocation." *Young Children* 54, no. 1 (1999): 5-10.

Jordan, Ijumaa. "The Real Power of Mentoring: An Interview with Ijumaa Jordan." Interview by Margie Carter. *Exchange*, March/April 2013.

Katz, Lilian. *Helping Others with Their Teaching.* Urbana: ERIC Clearinghouse on Elementary and Early Childhood Education, 1993.

_____. *Second Collection of Papers for Educators.* Urbana: ERIC Clearinghouse on Early Childhood Education, 1975.

Katz, Lillian, and Sylvia Chard. *Engaging Children's Minds: The Project Approach.* Greenwich: Ablex, 1989.

Khattar, R., and Callaghan, K. "Beyond Professionalism: Interrogating the Idea and the Ideals." *Canadian Children* 40, no. 1 (2015): 5-19.

Kingston, Maxine Hong. *The Fifth Book of Peace.* New York: Vintage Books, 2003.

Kissinger, Katie. "Wings of the Same Bird." In *Anti-Bias Education in the Early Childhood Classroom: Hand in Hand, Step by Step.* Abingdon: Taylor and Francis Group LLC Books, 2017.

Kohl, Herb. *Should We Burn Babar? Essays on Children's Literature and the Power of Stories.* New York: The New Press, 2007.

Kolbe, Ursula. *It's Not a Bird Yet: The Drama of Drawing.* Sydney: Peppinot Press, 2005.

Kozol, Jonathan. *Death at an Early Age.* Boston: Houghton Mifflin, 1967.

_____. *Letters to a Young Teacher.* New York: Crown Publishers, 2007.

_____. *On Being a Teacher.* New York: Continuum, 1981.

_____. *Ordinary Resurrections: Children in the Years of Hope.* New York: Crown Publishers, 2000.

Lamott, Anne. *Bird by Bird: Some Instructions on Writing and Life.* New York: Anchor Books, 1994.

Lohmann, Jeanne. "Questions Before Dark." *The Light of Invisible Bodies.* McKinleyville: Fithian Press, 2003.

Lopez, Barry. "The Contemporary Writer and Social Responsibility." *The 2016 Maxine Cushing Gray Distinguished Writer Award Lecture.* Seattle: University of Washington, October 27, 2016.

Machado, Antonio. *Antologia Poetica de Antonio Machado*, edited Andres Sorel. Madrid: XYZ, 1975.

Malaguzzi, Loris. "History, Ideas, and Basic Philosophy: An Interview with Lella Gandini." In *The Hundred Languages of Children: The Reggio Emilia Approach to Early Childhood Education*, edited by Carolyn Edwards, Lella Gandini, and George Forman. Greenwich: Ablex, 1998.

McDonald, Joseph P., Nancy Mohr, Alan Dichter, and Elizabeth C. McDonald. *The Power of Protocols: An Educator's Guide to Better Practice.* New York: Teachers College Press, 2004.

Meier, Daniel, and Barbara Henderson. *Learning from Young Children in the Classroom: The Art and Science of Teacher Research*. New York: Teachers College Press, 2007.

Miller, Henry. *The Wisdom of the Heart*. New York: New Directions, 1941.

Modlin, Brad Aaron. "What You Missed that Day You were Absent from Fourth Grade." *In Everyone at this Party has Two Names*. Springfield: Southeast Missouri State University Press, 2016.

Montessori, Maria. *The Absorbent Mind*. New York: Holt, Rinehart, & Winston, 1967.

———. *The Discovery of the Child*. New York: Ballantine Books, 1967.

———. *The Montessori Method*. Mineola: Dover Publications, 2002.

Moss, Peter. "Micro-project and Macro-policy: Learning Through Relationships." In *The Hundred Languages of Children: The Reggio Emilia Experience in Transformation*, 3rd ed, edited by C. Edwards, L. Gandini, and G. Forman. Santa Barbara: Praeger, 2012.

———. "Structures, Understandings and Discourses: possibilities for Re-envisioning the Early Childhood Worker." *Contemporary Issues in Early Childhood* 7, no. 1 (2006).

———. *Transformative Change and Real Utopias in Early Childhood Education: A Story of Democracy, Experimentation and Potentiality*. New York: Routledge, 2014.

———. "We Cannot Continue as We Are: The Educator in an Education for Survival." *Contemporary Issues in Early Childhood* 11, no. 1 (2010).

Nhat Hanh, Thich. "The Good News." In *Call Me By My True Names: The Collected Poems of Thich Nhat Hanh*. Berkeley: Parallax Press, 1999.

O'Connor, Flannery. *The Habit of Being: Letters of Flannery O'Connor*, edited by Sally Fitzgerald. New York: Farrar, Straus and Giroux, 1988.

O'Donahue, John. "For Longing." In *To Bless the Space Between Us: A Book of Blessings*. New York: Doubleday, 2008

Oken-Wright, Pam, and Marty Gravett. "Big Ideas and the Essence of Intent." In *Teaching and Learning: Collaborative Exploration of the Reggio Emilia Approach*, edited by Stremmel, Fu, and Hill. Upper Saddle River: Pearson Education, Inc., 2002.

Oliver, Mary. "Listening to the World: An Interview with Krista Tippett." *On Being*, October 15, 2015.

Olsson, L. M. *Movement and Experimentation in Young Children's Learning: Deleuze and Guattari in Early Childhood Education*. New York: Routledge, 2009.

Palmer, Parker. *The Courage to Teach: Exploring the Inner Landscape of a Teacher's Life*. San Francisco: Jossey-Bass, 1998.

———. *The Courage to Teach Guide for Reflection and Renewal*. San Francisco: Jossey-Bass, 2007.

Pelo, Ann. *The Language of Art: Inquiry-Based Studio Practices in Early Childhood Settings*. St. Paul: Redleaf Press, 2017.

Powell, John Wesley. "Down the Colorado: Diary of the First Trip through the Grand Canyon." In *The Early Grand Canyon: Early Impressions*, edited by Paul Schullery. Niwot: Colorado Associated University Press, 1981.

Rinaldi, Carlina. "The Relationship between Documentation and Assessment." *Innovations in Early Education* 11, no. 1 (Winter 2004).

———. "The Teacher as Researcher." *Innovations in Early Education: The International Reggio Exchange* 10, no. 2 (Spring 2003).

Roy, Arundhati. *The Ordinary Person's Guide to Empire*. New Delhi: Penquin, 2005.

Schwartz, Louisa, and Janet Robertson. "Materials Matter." In *Conversations Behind Early Childhood Pedagogical Documentation*, edited by Alma Fleet, Catherine Patterson, and Janet Robertson. Mt. Victoria, New South Wales: Pademelon Press, 2012.

Snyder, Gary. "For the Children." In *Turtle Island*. New York: New Directions, 1974.

Stafford, Kim. *The Muses Among Us: Eloquent Listening and Other Pleasures of the Writer's Craft*. Athens: The University of Athens Press, 2003.

———. "Nest Filled." In *The Flavor of Unity: Post-Election Poems*. Little Infinities, 2018.

Stafford, Victoria. "The Small Work in the Great Work." In *The Impossible Will Take a Little While: Perseverance and Hope in Troubled Times*, edited by Paul Rogat Loeb. Philadelphia: Basic Books, 2014.

Stafford, William. "The Way It Is." In *Ask Me: 100 Essential Poems*. Minneapolis: Graywolf Press, 2014.

Strachota, Bob. *On Their Side: Helping Children Take Charge of Their Learning*. Turners Falls: Northeast Foundation for Children, 1996.

Strayed, Cheryl. *Tiny Beautiful Things: Advice on Love and Life from Dear Sugar*. New York: Vintage Books, 2012.

Towle, Bridgette, and Angela Heape. *Cup: A Vibrant Vessel of Learning and Creativity*, edited by Ann Pelo and Margie Carter. Lincoln: Exchange Press, (in press).

Vecchi, Vea. *Art and Creativity in Reggio Emilia: Exploring the Role and Potential of Ateliers in Early Childhood Education*. New York: Routledge, 2010.

Weil, Simone. *Gravity and Grace*. London: Routledge, 2002.

Wheatley, Margaret. *Finding Our Way: Leadership for an Uncertain Time*. Oakland: Berrett-Koehler Publishers, 2005.

Wheatley, Margaret J., and Myron Kellner-Rogers. "Self-organization: The Irresistible Future of Organizing." *Strategy & Leadership* 24, no. 4 (1996).

Whitebook, Marcy, Elizabeth King, George Philipp, and Laura Sakai. *Teachers' Voices: Work Environment Conditions That Impact Teacher Practice and Program Quality*. Berkeley: Center for the Study of Child Care Employment Institute for Research on Labor and Employment, University of California, Berkeley, 2016.

Wien, Carol Anne. *Developmentally Appropriate Practice in "Real Life": Stories of Teacher Practical Knowledge*. New York: Teachers College Press, 1995.

van Wijk, Nikolien. *Getting Started with Schemas: Revealing the Wonder-full World of Children's Play*. Christschurch, NZ: Playcentre Federation, 2008.

Williams, Terry Tempest. "A Letter to Deb Clow." In *Red: Passion and Patience in the Desert*. New York: Pantheon Books, 2001.

Bibliography

Contributors

Christina Aubel has been in the early learning field for over 30 years; she's taught infants and preschool children, and college students. She's also worked as an art studio consultant, education coordinator, and mentor teacher. In addition to pursuing early learning, Christina studied law and art; the law deepened her sense of social justice, and the arts awakened a passion for the creative process. Currently, Christina is a member of the Child Studies faculty at Bates Technical College in Tacoma, WA. She is a proud member of Harvest Educators Collaborative. Christina is inspired by her students, and holds strong to her belief in the potential for all humans to be creative thinkers.

. . . .

Nicky Byres *(center)* has been the visionary leader of the Society of Richmond Children's Centres (SRCC) for almost two decades, overseeing the growth of the SRCC from two centres to six and leading a pedagogical shift that resulted in the creation of the formal administrative team position of *Pedagogical Leader.* **Jennifer Chen** *(right)* and **Helen Lo** *(left)* are both Early Childhood Educators who have worked in a variety of programs and in program leadership; they are now Directors with specific responsibilities for leading the curriculum work and mentoring educators in all six SRCC centres. Together, Nicky, Jennifer, and Helen form ¾ of the SRCC Executive team, and are ably assisted by an HR/Admin. Director.

Karyn Callaghan is a public learner who has been a professor in college and university ECE programs for over thirty years and founded and coordinated the Artists at the Centre project. She is president of the Ontario Reggio Association, a board member of the North American Reggio Emilia Alliance, and represents Canada on the Reggio Children International Network. Karyn has been a keynote speaker at conferences across North America, and in Asia and Australia, and consulted with Ontario's Ministry of Education as it developed its pedagogy for early years document, *How Does Learning Happen?*. Karyn is the co-author, with Carol Anne Wien and Jason Avery, of *Documenting Children's Meaning: Engaging in Design and Creativity with Children and Families.*

• •

Shaquam Urquhart Edwards is a full time Early Childhood Education faculty member at the College of Marin, in Kentfield, CA, and an Educational Consultant. Beginning as a preschool teacher, she found a fascination with young children and began to study the art and science of teaching. Shaquam earned her B.A. in Liberal Studies from Cal State East Bay, and an M.A. in Education from Mills College in Oakland, CA. Over more than 34 years, Shaquam has enjoyed various roles in teaching, consulting, and preschool administration, which led to a well-rounded understanding of the needs of children and families. Shaquam takes particular interest in issues of diversity, social justice, and equity; anti-bias education; compassion; social emotional learning; teacher development; team facilitation with an emphasis on positive, effective communication; in-class coaching; curriculum development; and creating engaging environments for children.

Eliana Elias has been working as an educator for the past 30 years. In her early 20's, she worked as a teacher in her home country, Brazil, before moving to the U.S. to attend graduate school at Mills College, in Oakland, CA. After graduate school, she worked as an instructor at The Mills College Children's School, a laboratory school dedicated to teacher development where she experienced firsthand the power of a learner-centered philosophy. For the past 12 years, Eliana has worked as a consultant, professional development presenter, coach, and college instructor. Eliana is member of Harvest Educators Collaborative, a group of Early Childhood trainers who place social justice at the center of their work. Eliana's areas of interest include cultural competency, dual language learners, social and emotional development, curriculum development, professional development, and equity issues.

Kristie Norwood is currently an Education Manager at Ounce of Prevention Grantee Support Services in Chicago where she integrates pedagogical leadership into all her work with Education Coordinators, Family Service Coordinators, and teachers. Previously, Kristie worked at Chicago Commons alongside Karen Haigh and other committed educators transforming their work to embrace new principles and flourished under them. Kristie is committed to developing educators and the field of early education as a whole.

Pam Oken-Wright is a pedagogical consultant and author who worked with young children as a teacher researcher for 36 years. She has studied the Reggio Emilia philosophy since 1990 and enjoys supporting teachers on their journeys exploring this most joyful (and complex!) way of teaching and learning. At present, Pam is working with a Pilot program to bring elements of the Reggio approach to a public Title One school. Pam travels nationwide to consult and give workshops and keynotes. She has contributed to a number of books, including *Teaching And Learning: Collaborative Exploration of the Reggio Emilia Approach*; *Next Steps Toward Teaching The Reggio Way*; and *Authentic Childhood and Early Childhood Education: An International Encyclopedia*. Her most recent work is published in her blog for educators, "The Voices Of Children: Lessons Learned While Listening" at pokenwright.com.

Nadiyah Taylor has been a professional in the early care and education field since 1994. She has worked in a variety of roles, including preschool teacher, parent educator, and diversity consultant. She is currently the Discipline Coordinator of the Early Childhood Development Department at Las Positas College in Livermore, CA. Nadiyah earned her Master's degree in Human Development, with a specialization in Bi-Cultural Development, from Pacific Oaks College. Her thesis, *The Motivation of Anti-Bias Educators*, focused on teachers who use the principles of anti-bias education in their classrooms. She was an adjunct faculty member at Pacific Oaks College for three years, teaching core classes in diversity and equity, and taught at Merritt College in Oakland for two years. In addition to her teaching, Nadiyah is a consultant, with a particular focus on the continuing need for inclusion of anti-bias principles in early childhood settings and in childrearing.

About the Authors

Ann Pelo is a teacher educator, program consultant, and author whose primary work focuses on reflective pedagogical practice, social justice and ecological teaching and learning, and the art of mentoring. After receiving a Masters in Child Development and Family Studies from Purdue University, Ann taught three-, four-, and five-year-old children at Hilltop Children's Center in Seattle for twelve years. That teaching evolved into the role of pedagogical leader; the thinking, learning, and questioning that she did in that context have informed her work since leaving Hilltop. Ann travels in the United States, Canada, Australia, and New Zealand to think together with early childhood educators and leaders about teacher research, and the pedagogical practices and organizational structures that support inquiry. Her work is anchored by a commitment to the right of educators to be intellectually, emotionally, and spiritually engaged by their work. This is Ann's sixth book.

• •

Margie Carter has worked as a kindergarten teacher, child care director, and adjunct faculty at Pacific Oaks College N.W., and Seattle Central Community College. Margie received her B.S. in Education from Northwestern University, and her M.A. in Human Development and Leadership from Pacific Oaks College, and has served as a long time contributing writer for *Exchange*. As the co-author of numerous professional learning books with Deb Curtis, Margie's speaking and consulting work as a teacher educator has her traveling along the same North American and international routes as Ann. Margie has a deep commitment to unpacking and changing the dynamics of race-power-and-white-privilege in the early childhood field and our wider world, which more than once has gotten her in a pickle. With social justice as a lens, she is concerned about play as an equity issue, cultural and linguistic democracy, and uplifting the leadership, respect, and compensation of a diverse body of educators.

Ann Pelo *(left)* and Margie Carter *(right)*

Acknowledgments

Gratitude—Ann

How to begin my thanks? With Margie, of course. From our first meeting decades ago to our celebratory champagne as we sent this book off into the world, Margie has been mentor, companion, friend. Margie's questions and challenges, her insights and encouragement, her generous collaboration have sustained me, heart, soul, and mind. Gratitude, Margie, and more gratitude.

My thinking in this book has been sharpened by my work with a range of people and organizations. I've had the good honor of working as a pedagogical companion to educators and program directors in residencies and institutes; I've learned from them about the dance between theory and practice, and the steadying consistency of protocols, and the potent resonance of stories. Gratitude to Nicky Byres and Team SRCC; Kim Bertino, Melodie Glass, Fran Bastian, Keran Elgie, Bonnie Te Ara Henare, Christine Legg, and the educators at KU Children's Services; Carrie Melsom, Jane Cawley, Susan Willis, and the directors and educators at NSCECE lab schools in Halifax, Nova Scotia; John Nimmo and the staff at the University of New Hampshire Child Study and Development Center; the participants in the Pedagogical Leaders group at Sound Child Care Solutions; Anita Morgan and the participants in the Reflective Practices Institute; and the educators at Hilltop Children's Center, where I began my journey as a pedagogical leader.

A bow of gratitude to the thinkers and comrades who have shaped my understanding of what it is to belong to a community that learns: Karyn Callaghan; Randa Khattar; Will Letts; Kate Dawson and Emily Vera at Terra Nova Nature School; Chris Bayes, Lorraine Manuela, Therese Visser, Helen Aiken, Lesley Puhio, Karen Liley, Brenda Souter, Prue Crarer, and Diti Hill, who are the remarkable leaders of Reggio Emilia Aotearoa New Zealand; Anne Marie Coughlin at London Bridge; Laurie Kocher and the Board of the Vancouver Reggio Consortium Society; Matt Karlsen and Susan MacKay at the Opal School; Bill Bigelow at Rethinking Schools; and Tenneson Woolf. Thanks to Sean Forsha at Little Owl Preschool for fossicking.

And to my best and dearest thinker and comrade, Eli: our life together is a glorious invitation to be as human as we can be. Gratitude and love, on and on.

Extended Acknowledgments and Appreciation—Margie

For Ann: our years of friendship and mutual learning together are indeed at the center of what makes me glow. Your writing cross pollinates so much of what is beautiful in the world, prodding me with quivers, questions, and revelry.

For our valued colleagues Pam Oken-Wright, Shaquam Edwards, Nadiyah Taylor, Christina Aubel, Karyn Callaghan, Kristie Norwood, Eliana Elias, Nicky Byres, Jennifer Chen, and Helen Lo: with a very short time frame you cheerfully read our initial manuscript, and took up the invitation to reflect on and write about what our ideas might mean for your thinking and work. Our conversations—some in person, others via Skype and email, were quite a gift to Ann and me as we wrestled with how this book could offer a range of voices and perspectives. Each of you have a multitude of commitments, yet made time for one more. Your contributions make this book more resonant, more solidly anchored, and more immediate. It's a better book because of your voices.

For Luz Casio: valued colleague and remarkable leader with steady determination and tenacity to make cultural and linguistic democracy come alive in her program. Busy as she always is, Luz has gifted me with wonderful insights, hospitality, and generosity of time and stories. Without knowing it, Luz's hungry, creative mind provided inspiration for me as I worked on this book.

For Ijumaa Jordan: a steady colleague and continued source of learning to deepen my understandings of the dynamics of race, power, and privilege. Ijumaa generously took time to review and offer feedback for portions of this book.

For Deb Curtis and David Heath at Redleaf Press: our extended journey of writing together has deeply shaped and expanded my career. Though you weren't directly part of this book, I felt your companionship and perspectives helping me to clarify my thinking during this writing endeavor.

I share gratitude to a number of the folks Ann mentions above, our paths crisscrossing the globe, fertilizing ideas and friendship. To the list of remarkable leaders in Aotearoa New Zealand that Ann calls out, I add my appreciation for Wendy Lee with whom I've shared deep conversations about professional learning, social justice, and the power of Learning Stories to shape identities. Many other tenacious teachers and administrators, colleagues, mentors, and organizations have inspired and sustained me in my work, far too many of you than I can acknowledge here. If you think you might be one of these, you most likely are. Soak in my genuine appreciation as a source of sustenance for yourself.

For both Ann and me, the experience of working with the team at Exchange Press/Dimensions Foundation was convivial and rewarding. Soon after our initial conversation about this book, we added a proposal for a collection of stories, under the series name of *Reimagining Our Work* (ROW), building on the foundation of *From Teaching to Thinking* and told by educators who are actively doing the daily work of reimagining early childhood education; the crew at Exchange was wonderfully willing to put their oars in and row forward with us for the whole adventure. For your solid support with editing, choosing a title, and creating a design that gorgeously captures our vision, we offer deep gratitude to Emily Rose, Tina Reeble, Kaitlyn Nelsen, and Stacy Hawthorne.

Finally, we want to pay a special tribute to song writer/troubadour Tom Hunter, whose life, humor, and deep respect for teachers nourished us for many years before his untimely death. You hear the reverberation of one of his last songs, "As Human as They Can Be," throughout this book.

ROW
COLLECTION

Companion Reading for *From Teaching to Thinking*

From Teaching to Thinking: A Pedagogy for Reimagining Our Work is the foundation text for a companion collection of stories written by educators illuminating the pedagogical principles and practices we describe in this book. This foundation text and the books in the companion collection, *Reimagining Our Work* (ROW), can be read independently. But when studied together, they become a powerful conversation between theory and practice, demonstrating the ways in which theory shapes practice and practice shapes theory. This combination of texts lends itself to professional learning and teacher education.

Building on the foundational text, the ROW collection offers stories in which children and educators take up ideas of substance, and pursue questions in ways that are unscripted and original. They braid fluid imagination and expansive awareness into their collaborative inquiry. The children in these books aren't "gifted" or privileged—except by the gift and privilege of their educators' potent regard for their capability, and their concomitant willingness to bring their best minds and hearts to the table.

Which is just what you see the educators do in this collection of stories.

You hear educators reflect—in their unique voices and contexts—on their evolving understandings of children's capacities, and their roles as educators, and the meaning and practice of teaching and learning. The educators in these books hold assumptions and visions different from the dominant paradigm in our field, and we have much to learn from them.

We offer the stories in the ROW collection as a contribution to advance the conversation among early childhood educators and administrators, community college and university educators, policy makers, and funders about the nature and practice of early education. With both the foundation book, *From Teaching to Thinking*, and the ROW collection, our aim is to energize a new and renewing understanding of early childhood education, one that carries us far beyond standards and accountability, as we reimagine our work.

—Ann Pelo and Margie Carter
Editors of the *Reimagining Our Work* (ROW) Collection
Authors of *From Teaching to Thinking: A Pedagogy for Reimagining Our Work*

For more information on the ROW collection and upcoming titles please visit ExchangePress.com/ROW